Pelican Books

KT-140-206

Style and Civilization | Edited by John Fleming and Hugh Honour

Early Medieval *by George Henderson*

George Henderson was born in Old Aberdeen in 1931 and educated at the Universities of Aberdeen and London. He did research for his doctorate at Trinity College, Cambridge, and further research on medieval pictorial art and imagery, first as Research Fellow at the Barber Institute of Fine Arts in Birmingham and then as Graham Robertson Research Fellow at Downing College, Cambridge. He was lecturer in the history of art at Manchester University from 1962 until 1965, when he joined the Fine Art Department at Edinburgh University, where he is now Reader.

George Henderson has published articles on various aspects of medieval art in learned periodicals; he is author of *Gothic* in the same Style and Civilization series and of *Chartres* in the Pelican Architect and Society series. He is married and has two children.

George Henderson

Style and Civilization

Early Medieval

Penguin Books

Penguin Books Ltd, Harmondsworth,
Middlesex, England
Penguin Books Inc., 7110 Ambassador Road,
Baltimore, Maryland 21207, U.S.A.
Penguin Books Australia Ltd, Ringwood,
Victoria, Australia

First published 1972
Copyright © George Henderson, 1972

Made and printed in Great Britain by
Hazell Watson & Viney Ltd, Aylesbury, Bucks
Set in Monophoto Garamond

Designed by Gerald Cinamon

FOR NORA KERSHAW CHADWICK

Contents

Editorial Foreword

The series to which this book belongs is devoted to both the history and the problems of style in European art. It is expository rather than critical. The aim is to discuss each important style in relation to contemporary shifts in emphasis and direction both in the other, non-visual arts and in thought and civilization as a whole. By examining artistic styles in this wider context it is hoped that closer definitions and a deeper understanding of their fundamental character and motivation will be reached.

The series is intended for the general reader but it is written at a level which should interest the specialist as well. Beyond this there has been no attempt at uniformity. Each author has had complete liberty in his mode of treatment and has been free to be as selective as he wishes – for selection and compression are inevitable in a series such as this, whose scope extends beyond the history of art. Not all great artists or great works of art can be mentioned, far less discussed. Nor, more specifically, is it intended to provide anything in the nature of a historical survey, period by period, but rather a discussion of the artistic concepts dominant in each successive period. And, for this purpose, the detailed analysis of a few carefully chosen issues is more revealing than the bird's-eye view.

Acknowledgements

I am grateful to Professor Donald Bullough, Professor David Talbot Rice and Professor Francis Wormald for reading the text and for making many helpful suggestions and criticisms.

For the earlier phases of the period covered by this book I have found the *Early British Studies* volumes, edited by Mrs N. K. Chadwick, and her book, *Poetry and Letters in Early Christian Gaul,* particularly useful and illuminating. By dedicating this book to Mrs Chadwick I want to express my more general indebtedness to her for the friendship and the intellectual stimulus which she has given to me and to my family over many years.

Early Medieval

1. Portable altar and reliquary of St Andrew, Trier, 10th century

I

Introduction

Among the church treasures preserved in the Cathedral of Trier, in Germany, is one whose fabric provides a summary chart or diagram of the changes and developments which go to make up the history of early medieval art [1]. This object is a portable altar containing relics, dedicated in honour of St Andrew the Apostle and made of ivory and gold, inlaid with enamel plaques and encrusted with pearls and gemstones. Above four recumbent lion-supporters, the rectangular altar-shrine is like the base of some lost *kouros* figure where one firmly planted foot alone survives of the statue, broken off at the ankle. The effigy of a human right foot rests on the top of the Trier shrine, overlaid with gold and decorated with four strands of gems to represent the straps of a sandal, the principal relic within the casket being a reputed sandal of St Andrew. As a cult object the altar-shrine with its one slim stationary foot may appear to modern eyes as grotesque and alien as the mummified cats and ibises of Ancient Egypt. It dates, however, from the late tenth century of the Christian era, and along with other famous relics of Christ and his saints brought prestige to medieval Trier, winning it the name *sancta civitas Treverorum*.

The altar-shrine was made by goldsmiths employed by Archbishop Egbert, a powerful churchman and notable art patron in Germany in the time of the Emperors of the Ottonian line. Not all the decoration of the shrine is of local manufacture or contemporary with Archbishop Egbert. At the heel end, the tenth-century goldsmiths embedded a much older jewel, a large fibula or brooch of a very distinctive design made for some leader of the Franks in the seventh century. The maker of the Frankish fibula, in his turn, had shaped his jewel about an earlier exotic kernel, a sixth-century gold medallion bearing the likeness of the Emperor Justinian, imported from the Eastern Roman Empire. Thus the back of the Trier altar-shrine is composed of a number of elements drawn from widely varied cultural contexts, strangely bonded together by the chances and processes of history, associated like the successive layers of some geological concretion which gather round a primary nucleus.

Although the six-hundred-years-long development of early medieval art, from roughly A.D. 550 to 1150, can reasonably be interpreted as a steady piling up of styles and traditions, stratification on stratification, this is not by any means the whole story. There is unconformity in art, as in Nature. Certain eruptive forces distort the orderly superimposition of successive cultures. Then again certain salient features may resist the attrition of the centuries, or a melting and mingling of contrary elements may take place. This last phenomenon of metamorphosis, fusion and change, is worth considering briefly, because it confronts us with one of the real problems in connection with the art discussed in this book. Although the period with which we are dealing is very extensive, on occasions, in certain circumstances, we find a remarkable resemblance between works of art produced very far apart in time. When, for example, the Romans introduced notions of naturalistic representation to the Celts of Gaul and Britain in the last century B.C. and the first century A.D., native Celtic artists approached the new business of depicting the human likeness by way of an old-established artistic tradition of their own, basically a non-representational linear decorative style. The fusion of classical and Celtic forms can be seen in a number of miniature second-century bronze heads of emperors

2 (*above left*). Head of the Emperor Hadrian (?), 2nd century

3 (*above right*). Head of St Luke, the Lichfield Gospels, 8th century

4 (*opposite*). Monument to Abbot Clement, Sherborne, *c.* 1160

found in the English Fenland, evidently intended to be mounted on top of sceptres or batons [2]. The provincialisms intruded by native craftsmen into these works, the ridged and linear construction of eyes, brows, noses, lips, the symmetrical nodules and formalized recessed panels on hair and beards, condition the whole character of the heads. What they lose in human-ness and normality they gain in decorativeness and numinousness. Not so much portraits as symbols, they could not be mistaken for genuine Roman productions, but if it were not for certain tricks of costume which confirm their early date, these heads could easily, from the stylistic point of view, be attributed to medieval artists. Similarly, mysterious rapt or glaring mask-like heads, crowned with elaborate patterned curls of hair, each feature turned into a formal design, recur in seventh-century monastic art in England, in illuminated manuscripts [3]. In the twelfth century an abbot of St Mary's Abbey at Sherborne in Dorset was memorialized by an identical image, in sculptured relief, the head reduced to a stark egg-shape, the ears, hair and beard carved as a springing linear pattern of lobes, the cheeks grooved and furrowed, the mouth a slit [4]. Early medieval art gains an illusionary consistency of stylistic outlook by the conflation, brought about afresh every now and then by changing

circumstances, of rational and irrational artistic traditions, of representation and abstraction.

On the other hand, many medieval works of art show no mixture or adulteration, but represent purely one or other of the particular stylistic traditions which contribute to the general tenor of medieval art. This integrity of style can be met with throughout the entire period under review, and consequently we again find stylistically identical monuments which in fact were produced centuries apart. Occasionally this leads to disputes as to the date of a given monument. A case in point is the pulpit in the church at Gropina in Tuscany carved with powerful designs which breathe the air of Barbarian, not Antique classical, Europe [5]. The supporting columns have capitals sculpted with rows of flat skull-faced squat-bodied figures, and the columns are weirdly linked by a massive worm-like knot of stone. Panels of reiterated spirals, or shallow symmetrical patterns of acrobatic men and rubbery monsters form the ornaments of the pulpit itself. Such a work seems at first sight to belong naturally to an age when Italy's classical heritage had been swamped by the crude vigour of the Germanic invaders. The Gropina pulpit has been attributed to the eighth or ninth centuries. But it has also been regarded as backwater workmanship of as late as the twelfth century, and the prevalence of fantastic and semi-abstract designs in mature Romanesque sculpture gives credit to this view.

The opposite tradition, that of Antique classicism, makes itself felt erratically during our period, giving again an effect of stylistic consistency to certain areas of early medieval art, though the breaks and lapses in the tradition are at least as marked as its continuation. The dissemination throughout Europe of Roman artistic standards in the first centuries of the Christian era formed the groundwork of much medieval art. Particularly important in this respect was the trade in sarcophagi during the late Antique period. These objects were mass produced and exported to all parts of the Empire, so that examples of a fairly uniform sculptural style and decorative programme were available as models to the later occupants of widely scattered parts of Europe, from Pisa to Ely, and remained influential, as we shall see, because of the later association of Roman sarcophagi with the burial of local saints. But Antique art was only one aspect of Antique civilization. In politics Antique civilization was looked back to as having a peculiar attractiveness and prestige, so that any large-scale coordinating regime which

emerged during the early medieval period tended to pose as the successor to the Roman Empire. Just about the time when the Trier altar-shrine with its old Frankish jewel enclosing a medal of Justinian was being made for Archbishop Egbert, the German Emperor Otto III was celebrating in his own person and in the state which he governed a *restitutio rei publicae* and *renovatio imperii Romanorum*. This late tenth-century renaissance of Romanism was profoundly influenced by a still more famous but equally short-lived revival, that promoted by Charlemagne and his successors in the ninth century. Charlemagne's palace at Aachen, begun shortly before 800, with its apsed throne

6. Interior of Palatine Chapel, Aachen, 792–805

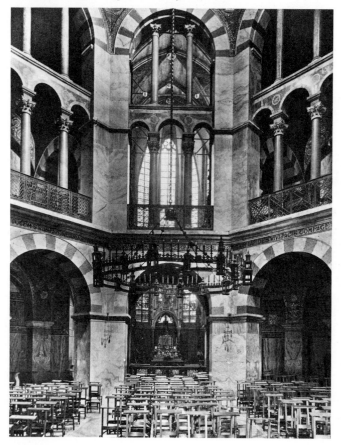

room and its finely proportioned church [6] set at opposite ends of an enormous courtyard, reflects the influence of one of the greatest Roman imperial monuments in northern Europe, the basilica or *aula palatina* at Trier. A renewed interest in classical visual values tends to accompany these and other similar political experiments, so that every so often throughout our period Antique forms emerge in a rather special role. The deliberate emulation by medieval rulers of the styles and monuments of the glamorous Roman past makes for artistic unity in Europe and helps to give vision and direction to the development of medieval art.

Quite apart from the Antique element in the constitution of the Carolingian and of the later Ottonian Empire, the actual establishment of large territorial and administrative blocks by Charlemagne, Lothair I, and Charles the Bald, and again by the German Ottonian emperors, had practical consequences in internationalizing art, encouraging contacts between patrons and workshops in different countries. This produces problems not so much regarding the date of art objects as regarding their place of origin. In the treasury of the Cathedral of Milan, for example, is a handsome liturgical object, a holy water stoup, or *situla*, carved out of ivory for Archbishop Gotfredus of Milan early in the last quarter of the tenth century [7]. The quiet grave stolid figures of the frontally enthroned Virgin and the seated Evangelists with their high crowns of hair, long flattened faces and soft simplified draperies, have roots in the Early Christian period, and have relations, too, with Carolingian art [8]. It is uncertain if the Milan *situla* was created locally or if it was made by artists in Switzerland or Germany. It undoubtedly comes from a highly productive workshop with Ottonian connections, which might arguably be Reichenau as easily as Milan, or vice versa. The patronage of Otto III 'took away from the cradle of my Fatherland' at least one Rome-trained painter, Johannes Italicus, who worked in northern centres such as Aachen and Liège. The re-establishment of a western Empire was therefore important for developing the trade routes of art, and supplemented the constant movement of men and ideas promoted by the international society of the Church from the earliest Middle Ages onwards.

The growth of international society not only gave scope and scale to the indigenous arts in Western Europe. It put Western Europe in touch with other parts of the civilized world. The territories of Islam and of the Byzantine Empire impinged on

7. Situla of Archbishop Gotfredus, 974/5-80

8 (*opposite*). Archbishop Angilbert presenting the golden altar to St Ambrose, S. Ambrogio, Milan, *c.* 850 (*cf.* illustration 94)

the frontiers of Latin Catholic Europe throughout our period, and both the tendency towards pure ornament, pattern, line, colour, and the tendency towards classical naturalism were refreshed by contacts outside Europe to the south and to the east. The example of Byzantine civilization was particularly important as a source of technical, formal, and iconographic ideas. It was to Byzantine art and Byzantine artists that Desiderius,

Abbot of Montecassino, in the eleventh century, turned for inspiration, when he despaired of the state of the arts at home in Italy. 'Mistress Latinitas', says his contemporary biographer, 'has been wanting in the skill of these arts . . . for five hundred years and more, and by the efforts of this man . . . merited to regain it in our time.' These extraordinary sentiments should make us wary of regarding Italian artistic developments as typical of early medieval Europe as a whole. Italy was an endlessly exciting mixing bowl of cultures and visual traditions, but other countries, Britain, France, Germany, even northern Spain, provide us with rather more coherent evidence for the progressive evolution of medieval art. However, by the time we reach the last stages of the period discussed in this book, that most composite of styles, Romanesque, has settled into a consistent enough shape over the whole of Europe, including Italy. The great church of S.Michele at Pavia [100], erected between about 1100 and 1160, has a west front as broad and high as a cliff which ends at the top in a magnificent stepped open gallery and single vast shallow gable. Across the lower part of the façade are friezes of foliage interspersed with figures, men strangling monsters, knights pursuing dragons, huntsmen returning with the trophies of their sport, confronted birds, lions couchant and rampant, in inconsequential profusion, while the three doorways are framed by shafts and arches busy with coiled stems and leaves and twitching eager little men or animals engrossed in strange meetings and wrestlings. The same frieze layout, the same abrupt changes of scale between the participating figures, the same repeated textile patterns transmuted into stone, are displayed on the twelfth-century wide flat front of the monastic church of Ripoll in Catalonia [9]. The tangled ornaments which crowd the voussoirs of the portal of the twelfth-century church at Dalmeny on the Forth estuary near Edinburgh, and, in the churchyard, a massive mouldering Romanesque sarcophagus carved with rows of figures and scrawny lions, assert the kinship of the far north with the far south of Europe, in art, culture and piety. The great pulpit of the church of S. Ambrogio in Milan summarizes in itself the range of Romanesque iconography and ornament, the scenes from the Old and New Testaments, the scenes of human seasonal labour, the inevitable drift into foliage chains and meshes, and swathed and plunging animal forms. At one of the corners, a column is crowned with a capital decorated with broad-

9. West front of abbey church of S. Maria de Ripoll, *c.* 1150

10. Detail of pulpit, S. Ambrogio, Milan, early 12th century

11 (*opposite*). Durham caryatid, *c.* 1140

breasted eagles, with heavy wings spread and a fine texture of carved feathers, petal-shaped above, stem-shaped below [10]. Identical eagles perch and stiffly spread their wings on a capital of the cloister of the Abbey of Moissac in Languedoc, of about 1100. Over the eagle capital on the Milan pulpit stands a robed human figure, his feet and knees turned in, his head drooping, his shoulders hunched, and his tube-like arms bent and raised to support the weight of a frieze of opposed lions and lush foliage interlace. Similar strained and stooping weight-lifters, Atlantes in medieval dress, support the giant ribs of the vault of the chapter house at Durham Cathedral, of the mid-twelfth century [11]. Thus a twelfth-century traveller, far from home,

in whatever region of Europe he might find himself, would recognize in the churches which he visited the same details and the same general character of design with which he was familiar in his native city.

The long period whose art is the subject of this book is unified by one dominating factor, the Christian religion. Christianity gave to medieval art its basic sense of purpose and its specific imagery. In the early Middle Ages Christianity was most actively promoted, privately and publicly, by the monks, members of the great institution founded by St Benedict in the sixth century. Indeed the early Middle Ages have been named 'the Benedictine centuries'. One of the preoccupations and duties of the medieval monk was the liturgy, the Divine Office recited with chant and ceremonial. The celebration of the sacred liturgy forms a girder-like bond of continuity throughout our period. St Gregory the Great, who set the monastic stamp on the Church over which he presided, launched the mission for the conversion to Christianity of the English people at the close of the sixth century. The elaborate liturgical practices of the great monastic basilicas of Rome in St Gregory's time were passed on to the English as a central element in the monastic institution. John, the archcantor of St Peter's in Rome, personally instructed the monks of seventh-century monasteries in Northumbria, Jarrow and Wearmouth, 'in the Roman mode of chanting, singing, and ministry in the church', and left behind his music books as a guide to future generations. With the withering of English monasticism, a result of the attacks of the pagan Norsemen from the late eighth century onwards, the grand liturgical tradition conveyed from Rome to England was not lost, for it passed to Germany and to other parts of Europe through the missionary activities of the Anglo-Saxons in the eighth century. It became enshrined as a prime expression of monastic life and service in the Carolingian church law books – in the *capitula* decreed as binding for the whole Carolingian Empire at a council of Abbots at Aachen in 817. The precarious political and ecclesiastical structure of the Carolingian Empire soon collapsed, but the *capitula* survived and preserved an ideal of conformity, dignity and sumptuousness in the ceremonies of the monks. In the tenth century the great independent reformed Benedictine monastery of Cluny in south Burgundy and the royal monasteries in Germany and England gave practical expression in various ways to the Carolingian regulations, filling them out with greater and greater emphasis on ceremonial and psalmody. The solemn choral devotions of the monks in the Old Minster at Winchester around 1000 were the natural descendants of the brilliant musical and processional spectacles of Charlemagne's time, at the monasteries of Aniane or St Riquier. At Cluny in the twelfth century the monks lived a wholly liturgical life, occupied continuously in grandly conceived ceremonies of praise and prayer. The scale and elaboration of this liturgical observance was reflected in the heroic proportions and noble design of the Abbey church, and in the massive tunnel vaults, which echoed and redoubled the glorious sound of the chant [103]. Here we have a history of growth, elaboration, renewal and invention, within a remarkably consistent basic tradition. Romanesque Cluny fully realized all that was inherent in monastic corporate devotion and music-making and ritual over six hundred years. The faithful preservation of traditional forms, never atrophying for long, frequently rediscovered and expanded by new minds, is characteristic not only of the history of monastic observance, but equally of the early medieval visual arts.

There is in medieval life, in its religious expression, much that is recognizably the same from start to finish of our period. But each generation offers its interpretation and colours the tradition which it inherits and in turn passes on. What the monastic communities represented and conserved were not merely formal rites and ceremonies, and constitutional laws and customs attractive to legal minds, but a way of life which offered indestructible benefits to its adherents and through them to the entire world. The religious traditions of the Middle Ages had the compulsion of absolute truths, absolute values, which for centuries kindled enthusiasm and creative talent. In those special monastic communities which grew up as custodians and witnesses around some venerated shrine, the corporate life of the monastery would inevitably be interpreted, in times of danger and depression, and in times of prosperity and expansion, as an aspect of the immortal life of the saint. Montecassino in south Italy, and Fleury on the Loire, both famous Benedictine houses and centres of reform, were St Benedict's peculiar devotees not only because they followed his authentic Rule, but because they preserved his relics in their midst and bore active witness to the unimpaired spiritual power which radiated from his shrines. St Benedict is represented on the splendid gold altar frontal donated by the German Emperor Henry II to Basle Cathedral in 1019 [12]. The saint stands under the arch of a arcade, clad in monastic dress and holding a staff, as a companion of Christ, along with the archangels Michael,

Gabriel and Raphael. This is not a memorial portrait of the ancient monastic founder, now a remote figure, long ago elevated to the celestial regions, but is, as it were, a contemporary portrait of an active participant in human affairs. Henry II presented the golden frontal to Basle partly as an act of personal gratitude to St Benedict, who had appeared to him in a dream, in answer to his prayers, and had cured him of a painful infirmity. The inscription above the arcade recalls St Benedict's name and thaumaturgical powers as an aspect of Christ's healing mercy: QUIS SICUT HEL FORTIS MEDICUS SOTER BENEDICTUS, 'Who is like God, a powerful physician, a blessed Saviour.'

12. Golden altar frontal of Basle, 1019

The saints' shrines of medieval Europe were not monuments to the famous dead, but were gateways into the supernatural world. Medieval monastic annals are full of stories of their patron saints beckoning dictatorially or stepping in and out of their high canopied shrines, magically slaying or deranging the wits of looters or secular oppressors, harrying their communities into new building projects or commanding the translation of their relics into positions of greater honour. The continuing vitality of, for example, St Denis in northern France and St Cuthbert in northern England, expressed in hagiographical narratives and embroidered with legends, are important factors in the history of medieval art. About their potent bodies great

13. Interior of nave, Durham Cathedral, 12th century

archives of treasures accumulated, products of art and piety, representing all the styles and techniques practised or admired by medieval craftsmen [67, 136]. The saint in whose honour the Lindisfarne Gospel Book was written in the late seventh century [32, 59, 74] is the same saint for whom Durham Cathedral was begun in the late eleventh century [13]. The personality of St Cuthbert does, it is true, show signs of modification with the passage of time. The real man of whom the historian Bede writes, intelligent, sensitive, patient and persevering, exerting his charm even over the wild sea otters which lay down at his feet on the shore near St Abb's Head, has become in the twelfth century *Libellus* of Reginald of Durham an awesome martinet, who lies encased but conscious and irritable in his wooden coffin, with growing nails which have to be pared and growing hair which has to be combed, at whose feet, within the coffin, by some horrid perversion of the beautiful story of the otters, a weasel brings forth its young. The 'undead' St Cuthbert of the twelfth century is a recognizably Romanesque interpretation, with that infusion of militancy and grotesquery which is charac-

14. Miracle at the tomb of St Cuthbert, *c.* 1200

teristic of the Romanesque style. But the hand which emerges from beneath the coffin lid in a late twelfth-century picture of a miracle at St Cuthbert's tomb is still obviously the big strong hand of the athletic saint whom Bede authentically described in the eighth century [14], and the shrine of St Cuthbert at Durham provides a genuine link with the Early Christian period of England, a bond between Norman monasticism and the first simple golden age of English monasticism. In the same way, all over Europe, the showplaces of the confessors and martyrs of the Christian faith, the material symbols of the Communion of Saints, comprise visible records of the growth of European culture and art, magnets of devotion and creative skill, psychic centres of inspiration for many generations. They are typical of early medieval civilization in representing rooted traditions which themselves continually exercise a fresh creative influence.

Early medieval art, then, is marked by consciously maintained traditions, but also by constant shifts and gradations in tone and outlook, productive of a fascinating plethora of artistic monuments, full of life and meaning for their own time. In the following chapters I have chosen a number of topics or lines of inquiry which I hope will reveal something of what stimulated early medieval artists and their patrons. The grandeur of the historical period, the changes of fortune experienced by so many European peoples, the huge forces at work throughout society, the genius of innumerable great men, make this a memorable, difficult and challenging area of art to study. Despite the difficulties, the effort to probe the wider causes of artistic creation is worth while, since it deepens immeasurably our appreciation of the individual works of art themselves.

15. Medallion of the Emperor Gratian in Gothic mount, *c.* 400

2

The Barbarian Tradition

'Treasure, gold in the ground, may easily madden any man, conceal it who will!' In these words the Old English poet of the epic *Beowulf* pays his own sombre tribute to what Virgil had called *auri sacra fames*. The lure and glamour of gold lies heavily over the early history of the Germanic tribes of the north and east of Europe who in the late fourth century were pressing irresistibly through the sagging frontiers of the Roman Empire:

> . . . a nation straung, with visage swart
> And courage fierce, that all men did affray,
> Which through the world then swarmd in euery part,
> And ouerflow'd all countries farre away,
> Like Noye's great flood, with their importune sway . . .

Gold was the price which they extorted for preserving the fiction of the *Pax Romana*, and gold also poured into their hands as access to southern markets was yielded to them by the weakening Roman state. Roman *solidi* carrying the emperor's portrait reached the remote and legendary lands around the Baltic in the fourth and fifth centuries, in such bulk that in certain areas they comprised an active currency. The top-soil of the Baltic Islands and southern Sweden was strewn thickly with treasure, like a pirate's map of the Caribbean, as large and lesser hoards were temporarily hidden when local war broke out, and never retrieved, or perhaps were offered in the ground to some god. A cache of forty-eight coins bearing the heads of emperors from Aurelian to Constantine II, found at Brangstrup on Fünen Island, Denmark, seems to represent a sample of the coins available in the Roman world around the mid-fourth century and is perhaps the pay of some returned Scandinavian-born mercenary, secreted at a time of peril with other trinkets gathered on his foreign campaigns and then lost.

In the year 375 the nomadic Huns rode out from the Asiatic Steppes and smashed into the Gothic kingdoms of the Ukraine and the eastern Balkans, setting in motion the huge collapse of the Western Roman Empire and its repopulation by the Germanic peoples. The treasure discovered in a field at Szilágy-Somlyó in Rumania was evidently buried by its Ostrogothic owner in response to war or rumours of war around the year 400. It consists of gold ornaments and coins, including seven Roman *solidi* and seven imperial medallions, those great plaques three or four times the weight of normal coins, struck by the emperors as diplomatic and personal gifts. One of the medallions, of the Emperor Gratian (367–83), struck at Trier, was mounted by a Gothic goldsmith as a pendant with a broad frame covered with filigree spirals and a row of fifteen small mask-like frontal heads [15]. The projecting stylized human faces, glum yet intense in expression, invest the smooth profile portrait of the Roman ruler with god-like grandeur, so that the whole jewel takes on the significance of a potent charm or amulet. A few Roman imperial medallions, similarly adapted as pendants, have been unearthed in the Scandinavian countries, and the influence of the Roman medallions is strongly felt in the great gold pendant disks called bracteates, made in their hundreds by Scandinavian goldsmiths in the fifth and sixth centuries, which are stamped on one side only with a head,

6 (*opposite*). Gerete bracteate, 6th century

7. West front of church at Échillais, *c.* 1135

modelled ultimately on that of the Roman emperor but gradually distending and dissolving, the likeness taking on the blank stare of the framing heads on the Gratian pendant, the hair sprouting and the ornamental diadem scattering off into geometrical symbols. In some bracteates such as one from Gerete, Sweden, the great balloon-like face with its spiral ears rests directly on the back of a monstrous beast, a horse perhaps, but with a goat's beard and bull's horns and hooked claws like a griffin [16]. The emperor's head has become that of a magic-working Scandinavian god, Odin or Tyr, encircled with a huge nimbus of beaten gold, stamped with chevrons, peltae, rope and spiral motifs, and with a great company of jawless profile heads. Soldered on to the V-shaped base of the loop of the Gerete pendant is a cluster of human heads, the victims or acolytes of the god, who in their fixed relentless stare, their air of a guarded secret, anticipate the visual language of eleventh- and twelfth-century Romanesque corbel tables and voussoirs where human and animal heads project in grim and inscrutable rows [17].

The gold hoards of the Age of the Migrations were not bloated only with Roman coins and with classical figurative art and its derivatives. Gold worked in other traditions swept into Europe in advance of, and forcibly behind, the Hunnish inroads of the fourth century – gold shaped into strips and cells to display formal geometric patterns of brightly coloured stones, notably garnets from India. The spectacular treasure from Petrossa in Rumania, buried and inadvertently abandoned sometime around 375, includes a gold circlet bearing a runic inscription which appears to proclaim the treasure as the sacred property of the Goths – probably a Visigothic semi-religious

18. Twelve-sided Gothic vessel
from Petrossa, 4th century

royal hoard. The fibulae, collars, and cups [18] represent polychrome and cloisonné metalwork of an early authentically Iranian kind, with broad gold frames, formed into regular rows of rectangular compartments and other simple circular and heart-shaped cells. The Ostrogothic treasure of Szilágy-Somlyó contains, as well as its Roman coins and medallions, a heap of ornamental brooches worked in gold cloisonné with infillings of enamel and precious stones. The Ostrogoths carried this taste for eastern-type polychrome jewellery into Italy, which they invaded under their leader Theodoric's command in 488. Theodoric the Ostrogoth was officially licensed in this invasion by the Byzantine government, as a distraction from his campaigns nearer Constantinople itself. Italy had already succumbed to wave after wave of Germanic invaders, Visigoths, Huns and Vandals, and so could cheerfully be committed to the mercy of yet another barbarian. Theodoric having personally, as later tradition states, split Odoacer, the German ruler of Ravenna, from head to foot with a stroke of his sword, established himself at Ravenna in conscious imitation of the Eastern Roman emperor. In 497 the emperor grudgingly transmitted to Theodoric the regalia of a Roman ruler, the *ornamenta palatii*. These Roman jewels and Roman thoughts did not, however, drive out the Iranian fashions from Gothic metalwork. The gold and garnet jewellery dating from Theodoric's time, found in various parts of Italy, is dominated by ladder, chevron, diamond and circle cloisons, lighter and more pliant than those from Petrossa, so that the continuous surface of the red garnets is, as it were, scored and patterned by gold lines, rather than having a continuous golden surface interspersed with coloured cubes and spots. The grandest of the Italian Ostrogothic jewels are a pair of fibulae found at Domagnano, shaped like eagles, with thick necks and long flecked tails outstretched and diminutive wings half-opened [19]. Eagle brooches were particularly favoured by the Germanic inhabitants of Dark Age Europe, examples close in design to the Domagnano version having been found in treasure hoards in France and Spain. The outline of the Domagnano eagle is filled up methodically by an accumulation of rows of small cells, on an additive principle of design, not organic or naturalistic. This mathematical and segmented quality was to remain characteristic of medieval art, whether a fibula or a church ground-plan [97], until that great shift in emphasis and

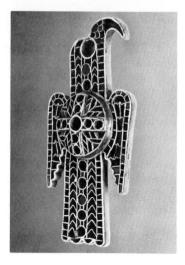

19. Eagle fibula,
Domagnano, c. 500

outlook which occurred around the middle years of the twelfth century, resulting in the style which we now so strangely call 'Gothic'.

All across Europe, from the south to the extreme north, gold was worked into many strange and elaborate forms in the early Dark Ages, but as impressive as any of these are the great bars, ingots, rings and coils of gold wire which are a feature of Swedish material culture in the sixth century. Fifteen pounds of gold from Timboholm in Västergötland, Sweden, are composed of ingots and dense tangles of gold loops, strung together to form a rough irregular chain [20]. This is ring gold, the raw material of state and personal finance and of the goldsmith's craft. In the late sixth century in North Britain, gilt silver, booty seized long before from the old Roman province of Britain, was reworked by Pictish metalworkers to form massive silver chains, of which ten have so far been discovered in Scotland [21]. The Pictish chains, varying in girth and weight but not markedly in length, have double links which look like a rationalization of the haphazard festoons of the Timboholm ring money. The chains are secured by separately sliding the pair of rings at either end on to a broad terminal ring, resembling a napkin ring and engraved with formalized designs or symbols of unknown significance. The chain, so secured, would be worn as a collar, and may also have served as a readily accessible source of currency and reward. Of the Swedish gold hoards

20. Ring gold and ingots, 9th century

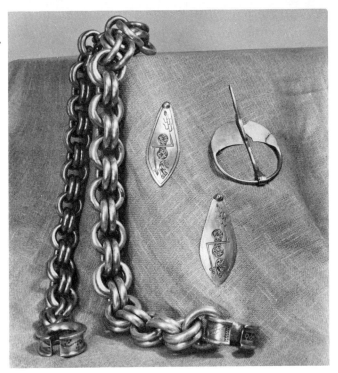

21. Pictish chain and other ornaments, c. 600-700

of the sixth century, the greatest was that found at Tuna in Västergötland, which contained both ingots and gold manipulated by a goldsmith one stage beyond the incoherent looped chains of Timboholm into a grand gold collar, two pounds in weight, a fortune carried round its owner's neck, a prize for a hero.

Such gold collars, of fame and ostentation, are a feature of Germanic Dark Age literature. For example, the Anglo-Saxon poem *Widsith*, composed in the seventh century but looking back at the period of the invasions of Italy and even earlier, first pictures the poet in the service of Hermanric, King of the Goths, who died in 375 when his kingdom collapsed before the onslaught of the Huns. 'Then the King of the Goths treated me well. He, prince of city dwellers, gave me a circlet (collar) in which there was reckoned to be six hundred pieces of pure gold . . .' After his adventures and victories in the service of Hrothgar, King of the Danes, the hero Beowulf is presented with two armlets, a corslet, and 'rings, greatest of necklaces that I have ever heard of on earth'. Again Hermanric the Goth is associated with this kind of ornament, for Beowulf's collar is compared with the most noted of all the fabled collars of Germanic literature. 'I have not heard', says the poet, 'of any better hoarded treasure of heroes under the sky, since Hama carried off the necklace of the Brisings, the ornament and treasure. He fled from the malevolence of Hermanric . . .', that is, the unknown hero Hama steals the famous collar from Hermanric. In the tenth-century Norse *Lay of Thrym* the 'Brisings' necklace' is worn by the goddess Freya herself. When the goddess hears that the Etin, or giant, Thrym aspires to have her as his bride she foams at the mouth with fury, causes the shining halls to tremble, and bursts asunder the great necklace.

These wonderful ornaments thought worthy to be the attributes of the gods and of heroes can be visualized in the shape of those supreme relics of the Scandinavian Iron Age, the massive gold collars from Ålleberg and Möne in Västergötland, formed of row upon row of gold ropes or tubes set side by side, and bound with threads of filigree [22]. The gaps and hollows between the ropes are filled up with crouching and creeping fantastic animals formed from filigree and gold beads, and with golden human masks like those of the Gerete bracteate. The thick clotted design of the collars, the many strands ridged and looped and strapped together, the variety of motifs,

22. Ålleberg gold collar, 5th century

23. Portal of Riccall church, Yorkshire, 12th century

the scattered human and animal and abstract forms, astonishingly parallel the construction of provincial Romanesque doorways, with their thick mouldings and accumulated ornaments, for example at Riccall in strongly Norse Yorkshire [23] or at Kilpeck in remote Herefordshire [24].

In all the struggles, dangers and sudden reversals which swayed the fortunes of the infant states of medieval Europe, the loyalty of the warrior to his lord, and the lord's power to protect and generously reward those who served him well were vitally important stabilizing forces. A letter issued from the

24. Portal of Kilpeck church, Herefordshire, c. 1140

court of Theodoric the Ostrogoth summons the German warriors settled in the south of the Italian peninsula to attend the
King's court so as to enjoy his 'royal largesse', for a warrior 'is
as one dead who is unknown to his Lord'. The heroic literature
of the Dark Ages often movingly depicts the feelings of the
warrior towards his lord, as the source of honour and of direc-
tive purpose in life as well as of material reward. In *The Wanderer*
the poet speaks of himself in exile, a lonely survivor far from
his kinsmen, and thinks sorrowfully 'of retainers in hall and the
receiving of treasure, of how in his youth his gold-friend was

courteous to him at the feast. It seems to him in his mind that he clasps his Lord and lays hands and head on his knee, as when formerly in past days he was near the gift-throne.' The collar of Widsith was an example of the royal generosity of Hermanric. Beowulf's great collar was another royal award, for gallant service. Hrothgar, King of the Danes, is called 'the keeper of ring-treasures', 'an excellent giver of rings', 'the treasure guardian of heroes'. Beowulf is spoken of by the young hero Wiglaf as 'our Lord who gave us these rings', to whom loyal service in battle is due. As a consequence of the terrible set-back to English civilization brought about by the Viking invasions and the perpetual local and international warfare that ensued for many centuries, the same primitive description of the king is still spontaneously used in the *Anglo-Saxon Chronicle*, commenting on the wars of Athelstan. I will refer in a later chapter to the lavish diplomatic gift of an Antique vase, jewels, horses, and sacred relics, sent to Athelstan by Hugh the Great, Duke of the Franks. On that occasion England received a portion of the noble heritage of the Carolingians, and so moved tentatively towards the grand monastic culture of the High Middle Ages. But marching through the north country to meet the Norse King of Dublin, the King of Scots, and the King of Strathclyde in 937, Athelstan is still described as a king in the tradition of Beowulf and Hrothgar.

> In this year King Athelstan, Lord of warriors,
> Ring giver of men, with his brother the Prince Edmund
> Won undying glory with the edge of swords
> In warfare around Brunanburh.
> With their hammered blades, the sons of Edward
> Clove the shield wall and hacked the linden bucklers
> As was instinctive in them, from their ancestry,
> To defend their land, their treasure, and their homes,
> In frequent battle against each enemy.

Historical and literary records, and the evidence of archaeology, provide many examples of royal treasures, the accumulation of gold, coins and plate and weapons, with which the royal office was upheld and the service of the king's thegns was honourably purchased. We have already witnessed the treasure of Petrossa, lavish and brilliant in the extreme, buried in a remote mountain refuge and through war and death never reclaimed, its secret undiscovered until 1837. The last portion of the poem *Beowulf* celebrates just such a royal treasure. 'There in the cave were many ancient heirlooms, which in days long gone by some men carefully hid there, great riches of a noble race, precious store. Death carried them all off in past times . . .' The last veteran, before his death, laments over the treasure: 'Now, O Earth, do you hold, now that heroes cannot, the riches of nobles. Behold, valiant men formerly took it from you. Death in battle, sweeping slaughter, took away each of the men, my own people. I have no one to bear up the sword or to polish the golden vessel . . . the hoard of rings, the ancient work of men.' The old treasure, the goblets, flagons, dishes, the 'armlets cunningly bound', the 'standard all gilt, standing high above the hoard', is won for his people by Beowulf, in his last great fight. But the treasure is accursed, and proves fatal to its new owner. 'The famous princes who stored it there, laid a heavy ban upon it until Doomsday, so that the men who should plunder the place should be guilty of sin, and should be confined in cursed places, kept fast in the bonds of Hell, smitten with plagues . . .' Here we may have preserved some echo of the kind of sacred oaths and imprecations which kept all tongues silent about the whereabouts of the treasure of Petrossa and the like, royal hoards concealed through necessity of war, and an echo also of the ban laid by Dark Age pagan and Early Christian society upon treasures officially discarded as a generous offering to the dead, for example in the burial mounds of Sweden and East Anglia. But the vocabulary of the ban in *Beowulf*, 'until Doomsday . . . guilty of sin . . .', is manifestly modified and coloured by Christian concepts familiar to the author or redactor.

In Abbot Suger's account of the treasures of St-Denis, written in the 1140s, he records with satisfaction that his new gold cross, studded with gems, was guarded by a ban pronounced by Pope Eugenius III at St-Denis at Easter 1147. 'Publicly, in the presence of all, he anathematized, by the sword of the blessed Peter and by the sword of the Holy Ghost, whosoever would steal anything therefrom and whosoever would raise his hand against it in reckless temerity; and we ordered the ban (*anathema*) to be inscribed at the foot of the cross.' Very different from this matter-of-fact and tidy label on the St-Denis cross is the tragic unavoidable doom which hangs over the greatest treasure of Germanic herioc literature, the gold of the Niflungs or Nibelungs. The story of this fatal treasure is told in the tenth-century Eddic Poems and in the prose *Völsunga Saga*, written down in Iceland in the thirteenth century, but it was familiar throughout Europe at an early date, a primitive version being known in

England in the eighth century. The gold was taken by the gods Odin and Loki from the dwarf Andvari, from under the water-fall. On delivering it up, the dwarf cursed his gold. The gold fell into the hands of the giant Fafnir, whom it possessed, mind and body. When Sigurd fatally wounded him and seized his gold, Fafnir cursed the treasure a second time. 'That same gold shall be thy bane, and every other man's bane who owns it.' When Sigurd returned with his booty, 'four men lifted the gold from his horse. There were many rich and beautiful treasures to see there, and it was thought great pleasure to gaze on the body armour and helmets and great rings, the golden vessels and weapons . . .' After the murder of Sigurd, the brothers Gunnar and Hogni inherit his gold. Omens warn them that their doom is coming upon them. In a dream an eagle is seen to fly through the hall, showering everyone with blood, like the eagle in illustrations of chapter 8 of the Book of Revelation, which flies through heaven crying 'Woe! Woe! Woe!' Hogni and Gunnar are tortured to death by Attila, King of the Huns, in his frenzy to discover the hiding place of the gold. 'I say', says Gunnar stubbornly before his death, 'that the River Rhine shall have all the gold, rather than have it fall into the hands of the Hun.' The gold from the waterfall of Andvari, having worn a deep track through many men's lives, returns to the waters from which it rose.

The *Völsunga Saga*, as well as celebrating the legendary Niflung gold, reflects the Age of the Migrations in its references to other vast royal treasures, which change hands as the chance of war ordains. The treasure of Sigmund, hidden before his disastrous battle with his enemy King Lyngvi, is recovered by a passing band of Danes, to whom Sigmund's widow reveals its hiding-place. 'There they found great wealth, so that they thought that they had never before seen so much gathered together in one place.' This they conveyed to their ships, and carried off to Denmark. When Sigurd avenges his father Sigmund, and kills Lyngvi, he bears home 'great booty, which he had taken in this war'. In the Dark Ages precious ornaments and weapons, the regalia of Kings, suffered sudden changes of ownership. The poem *Beowulf* records the loss by the Geats of the great gold collar presented to Beowulf at Hrothgar's court. Beowulf had given it to Hygd, Queen to Hygelac, King of the Geats. Hygelac 'had the circlet on his last expedition, when beneath his banner he defended the treasure . . . the mighty prince bore the ornament, the precious jewel over the sea; he fell under his shield. Then the King's body passed into the power of the Franks, his breast armour and the circlet also . . .' We can imagine a collar like that of Ålleberg passing into the Frankish royal treasury. Treasures might also be exchanged between peoples deliberately, generously, to promote peace. The Gothic historian Jordanes records a letter sent by Theodoric to the King of the Heruls, offering him alliance against the growing power of Clovis, King of the Franks. 'We bestow upon you horses, swords, shields and other weapons of war. But more important still we also bestow on you our favour. Take then these weapons, let them serve both you and me . . .' Hrothgar, King of the Danes, tells Beowulf how he brought about peace with the Wylfings: 'Afterwards I ended the feud with money. I sent ancient treasures to the Wylfings over the back of the waters.' He imagines a future time of general peace. 'Treasures shall be in common. Many a man shall greet another with gifts across the gannets' bath. The ring-prowed ship shall bear offerings and love-tokens over the sea . . .' This exchange of treasure, by accident of war or peaceful diplomacy, promoted diffusion of artistic motifs, and consequent cultural cross-fertilization which was of such great importance in the development of both court and ecclesiastical art in early medieval Europe.

The rulers of the many different nations who occupied the British Isles in the sixth and seventh centuries were certainly well-endowed with royal treasure. From Adomnan's *Life of St Columba,* written about 700, we hear of *thesaurus regis,* the Treasury of the sixth-century Pictish King Bridei, in the royal residence situated probably near Inverness. This treasury must have contained old Romano–British silver plate, of the kind from which the Pictish chains were made, and doubtless examples of the double-linked chains themselves, since these may well be royal regalia, on the evidence of the ninth-century Welsh kings who wore not crowns but golden 'gyves' or 'fetters'. But the most distinguished treasure of Dark Age Britain has not survived to us. It formed the centre and subject of an incident long famous among the Britons of Strathclyde, Cumberland, and Wales. In 651 the English King Penda of Mercia and his British allies appear to have trapped King Oswy of Northumbria in his most northerly outpost of 'Iudeu', probably Stirling. Oswy was forced to cede to his besiegers 'all the riches which he had in the town', and these treasures were distributed by Penda to his British allies. Since the Welsh ninth-century historian Nennius called this event by its seventh-century traditional name '*Atbret Iudeu*', 'the Restitution of Iudeu', it appears that Oswy was forced to hand back treasures which he had formerly seized from the British. The English historian Bede tells a story of how Oswy was compelled by the threats and invasions of Penda to offer as tribute a great treasure, 'ornamenta regia', as the price of peace. There may be some truth in this description of the treasure, since the fame of the incident among the British suggests that important treasures, royal honours, were at stake. Bede's words echo the 'ornamenta palatii', the official regalia delivered by the Byzantines to Theodoric. Shortly afterwards, near Leeds, Oswy fought a battle against his united enemies, and killed Penda of Mercia, Aethelhere of East Anglia, and all but one of the allied British kings, so that part at least of the royal booty may have passed back into Oswy's possession in 655. This bandying to and fro of sumptuous artifacts of British and English manufacture, at the extremities of Northumbria, north and south, provides an interesting background for that mixed visual culture which as we shall see characterizes Northumbrian manuscript illumination from the mid-seventh century onwards.

Around the time of the wars of Oswy, or not many years before, a superb royal treasure of gold ornaments, regalia, and weapons, was buried at Sutton Hoo in Suffolk [27, 28]. This treasure was not merely deposited in some secret place, in time of war, like the Petrossa hoard or the gold of Sigmund before his battle with King Lyngvi, but was officially buried as part of a solemn pagan funerary ritual, in loyalty and reverence to a dead king. A continental parallel for the burial of treasure in association with a royal funeral is provided by the grave-goods of Childeric, the last pagan King of the Franks, father of Clovis, the first Christian and Catholic King of the Franks. Childeric died in 482, and was buried at Tournai, where his grave was accidentally discovered in 1653. It contained the king's signet ring, with his name and portrait, a purse loaded with one hundred gold and two hundred silver coins, three hundred gold cicadas, their folded wings inlaid with garnets, which were originally sewn in glittering profusion on the king's mantle, two swords, magnificently ornamented with gold cloisonné work with garnet inlay, the king's battle axe, the severed head of his horse with its harness, and a crystal ball, like the one which was once possessed by the fourth-century mercenary of Brang-

25. The treasure of King Childeric, 5th century

strup, Denmark [25]. The grave-goods of the King of Sutton Hoo, even more sumptuous than those of Childeric, were not laid directly in a grave in the earth but were set out at the bottom of a great open rowing-boat, nearly ninety feet long, with benches for forty rowers, over which was raised an enormous funeral mound. Royal interments in a ship under a mound are directly paralleled not in the Frankish area, from where the gold coins in the Sutton Hoo king's purse were derived, but in Sweden, in Uppland, at Vendel and Valsgarde, where from about 600 A.D. onwards the chief men of great families were buried in their boats, near the sea, splendidly equipped with arms and treasure.

The Anglo-Saxon poem *Beowulf* begins with a description of the funeral rites of a king called Scyld Scefing, who is placed with treasure in a boat, and then, perhaps symbolically, committed to the mercy of the sea. 'Then they laid down the beloved Lord, the giver of rings in the bosom of the ship, the famous man by the mast. Many treasures and ornaments were there, brought from far-off lands. I never heard of a ship furnished more nobly with weapons of war and battle-raiment, swords and corselets . . . Furthermore they set a golden banner high above his head . . .' The erection of a great golden banner in the imaginary description of the pagan burial recalls the historian Bede's report that the golden banner of King Oswald of Northumbria was placed at the order of his niece, the daughter of King Oswy, over the tomb of the dead king in the monastery of Bardney. The dead king of Sutton Hoo was equipped as befitted a Dark Age hero, with just those arms and symbols which Hrothgar awarded to Beowulf, 'a helmet and corselet and a famous precious sword'. The same arms are awarded by Duke William of Normandy to Earl Harold in the Bayeux Tapestry after the siege of Dinan [26]. The helmet of the King of Sutton

Hoo was 'brought from far-off lands', like Scyld Scefing's treasures – significantly from Sweden, perhaps a trophy of war but more likely a 'love-token (from) over the sea [27]. It is like Beowulf's helmet, "wrought by the weapon-smith in days long past, set round with boar images, the gleaming helmet . . . guarded his head so that no sword or battle blade could pierce

26 (*opposite*). Harold receiving arms, the Bayeux Tapestry, *c.* 1077

27. The Sutton Hoo helmet, 7th century

it".' The bronze and silver eyebrows terminate in small boars' heads, in gilt bronze. The crest was covered with silver, and the crown was decorated with gilt bronze plaques, like those on Scandinavian helmets of the seventh century, for example the 'beast-leader' plaque from Torslunda [55]. Such a helmet would be an heirloom of the royal house, as also would be the body-armour, of which only a rusted mass of metal survives, found under the great Byzantine dishes. Beowulf possessed 'the finest of corselets, the heritage of Hrethel (his grandfather), the work of Weland'. In the fragmentary Anglo-Saxon poem *Waldere*, when the hero is trapped and besieged after his flight from the court of Attila the Hun, he speaks of his noble body-armour as an heirloom, 'good and broadly woven, adorned with gold, no mean dress for a prince to bear . . .'

Most important of all the equipment of the Dark Age war-rior was his sword. A sword, of proven worth, might be of venerable age, and might be held in superstitious awe. A sword garnished with gold and garnet inlay, from Vallstenarum, Sweden, is composite work from the sixth to the eighth century, evidently an heirloom of great reputation, carefully tended and repaired. The famous smith of Germanic legend, Weland, made swords for heroes, each with its individual name, for example the sword 'Mimming', mentiones in *Waldere*. In the eleventh-century Old French epic the *Chanson de Roland*, Roland and his companions Oliver and Turpin have named swords, 'Durendal', 'Halteclere', and 'Almice'. In the *Chanson* the magical sanc-tity of the sword is rationalized by its having relics set into its hilt, hair of St Denis and a portion of a garment of the Blessed Virgin. Sigurd the son of Sigmund inherited his father's sword 'Gram'. 'When he passed through a full-grown field of corn wearing his sword Gram – which was seven spans long – the chape of its sheath grazed the top of the standing grain.' Beowulf was armed with a sword 'called Hrunting. It was an excellent old treasure . . . the sword, adorned with rings, sang a greedy war chant . . .' The sword of the King of Sutton Hoo, like his helmet, has foreign antecedents, and is splendidly decked with gold and garnet inlay on the pommel, hilt, and scabbard [28]. The scabbard bosses are among the finest cloisonné jewels in existence. They follow the same basic pattern as the medallion-shaped body of the Domagnano eagle fibula with its main cruciform motif and the radiating cells between the arms of the cross [19]. But the minute and delicate metal- and lapidary-work of the great craftsman of Sutton Hoo shows a technical

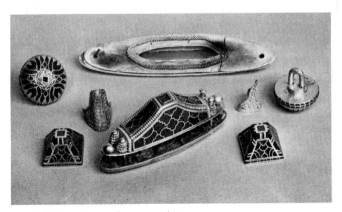

28. The Sutton Hoo sword mounts, 7th century

skill and finesse beyond anything found elsewhere in the German world of the Dark Ages, the climax of a style whose raw beginnings in Europe we witness in the Petrossa treasure.

We may compare the artistry of the Sutton Hoo goldsmith with that of his Continental contemporary Eligius, the master of 'verroterie cloisonnée', maker of saints' shrines and of other ornaments for churches [136]. In Eligius's work we see the centuries-old taste for gold cells and polychrome inlays being lavishly applied to the service of the Catholic Church. After the Germanic nations had overrun the Western Roman Empire, their early Christian art was erected on the basis of the art with which they were most familiar, namely secular jewellery. Precious secular ornaments made their way into ecclesiastical hands as consecrated offerings, especially when the pagan custom of grave-goods deposits gave way to endowments of altars and Masses. Oswald's royal banner was in the possession of the community of Bardney. Splendid eighth-century silver mounts of weapons, perhaps the relics of some donation, were found in 1958 along with ecclesiastical treasures buried beneath a thin stone slab, marked with a cross, on the site of a church on St Ninian's Isle off the mainland of Shetland. When King Athelstan marched through County Durham in 934 he offered treasures at the shrine of St Cuthbert at Chester-le-Street which included two horns mounted in gold and silver, two banners, two armills or bracelets of gold, and cups full of money, while his army commanders offered ninety-six pounds of silver. Abbot Suger writes of a most noble collar of the seventh-century Queen

29. The Eagle symbol, The Book of Durrow, 7th century

Nanthilda which was fixed to the cross of Charlemagne at St-Denis.

The transference of secular art styles into the ecclesiastical context was inevitable. A striking example is the page decorated with the evangelical symbol of the eagle in the magnificent Gospel Book of Durrow, illuminated in the third quarter of the seventh century, and now in Trinity College, Dublin [29]. The eagle symbol is framed by a massive border of interlace. This strap work, broad and flat in the individual strands, and arranged in loose knots laid diagonally on the page, is very similar to the strapwork ornamenting the spectacular gold buckle from the Sutton Hoo treasure. The Durrow eagle stands isolated, with its great penguin-like wings drooping to the level of its feet. Although the design is different from that of the Domagnano eagle, the resemblance to a hieratic bird fibula is striking. The thin double line which surrounds the eagle's body and the radical segmentation of its head and beak, reproduce the cloisons of the Dark Age goldsmith, and the texture of the short ruffled plumage of the breast and shoulders, and the long curved feathers of the wings recall the effect of variegated enamel inlay and incised gold sheets. The eagle of Durrow is a Christian evangelist symbol as conceived by a craftsman like the Sutton Hoo goldsmith, and has its nearest relatives among the ducks and pouncing eagles on the gold and garnet inlaid purse cover. One is tempted to attribute the Book of Durrow to East Anglia, as the luxury Gospel Book of a seventh-century church establishment at Burgh Castle or Felixstowe or Dunwich. But internal evidence may link the book with Northumbria, specifically with Lindisfarne, settled by Columban monks from Iona in 635, since a note by the scribe asking for the prayers of those who use his book appears to have been copied from a text written by St Columba himself. Doubtless King Oswald, who brought the monks to Lindisfarne, possessed splendid royal jewels. As we have seen, his brother Oswy had precious regalia through his hands in the 650s.

Another Gospel Book, close in style to that of Durrow, is now in the Bibliothèque Nationale in Paris. It was taken to the Continent around 700 by an Anglo-Saxon missionary named Willibrord, and deposited by him at his monastic foundation at Echternach. The symbol of St Luke in the Echternach Gospels, the *imago vituli*, paces on delicate hooves across the page, its large mild head and slim body drawn with a firm un-

30. The Calf symbol, the Echternach Gospels, 7th century

dulating outline [30]. The conjunction of the calf's cheek and throat is marked by a curved scroll, and a wedge-shaped decorative panel runs from the base of the ear to the breast. The shoulder and the haunch are articulated by long narrow scrolls,

31. The Ardross wolf, *c.* 600

which form a strong pattern of verticals running counter to the main horizontal accent of the design. This system of scrolls, not only enlivening the design but also accurately and economically describing the movement and anatomy of the animal, shows that the artist of the Echternach Gospels was influenced, not this time by Anglo-Saxon royal metalwork, but by sixth- and seventh-century Pictish art, as we know it from a few examples of silver jewellery and from a series of impressive standing stones carved with animal portraits and with mysterious formalized symbols. From Ardross in Ross, Scotland, comes a stone incised with the eager menacing body of a running wolf, with half-opened jaws, thick muscular throat and powerful shoulders, the strength and motion of the beast underlined by the elegant curve of the inner scrolls [31]. The Pictish animal sculptures abound in the area centred upon King Bridei's fortress and treasury near Inverness. They are strictly uniform in style and seem therefore to reproduce or represent the designs of a single artist. His designs have the vitality and mastery of the characteristics of different animals which we see in early Greek seals. Perhaps some such models, centuries old, helped to define the visual language of the Pictish symbol stones when these were erected for some sociological or political purpose unknown to us. But whatever the ultimate source of the Pictish designs, their influence was felt in the monastic scriptorium which produced the Book of Echternach and other illuminated Gospels, either by direct knowledge of the symbol stones or from silver ornaments like the chain terminals and the oval plaques found in a hoard at Norries Law in Fife [21]. The art of the illuminators of early Christian England was thus founded upon native art-styles, various traditions being fused and given new scope in the service of the Gospel of Christ.

In Northumbria among the first generations of Christians, the great central mystery of the new faith, the Incarnation of the Word, was celebrated in fantastically decorated monumental letters at the beginning of each of the four Gospels. In the Book of Durrow, the Book of Echternach, and most elaborately of all in the Gospel Book of Lindisfarne, written and illuminated by the Anglo-Saxon Eadfrith around or before 698, the first words of St Matthew's Gospel, *Liber generationis*, 'the book of the generation of Jesus Christ', are given physical presence and grandeur unparalleled and unthought of in earlier continental Gospel Books [32]. The densely-enmeshed strapwork and the interwoven animal forms are based not on principles of Christian art followed in Constantinople or Rome, but on the designs of Anglo-Saxon ornaments and weapons, wrought up to heights of firmly controlled complexity. But in the grand restless rolling terminals of the L, the I and the B, we see a design of British, not English antecedents. These broad rings, now tightening into rapid spirals, now diversifying and spreading out, with little oval vents placed on the thickness of the joints between the spirals, are descended by a long process of evolution from the flowing curvilinear designs used by native craftsmen on mirror-backs and harness and shields before the Roman invasion of Britain. When centuries later the eastern parts of the Roman province of Britain were seized by the Anglo-Saxon invaders, the long wars between the British and the Saxons brought objects of traditional British manufacture into English hands, as booty of war or tribute. Among the grave-goods of the King of Sutton Hoo is a great bronze hanging bowl, its sides ornamented with enamelled bronze disks or escutcheons, coloured green and red and filled with beautiful sinuous patterns of rings and spirals and trumpet-like swellings. These escutcheons are thought by many to have been made in a Celtic-speaking portion of the British Isles; the bowl, having passed by fortune of war into English possession, was handed down as a royal treasure, as an heirloom, carefully patched where it was worn, until its burial along with Byzantine dishes and Frankish coins, a Swedish helmet and English cloisonné jewels. Thus the treasury of the King of Sutton Hoo contained 'Celtic' trumpet-spiral patterns – yet another ingredient of the decorations of the great Gospel Books of the seventh century. King Oswy's treasury in the 650s was also provided with exactly the right models, British and English, from which the Christian scribes of Northumbria could derive inspiration for the Books of Durrow and Lindisfarne. Pictish influence, such as we see in the Echternach Gospels, would tend to reinforce the new English taste for spiral patterns, since such patterns were a natural part of the repertoire of Pictish craftsmen of the sixth and seventh centuries [21].

The glorious richness, cohesion, and vitality of the decorative language of the Book of Lindisfarne renders it one of the greatest monuments of abstract art in European history. The full astonishing repertoire is also displayed, to unforgettable effect, in the huge late eighth-century Pictish cross-slab at

32. Beginning of St Matthew's Gospel, Lindisfarne Gospels, *c.* 698

33. Nigg cross-slab,
c. 800

Nigg, Ross [33]. The abstract decorative forms here acknowledge, as it were, their origin in metalwork, by invoking the extra power and charm of plasticity, recession and projection. The arms of the cross, the uppermost one unfortunately broken and truncated, are filled with diagonally interlocked animal bodies. The centre of the cross consists of a square of fine woven strapwork, and the bosses on either side of the cross stem are also made of strapwork, matted into great rounded heaps. At the base of the cross the trumpet-spiral motif is displayed in two magnificent panels, full of diverse invention, which stir and bubble like boiling pitch. The monumental cross of Nigg in its noble height and breadth, in the mastery and range of its decorative forms and the superlative technique to which nothing seems too difficult, is one of the grandest representations of the Cross in early medieval Europe. Formally and aesthetically it stands at the opposite extreme from the Ruthwell Cross [140] being an illuminated carpet-pattern page or a metal book-cover design directly transferred to a monolith, not a free-standing cross column with emerging arms; the Nigg sculptor did not visualize the body of the cross as a sequence of narrative figurative scenes but as a dramatic juxtaposition of various abstract designs. He makes no use, consequently, of didactic inscriptions, such as crowd the borders at Ruthwell, although we might regard his cross as a kind of formal palindrome, identical if read from top to bottom to top, from left to right, or right to left. Together Ruthwell and Nigg represent the wide range of sources, and the wide range of interpretations employed in their celebration of the Cross of Christ by insular artists of the early Middle Ages.

The Dark Age insular style, of which the Lindisfarne Gospels and the Cross of Nigg are great authentic examples, had a profound influence on the development of Continental art. Northumbrian scholars such as Alcuin of York, and others trained in insular schools, were summoned by Charlemagne to help in his great intellectual campaign for the revival of culture in Europe. From Northumbria and other provinces came a flow of books, some of them illuminated with large decorative letters like those in the Book of Lindisfarne. Even in the Carolingian workshops most conscious of the forms and ideals of the classical past, the insular style made inroads and influenced the taste of eighth- and ninth-century Frankish scribes and artists. In the Utrecht Psalter, the masterpiece of the Carolingian Renaissance [92], the first initial to the first Psalm is insular in design. The great Gospel Books of the Court School, where Evangelists appear in the medallion-covered mantles of Roman consuls and where Canon Tables are framed by columns mottled and coloured like marble, crowned by grand Roman-type capitals, nevertheless bear the stamp of insular tradition in certain of the splendid inflated letters with which the gospel texts begin. In the early ninth-century Carolingian Gospel Book in the British Museum, Harley MS. 2788, the *Liber generationis* of St Matthew's Gospel pays tribute to the Durrow, Echternach, Lindisfarne tradition [34]. The fulsome sweep of the curved L is broken and penetrated by the vertical stem of the I. The remaining letters are strictly classical, with their origins in the noble inscriptions cut, for example, on the base of Trajan's Column, but in the outline of the first two great letters, and in their crisp strapwork, insular influence is clear enough, although the variety of insular forms is perceptibly muted. The animal interlace has vanished – two confronted lions alone inhabit the letter – and the terminals consist not of busy runs of spirals, but of high crests and knots of strapwork, ending in modest little coils. The process which we see at work here is again one of balance and compromise between divergent traditions, the fully mature insular style, itself an eclectic product, being rubbed off against new powerful traditions coming into France and western Germany from the south and east.

The presence of the strong influence of insular illuminations and metalwork in Carolingian art, at the very time when classical influences were being brought powerfully to bear on Carolingian workshops, and the resulting effort to absorb two diverse, indeed opposite, strains gives us an insight into the whole nature of early medieval art. Despite its profound respect for classical culture and classical forms, medieval art is seldom academically correct and respectable. It maintains a feeling for abstract ornament, for dense textures and linear rhythms, outside the visual range of classical art and expressive of experiences and attitudes unknown to the Romans. The ambivalent nature of early medieval art, and especially of the Romanesque, that extraordinary style in which the classical and the non-classical styles are combined in an uneasy but immensely fruitful partnership, is summed up in one detail from a Canon Table in the First Bible of Charles the Bald. Showing his knowledge of the illuminations of the Court School, the artist has constructed an array of handsome columns with Roman-type capitals and heavy block-like abaci. But at the two extremes

34. Beginning of St Matthew's Gospel, B.M., Harley MS. 2788, *c.* 800

of the page the great voluted capitals are not in fact solid, foliated and Antique, but consist of an open strapwork, of exactly the design of the terminals on the *Liber generationis* initials in the Gospels, Harley MS. 2788 [35]. Thus the outer skin, the basic structure of the classical capital, is filled in with a

35. Interlace ornament on capitals, Tours, 844–51

linear pattern of insular origin. The artist of the First Bible of Charles the Bald, of about 850, has in fact invented the Romanesque architectural capital, endlessly dragged to and fro between Roman bulk and structure, and barbaric surface pattern.

The traditions of the seventh- and eighth-century insular style remained a conditioning factor in the visual arts through

RIMO TEMPORE

ALLCUIATA EST

TERRA ZABVLON?

ET TERRAN EPTALM

36. Initial in Montecassino homilies, 11th century

many generations. In the late eleventh century, in the extreme
south of Europe, the illuminated initials produced in the great
Benedictine monastery of Montecassino during the reign of
Abbot Desiderius clearly reflect insular initials, or Carolingian
interpretations of them, in the metallic angular forms employed,
the inset panels of ornament, animal-head terminals and looped

and tangled animal bodies [36]. In the extreme north of Europe, thanks to contacts with Scotland and Ireland established by the Vikings from the late eighth century onwards, art was directed for centuries into the investigation of abstract or semi-abstract patterns, to which the tensions and rhythms of trumpet spirals, interlaced strapwork and attenuated yet energetic animal bodies have all contributed. At the Stave Church at Urnes, of the third quarter of the eleventh century, carved wooden panels decorate the walls and surround the doorways, filled with long animal bodies swathed together in a loose tangle [37]. Under

37. Portal of Urnes church, 11th century

and over the interwoven animals is a maze of figures-of-eight, formed of fine slender strands. The exciting contrast of thin and thick strapwork was already known to the illuminator of the Durrow Gospels in the seventh century and to the sculptor of the eighth-century Nigg Cross. At Urnes the hypnotic flow and ebb of sinuous snake-like necks and bodies and limbs, rubbery and smooth, has a chilly elegance and sumptuousness strangely akin to the spirit of *art nouveau*. On the leg joints of the animals on the Urnes door are deeply incised spirals, or rather coils, for the circle is not closed. Of all the insular motifs, the spiral, with

38a. Enlarged detail of figure of Christ, Vézelay, *c.* 1130

its trumpet-like extremity, made least headway on the Continent. Carefully imitated from Northumbrian models by eighth-century scribes at Canterbury in the Canterbury Psalter and the Stockholm Golden Codex, the trumpet-spiral seems to have been too idiomatic, too specific to insular art, to attract continental taste. We have seen the resistance to it in the *Liber generationis* page of Harley MS. 2788. Yet after centuries of neglect the spiral motif enjoys one last sudden momentary eruption in a major monument of Romanesque sculpture, the tympanum of the western portal of the church of the Madeleine at Vézelay, of about 1130 [38]. Here at the centre of an enormous encyclopedic relief sits a gigantic figure of Christ, shedding the rays of pentecostal fire from his outstretched hands, and with his shoulders and arms cascading streaming draperies like an Antique Jupiter Pluvius. Above the waist the figure is frontal. Below the waist, the legs are jerked round towards the right. On the right thigh and the left knee of Christ the parallel ridges of the drapery begin to spin in an ever-tightening spiral, while from the maelstrom of thin folds long curves of furrowed draperies shoot out, like the trumpet terminals of the old insular spirals. The sculptor of Vézelay, in his grand ecstatic image of Christ, God irradiating power, seated at the heart of the whirl-wind, has found his own way back to expressive rhythms and textures akin to those of the most creative age of insular art, and the foundation of the Romanesque aesthetic in old northern artistic traditions is once again underlined.

39. Pentecost tympanum, Vézelay, *c.* 1130

3

An Habitation of Dragons

The great tympanum of the priory of Vézelay in Burgundy represents the Ascension of Christ, out of sight of the Apostles into the clouds, as narrated in the first chapter of Acts, and the fulfilment of Christ's promise to his disciples that the power of the Holy Ghost would descend upon them, enabling them to heal the sick, drive out devils, and confirming them as Christ's witnesses before all nations, even 'unto the uttermost parts of the earth' [39]. In the box-like compartments set like cloisons on a Dark Age fibula about the rim of the tympanum, and in the long narrow lintel, the thaumaturgical and preaching mission of the Apostles has begun and the inhabitants of the earth have started up and are hurrying into the fold of Holy Church. In the Middle Ages theologians interpreted a number of passages in the Book of the Prophet Isaiah as referring to the mission of the Apostles and the coming into being of the Christian Church: 'I will say to the North, Give up; and to the South, Keep not back: Bring my sons from afar and my daughters from the ends of the earth. Bring forth the people who are blind, though they have eyes, and those who are deaf, though they have ears. Let all the nations be gathered together. . . . I will send unto the nations, to Africa and Lydia, who draw the bow, to Italy and Greece and the Isles afar off, that have not heard my fame, neither seen my glory. . . . Then the eyes of the blind shall be opened, and the ears of the deaf shall be unstopped. Then shall the lame man leap as an hart, and the tongue of the dumb sing . . .' In the third compartment upwards on the right of the tympanum at Vézelay a lame man is making his way to the summons, leaning heavily on a stick. In the equivalent compartment at the left, madmen with flaming hair stagger in the throes of their dementia, from which the curative word of the apostles will release them. Other debilitates suffer from moral illness. Above the outstretched right hand of Christ are two of the famous race of the Cynocephali, creatures with human bodies and dogs' heads. These are they who are dumb, though they have tongues, through their ignorance of God's truth. Representatives of another monstrous race, inhabitants of India, appear at the right of the lintel, with ears like enormous bracket fungi sprouting from their heads. These are the morally deaf, though there is no doubt that they have ears. Next to them come the Pygmies, the dwarfish race to whom an ordinary horse is like the huge horse of Troy, to be mounted only up a ladder. These represent the inhabitants of Africa, who with the Lydian archers at the left of the lintel, make their way to the feet of Christ.

The sculptor of the Vézelay tympanum, wishing to express the varieties of mankind and the vastness of the earth, has drawn inspiration from one of the many concoctions of monster lore, some in part of Antique origin, which were popular in the early Middle Ages and which formed the opinion of medieval men about the remoter regions of the globe. In the scientific writings of Isidore of Seville in the seventh century and Rabanus Maurus in the ninth, strange and savage peoples are described who inhabit large tracts of the earth, notably the vast and geographically vague land of Scythia.

Scythia is said to be named Gothia from Magog, the son of Japheth . . . it extended from India in the east, and from the north through the Maeotic Marshes, between the Danube and the Ocean as far as the borders of Germany. . . . This country has an equal number of tribes, which wander widely on account of the barrenness of the land. Some of them cultivate the fields, others inhuman and bloodthirsty live on human flesh and blood . . . There are many rich and many uninhabitable regions in Scythia. For while in most places these areas abound in gold and precious stones, they are for the most part inaccessible to men because of the fierceness of the griffins. Moreover, superb emeralds are found in this country.

On the thirteenth-century Hereford map, a compendium of medieval geographical and anthropological lore, the men who use their ears to cover themselves inhabit an island in the northern ocean. The Cynocephali are found to the east of the Scandinavian peninsula. Further east again stands a splendid griffin, threatening and being threatened by a company of armed men, the foremost of whom protects his body with a long shield, like the knight represented in the twelfth-century Seal of Richard Basset [91]. A relic of some such encounter was preserved in the Treasury at St-Denis, and was admired by the seventeenth-century diarist John Evelyn, 'The onely tallon or claw of a Griffon that ever I saw', as big as a cow's horn. In a great promontory of Asia on the Hereford map an inscription tells of the nature of the region: 'Besides being intolerably cold, it is filled with unimaginable horrors of every sort; for at certain times there is a very fierce wind from the mountains. . . . Here there are savages who feed on human flesh and drink human blood, accursed sons of Cain . . .'

The English audience for whom the poem *Beowulf* was composed back in the eighth century was familiar with the idea that monstrous beings inhabited the northern parts of the world, including Scandinavia. Beowulf set out for Hrothgar's court to fight Grendel, a demon of the moors and fens, who was one of the progeny of Cain the murderer. Grendel comes by night to Heorot, the hall of Hrothgar, greedy for men's flesh. Beowulf witnesses his last swift assassination. 'He quickly seized a sleeping warrior, suddenly tore him asunder, devoured his body, drank the blood from his veins, swallowed him with large bites.

40. Mamres at the mouth of Hell, *Marvels of the East, c.* 1025

41. The Snartemo
sword hilt, Norway,
6th century

Straightway he consumed all the body, even the hands and feet.' Beowulf wrestles mightily with the monster, and when it at last breaks free from his grasp and makes off, it leaves behind one of its colossal arms, torn off at the shoulder, the hand, armed with nails like steel, stretching up to the very roof of the hall. When Beowulf has pursued his mutilated enemy and has beheaded him in his lair beneath the waters of the mere, the demon's head, like the giant Goliath's, is carried home with difficulty by four warriors. We can visualize Grendel in terms of an illustration in an English eleventh-century manuscript of *The Marvels of the East*, where the magician Mamres stands at the mouth of Hell [40]. Before him is the vast strong and terrible figure of Satan, his mouth gaping, his ferocious teeth fixed in the naked body of a victim, while he scoops other bodies towards him with his huge clawed fists. The comparison of Grendel and Satan is justifiable. Grendel is called 'a fiend in Hell'. He is roused to his enmity of Hrothgar's household by hearing, in his lonely fen, the voice of the king's minstrel telling the story of the Creation, of the making of sea and land, and of the great lights in the sky, and of all living things. In the same way Satan, learning of God's great new works, is inflamed with envy and destructive rage against mankind. Grendel belongs to the family of 'ogres, elves and sea monsters, – the giants too, who struggled long against God'. Grendel's head is severed from his trunk with a magical blade, 'an old sword of giants'. This sword with its 'twisted haft and snake images' must have looked very like the great Snartemo sword, from a royal grave in southern Norway, of the late sixth century, decorated with distorted and dismembered animal shapes [41]. The silver pommel has two crawling stick-legged beaked monsters facing one another. The hilt is filled with gold plates, on which is a writhing mass of serpentine bodies, with awful teeth and claws rising occasionally into view. Beowulf's sword also had gold plates, inscribed in runes with the story of the ruin of the race of evil giants, drowned by God in the surging waters of the Flood.

At the root of such stories of a war between God and monstrous enemies lie the scriptural references to the conquest of Rahab, the great sea dragon. In Psalm 74 we read, 'For God is my King of old, working salvation in the midst of the earth. Thou didst divide the sea by thy strength, thou brakest the heads of dragons in the waters . . .'; and in the Book of Isaiah, chapter 51, 'Awake, awake, put on strength, O arm of the Lord;

awake, as in the ancient days, in the generations of old. Art thou not it that hath cut Rahab, and wounded the dragon? Art thou not it which hath dried the sea, the waters of the great deep; that hath made the depths of the sea a way for the ransomed to pass over?' In the early Middle Ages, among dwellers in lonely islands, desolate shores, remote mountains between river and sea, the omnipresent uncontrollable forces of nature were inevitably imagined in terms of active malignant intelligences, enemies of God and men. In the preface to his *Life of Columba* Adomnan records in two consecutive sentences the saint's miraculous ability to subdue the furious rage of wild beasts and 'the surging waves, at times rolling mountains high'. In Book II of the *Life* Adomnan tells of an incident which was reputed to have happened when St Columba was living in the province of the Picts, evidently close to the fortress of King Bridei. On the banks of the River Ness he saw a dead man being buried, who had been seized and fatally bitten by a monster which lived in the waters. Another swimmer is saved by the saint from a like fate, for as the monster pursued the man through the river 'with an awful roar and its mouth wide open', the saint, making the sign of the cross, commanded the monster to retire, which it did 'more quickly than if it had been pulled back with ropes'. This notable piece of hagiography must have been known in Northumbria, first in the Columban monastery at Lindisfarne and later in Jarrow-Wearmouth as a result of Adomnan's visits. The same picturesque adventures which animate the hagiographical literature of the age are found in the heroic vernacular poetry. In phrases which seem to echo the sonorous language of the Psalms quoted above, the poet of *Beowulf* speaks of his hero's exploits at sea, how he plies the ocean streams with his arms, throws aside the sea with his hands. For seven nights he 'toiled in the power of the waters'. 'Wild were the waves. The wrath of the sea monsters was stirred. A hostile deadly foe drew me to the depths, had me firmly and fiercely in his grip. Yet it was granted to me that I pierced the monster with my battle spear. The rush of battle carried off the mighty sea monster by my hand . . . the surges sank down, so that I could behold the sea capes, the windy headlands.' Beowulf slays nine sea monsters with his sword. Then at Grendel's mere he again suffers their assaults. 'They saw along the water many of the dragon kind, strange sea-dragons moving over the mere.' As Beowulf swims in the waters he is pursued and attacked by many monsters, who rend 'his war corselet with battle tusks'.

A fleet of Viking ships, each with its prow carved in the shape of a monster's head, and crowded with savage marauders, moving in round the Island of Lindisfarne in 793 and sailing up the Sound of Iona in 798, must have appeared to the inhabitants of these peaceful and venerable seats of Christian art and learning like a terrible embodiment of the popular imagery of sea-monsters. Much the same kind of dragon ships brought William the Norman and his army across the English Channel in 1066

42. The Norman Invasion fleet, the Bayeux Tapestry, c. 1077

[42]. The northern and western waters of Scotland were still coursed by dragon ships in the thirteenth century. An account of the campaign against Scotland undertaken by King Hakon of Norway in 1263 describes the royal galley as ornamented with heads and necks of dragons beautifully overlaid with gold. The writer comments on the great strength of the fleet and the army which it conveyed. 'No terrifier of dragons, guardians of the hoarded treasures, ever in one place beheld more numerous hosts.' By 'terrifier of dragons', in the traditional poetic parlance of the day, he means of course a warrior. The allusion to the dragon guarding treasure brings us again to the medieval folk-lore of monsters. The idea of the great and fierce guardian of treasure goes back to Greek and Latin classical authors such as Pliny, and was familiar to medieval cosmographers. In Scythia, as we have seen, the danger of griffins frightened men away from gold and jewels which abounded in that country. In Germanic literature the classical griffin is replaced by a beast of even more sinister shape and proportions. In the *Völsunga Saga* the giant Fafnir, transformed by greed into a huge and cruel dragon, guards the treasure of Andvari. The dragon leaves his den to drink at the water, making the earth shake and spewing

79

out poison before him. Sigurd conceals himself in a pit in the dragon's path, and as the monstrous beast rolls over him, pierces its heart [43]. In the poem *Beowulf,* this deed is attributed to Sigurd's father Sigmund: 'He killed the dragon, the guardian of the treasure. Under the grey stone he ventured alone, the son of a chieftain, on the daring quest. . . . The dragon died violently.' This story is narrated at Heorot, at the feast when Beowulf's victory over Grendel is celebrated. It foreshadows the dark ending of the poem, when a treasure, 'the great relics of a noble race', is won by Beowulf at the cost of his life in a

43. Sigurd killing Fafnir, Ramsund, 11th century

terrible duel with a fire dragon, 'a dread gleaming monster'. 'The guardian of the treasure was in savage mood. He cast forth deadly fire . . . he rushed at the mighty man when occasion offered, hot and fierce in fight, and enclosed his whole neck between his sharp teeth. Beowulf grew stained with his own life blood . . .'

The epic struggles of men and monsters which are such a feature of Dark Age literature are reflected in innumerable early medieval works of art. On a sixth-century silver fibula from Grönby, Schonen, Sweden, a man's face appears from amidst a thick tangle of dragons' bodies, his throat clutched by à monstrous beak, while rearing up behind him is the arched neck, gaping jaws, pointed fangs, and lolling tongue of a great dragon [44]. In a seventh-century Frankish buckle of vigorous open-work design, at Rouen, similar long-arched dragons' necks and mouths grope down at either side of a glaring bullet-

44. Grönby Fibula, 6th century

shaped human head perched on a diminutive body [53]. The
man himself undergoes transformation into a dragon. His short
curved arms end in huge beaked animal heads, while his legs
form a writhing scroll-work and end also in beasts' heads,
attacked and bitten by his own dragon-shaped hands. A fragmentary eighth-century sandstone relief from Rosemarkie in
Ross shows a bearded man's head, in profile, staring into the
open mouth and the great teeth of a gigantic wolf-like monster,
its jaws and throat emphasized by a double line and its ear-base
marked by a scroll, as in the wolf of Ardross [45]. Immediately
above the heads of the wolf and the man are the four trampling
feet of another beast. The tongue, muzzle and teeth of yet
another beast touch the back of the man's head, and a further
wolf's head bores into his chest. The man's head may not belong
to a human figure, but to the evil four-footed Manticora, a
monstrous creature familiar from the medieval *Bestiary,* a tiger

45. Fragment of a relief sculpture, Rosemarkie, 8th century

with a human face. A claustrophobic world of violence and menace is created by the Pictish sculptor in this small broken slab, less than a foot square.

On a gilt bronze plaque, now in the Museum at St-Germain-en-Laye, a similar mood is engendered [46]. At the left of the plaque a human head or human mask, expressionless, impassive, like the heads on the Gerete bracteate, is gripped in the widely gaping maw of a wolf. Both wolf's head and man's head

46. Bronze plaque, 8th century

are attached to long gently curved serpents' bodies which trail away, to meet and cross other snakes similarly terminating in human or wolves' heads, or with pointed snakes' heads which give a sudden deadly twist round, to sting or throttle some adjacent serpent. The sense of slow purposeful slithering, of a cold twining action, is brilliantly accentuated by the six shallow bosses irregularly arranged across the surface of the plaque. These bosses are decorated with tight patterns of concentric rings which seem to revolve like records on a turntable, while the huge snakes crawl to and fro. The masterly use of asymmetry, the richness and grandeur of the composition, the vitality and inventiveness of all the formal elements and the technical prowess, link the St-Germain plaque with the contemporary cross-slab at Nigg, where the matted strapwork bosses are similarly straddled and looped about with adders' bodies. The swift inner whorls on the plaque, and the long curves of the snakes sweeping off at a tangent, are also strikingly akin in feeling to the draperies of Christ on the Vézelay tympanum more than three centuries later, where oddly enough the chip-carving patterns of the recessed background of the St-Germain plaque are revived by the great Romanesque sculptor, on the skirts of an apostle at the left of Christ, as an extension of the superb range of textured surfaces.

The designs which we have considered so far have probably no specific meaning, though they reflect a taste for fantasy and radical stylization, and are clearly enough influenced by a picture of man's life as a struggle, epic, dangerous, uncertain, in a hostile environment. In the magnificently carved wooden cart from the ship burial of a ninth-century Norwegian queen, at Oseberg, however, the imagery of a man surrounded by

47. Detail from the Oseberg Cart, *c.* 850

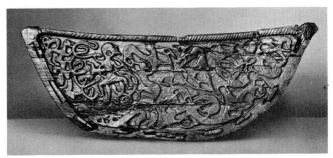

serpents rises to the level of narrative illustration. On the front of the cart, at the left, a man with a big head and small body squats amidst a mass of snakes, which drive their oval heads in upon him from all directions [47]. Two he grasps and fends off as they rush towards his throat. But others have already attacked his legs, a slim snake creeps up his body in front, and a toad-like creature has fastened itself to his right side. This carving must represent the death of a hero such as Gunnar, who in the *Völsunga Saga* refuses to betray the secret of the gold hoard to Attila, and dies in a pit full of loathsome snakes. In the Gunnar story, the hero's hands are bound but he plays a harp with his feet, and succeeds in charming all the snakes to sleep, except for one large ugly adder which crawls up to him and stings him in the very heart. These details are missing from the Oseberg carving. The snake pit story was doubtless applied as a fero-cious climax to many tales of violence and revenge as in the *Saga of Ragnar Loðbrók,* the famous historical Viking who obtained a tribute of seven thousand pounds of silver at Paris from Charles the Bald, and whose sons invaded and conquered half England. Ragnar meets his death in a snake pit, where he sits for a long time. When none of the snakes attack him, his uppermost garment is stripped off by his tormentors, and

48. Rune stone at Jelling, Jutland, 965-85

49. Crucifixion in St Gall Gospels, *c.* 750

'straightway all the snakes hung upon him with all their might. Fiercely the fangs of the snakes strike home.' Then says the hero, 'Among the beasts I shall soon lie dead . . .'

Sometime between 965 and 985 Harald Bluetooth, the first Christian King of Denmark, erected at Jelling in Jutland a grandiose sculptured memorial to his father and mother and to his own victories and achievements. One whole face of the stone, and the base of other two sides, carry a runic inscription which reads 'King Harald had this memorial set up to Gorm his father and Thyra his mother; King Harald who conquered all Denmark, and Norway, and who made the Danes Christian'. This last phrase appears beneath a representation of Christ crucified, one of the strangest versions of the subject to have come down to us [48]. In certain insular representations of Christ on the cross, for example in the eighth-century Gospels of St Gall [49], Christ wears a robe or *collobium* which is wound in bandage-like strands about his body, passing down his shoulders in diagonal strips, looped about his outspread arms and tightened across his chest, strapped horizontally about his waist, and again wound about his legs in a loose double loop. From some such stylized rendering of the *collobium,* perhaps, the sculptor of the Jelling stone has derived his sweeping pattern of broad bands slung over the outstretched arms and threaded through in a great chain system about Christ's waist and thighs. Beyond the outline of the frontal rigid figure there is no cross, only a thick coiling mass of tendrils, swelling occasionally into vast iron girders and knots. The Passion is here interpreted in terms of the ambiguous formal language of a Dark Age ornament like the Grönby fibula and the Rouen buckle [44, 53]. Christ is tethered with great chains, and the stony cavern of his captivity is infested with faceless snakes.

Already in the eighth century, in the poem *Beowulf,* we were aware of a strong theological element in the presentation and characterization of the monstrous enemies of mankind with whom the hero has to contend. I have remarked on Grendel's Satanic qualities. The traditional monster lore of the early Middle Ages, and the epic battles of men and monsters which are such a feature of Dark Age poems and sagas, inevitably coalesced in the popular Christian imagination in the literary and pictorial iconography of Hell. In the Old English poem *Christ and Satan,* for example, the fallen angel laments like an exiled thegn: 'Where has gone the glory of angels which we were wont to possess in heaven? Lo! in the presence of God we had delight formerly, singing in heaven in happier times, where now around the Eternal stand the noble ones about the throne . . .' Satan inhabits a sort of nether Scythia, full of horrors. 'At times heat and cold are mingled. At times I hear the creatures of Hell, the sorrowing race bemoaning the abysses under the headlands. At times naked men strive amid serpents. This windy hall is all filled with evil . . . Here is the hiss of adders, and serpents have here their dwelling. This tormenting bond is fast fettered.' Satan's malice is directed against mankind, whose souls 'he may bear to a home in bondage'. The drawing of Hell in the eleventh-century *Marvels of the East* shows the souls of the wicked wound round with snakes. Another memorable portrait of Hell was drawn by the artist of an eleventh-century Psalter in the British Museum, Cotton MS. Tiberius C. vi, in his representation of Christ raising the souls of the just patriarchs [50]. Christ tramples down the crooked snarling figure of Satan, naked, with pointed tufts of hair like the madmen of Vézelay, his clawed hands and feet ringed and fettered. He lies above a winged dragon, with open jaws and a long scaly

tail. Alongside Satan and the dragon is a vast inverted beast's head, out of which the redeemed souls are being lifted. This is the maw of Hell, ready to swallow up the souls of the damned, as Grendel ravenously devoured the warrior at Heorot.

In Romanesque art the motif familiar on Dark Age ornaments of the human figure lost in the strong folds of serpents or

87

51. Capital with man and monster, Chauvigny, 12th century

52. Capital with Miser's death, Besse-en-Chandesse, 12th century

menacingly pursued or pressed in upon by vast jaws, takes on the role of the soul, naked, at the mercy of devils. On a twelfth-century capital at the church of St-Pierre at Chauvigny, a human soul is clutched in the forepaws of an immense double-bodied dragon, with wings and coiled encrusted tail [51]. The monster's wide span of teeth is poised over the head of its victim, just as the human face on the St-Germain plaque was framed by the teeth and distended wolfish jaws of a dragon. On another twelfth-century capital in the church of Besse-en-Chandesse, Puy-de-Dôme, three brutish demons with roaring mouths grab and swing upside down, like a victim in some pre-historic pagan ritual, the naked soul of a newly expired sinner. His corpse lies upon its death-bed, and under the bed is his money-box, ironically guarded like the treasure hoards of legend by a long coiling worm, which will now punish the avaricious man in Hell [52]. The surface of the capital is cut away so that the bent interlocked arms and legs and thick-set

53. Frankish belt buckle, 7th century

bodies of the bull-headed devils and of their prey, stand out in high relief. The vivid pattern quality which results is strikingly close to that of the seventh-century open-work Rouen belt buckle [53], and the violence of the Romanesque theme and treatment seem like an extension into High Medieval didactic art of that generalized ferocity so prevalent in Dark Age weapons and jewellery.

The death and torments of a miser were also represented by the great sculptor of the porch of Moissac, about 1125. Here the iconographic programme is elaborate and allusive. On the left side of the porch is displayed the story of Dives and Lazarus, narrated in St Luke's Gospel, chapter 16. It shows the rich man luxuriating at his table while the beggar starves outside his closed doors, and then their changed fortunes in the after life [54]. The words of the Magnificat, 'He hath filled the hungry with good things, and the rich he hath sent empty away', form a link between the Dives and Lazarus theme and the Nativity cycle on the right side of the porch. The Dives and Lazarus theme also makes sense beside the vast representation of the Majesty of God in the main tympanum of the porch, illustrating the Book of Revelation, chapter 4, because of the moral and didactic content of the Letter to the Laodiceans at the end of chapter 3 of Revelation, which states 'Because thou sayest, I am rich, and increased with goods, and have need of nothing, and knowest not that thou art wretched and miserable and poor and blind and naked. . . . Behold, I stand at the door and knock. If any man hear my voice, and open the door, I will come in to him, and will sup with him, and he with me . . .'

The art of Moissac is grand and monumental, sophisticated and learned, yet we are still able to trace in the plethora of forms and their disposition aesthetic tendencies and habits of mind going back a long way into the deep past of European culture. In the hollows cut from the jambs of the portal, folded shell-like plants, stout little birds, and humped rodents crawl and edge their way upwards, producing an erratically embossed texture, and a curious effect of infestation, such as must once have appeared on the cicada-covered mantle of King Childeric. The sculptures on the left side of the porch terminate in a broad vertical panel, loaded with a Jelling-like strapwork, with leaf forms like the claws and mouths on the Snartemo sword hilt, and a row of grinning masks emerging from the matted gar-lands, reminiscent of the masks on the Ålleberg gold collar.

54. Sculptures on west inner wall of the porch of Moissac, *c.* 1125

Below the narrative scenes of Dives and Lazarus, two large-scale reliefs show a figure symbolizing Avarice and a figure symbolizing Lust, each accompanied by a demon. As in the seventh-century Torslunda beast-leader plaque, the human and animal figures stand side by side [55, 56]. In the horrid confrontation at Moissac the ancient theme of man versus monster reaches its climax. The demon who grasps the wrist of his victim is muscular yet insect-like, obese yet emaciated, human in outline yet with the clawed feet of a wolf or bear, and with a cruel, distorted, bestial head. Here is the authentic likeness of a denizen of Hell, he whom Marbodus, Bishop of Rennes, in his poem on the Legend of Theophilus, calls *Satanas rex, mortis imago*. Beside the demon stands Lust, a naked woman, grim and desolate, the arms bent and the hands flung up in a staccato gesture of despair, the fingers digging into the palms, the head

55. Man leading a bear, Torslunda, *c.* 600

tilted forward so that at first all that we can see is the hair in
long snakey locks, masking the skull-like face. This is Eve, the
Mother of all Living, after she has tasted death in obedience to the
Tempter's voice. In the eleventh-century Tongres ivory of the
Crucifixion, a personification of Mother Earth, *Terra*, sits holding a growing tree and a serpent, creatures of earth [149].
In other classicizing ivories of the Carolingian period *Terra*
suckles serpents at her breasts. At Moissac this classical image
of fruitful Nature has been subverted, transformed. The snakes,
heavy as pythons at the breasts of Lust and swagged over her
arms, torment and devour her, like the snakes closing in upon
the doomed hero on the Oseberg cart.

At Souillac, about 1125, the great tympanum of the church
portal was sculptured with the story of the pledge of service
given by the apostate Theophilus to Satan. Below, on the

56. A Demon and a personification of Lust,
Moissac, *c.* 1125

93

trumeau or central supporting column of the portal, a group of monstrous beasts are locked in furious combat [57]. Magnificent lions and griffins, those exotic guardians of treasure whom Marbodus of Rennes interpreted as the enemies of the human soul, stand in pairs, their bodies opposed and diagonally crossed to form a heraldic design originally suggested, perhaps, by some great Byzantine silk. The griffins thrust their necks round the slender shafts which mark the edges of the trumeau, rupturing them, tugging them out of position like stretched elastic, so that their architectural function is negated and the whole structure, packed from top to bottom with fantastic gymnastic animals, seems ready to topple. The back-turned heads of the griffins savagely bite the bodies of beasts and birds which slide and tumble past them down to the base of the trumeau. At the top, a naked man is trapped between two monsters. The parrot-like beak of a griffin bites his right flank, and his head is seized in the jaws of a shaggy wolf or lion. This energetic visual fantasy sums up many centuries of European art – the sustained inventive pattern-making, the delight in cumulative and complex interwoven linear and plastic forms, and that dark undercurrent of vehemence and tension most often expressed in the representation of the destructive teeth and talons of ferocious beasts.

Shortly before the Souillac trumeau was carved, St Bernard of Clairvaux, the great mystic and reformer of monastic life in western Europe, wrote his famous *Apologia ad Willelmum* in which he questions and repudiates certain aspects of the contemporary visual arts: 'In the cloisters', he writes,

under the eyes of the brethren engaged in reading, what business has there that ridiculous monstrosity, that amazing mis-shapen shapeliness and shapely mis-shapenness? Those unclean monkeys? Those fierce lions? Those monstrous centaurs? Those semi-human beings? Those spotted tigers? Those fighting warriors? Those huntsmen blowing their horns? Here you behold several bodies beneath one head; there again several heads upon one body. Here you see a quadruped with the tail of a serpent; there a fish with the head of a quadruped. There an animal suggests a horse in front and half a goat behind; here a horned beast exhibits the rear part of a horse. In fine, on all sides there appears so rich and so amazing a variety of forms that it is more delightful to read the marbles than the manuscripts, and to spend the whole day in admiring these things, piece by piece, rather than in meditating on the Law of God.

These words precisely describe the art of decoration inherited by the Romanesque world from its pre-Carolingian antecedents. At the end of a long uniform development, St

Bernard's strictures parallel those of Alcuin near its beginning, in 797, indignantly blaming the monks of Lindisfarne for their interest in songs about Ingeld, the epic hero mentioned in *Beowulf*. 'What', asks Alcuin, 'has Ingeld to do with Christ?' Either in consequence of St Bernard's criticism, or because the same ideas were in their minds, many enlightened men, patrons and artists around the middle years of the twelfth century, paused and gave thought to the problems of Christian art. One of these men was Abbot Suger, whose achievements as the promoter of Gothic art I have discussed in another volume of this series. As European civilization, and above all French civilization, began suddenly to advance on all fronts, economic, political, and intellectual, the need made itself felt for a clarification of visual imagery, for a disciplined presentation, for a consistent tone, for a sense in art – as in all periods of renaissance – of man's control and understanding of his environment, for a renunciation of the simple formulas of the epic past, and a consciousness of a new beginning.

4

The Uses of Antiquity

The sixth-century Byzantine Emperor Tiberius II was walking
one day in the Great Palace at Constantinople when he noticed
inset on the floor of a certain chamber a marble slab carved with
the sign of the cross. 'By thy Cross, O Lord', exclaimed the
Emperor indignantly, 'we defend our brows and breasts, yet
here we trample it under our feet!' He gave orders that the slab
should be removed and set upright. But the workmen who
levered it out found beneath it another slab likewise marked
with the cross, and when this in turn had been lifted, a third
identical slab lay exposed. At the Emperor's command, they
again went to work and raised the third slab. They found
beneath it a dazzling treasure, consisting of over a hundred
thousand pounds weight of gold, more than enough to offset
the Emperor's lavish almsgiving and to stabilize the finances of
the Empire.

Features of this anecdote, and of the story which immediately
follows it in Gregory of Tours's *History of the Franks* about the
golden hoard hidden by Duke Narses in a cistern, the secret of
which he confided to one old man, will put devotees of Dr M.
R. James's ghost stories in mind of *The Treasure of Abbot Thomas*.
From our present point of view, however, the interest of the
anecdote lies in the Emperor's scruples about the use of the cross
as decoration on a pavement. A century later, the Greek Church
Council of 692, known as the *Trullanum* after the circular apart-
ment in the Great Palace at Constantinople where it met, officially decreed as its seventy-third canon that no one, on pain
of excommunication, should inscribe the sign of the cross in a
lowly position, either on the earth itself or in mosaic inlay or on
marble paving stones. It is fortunate for historians of the British
church that Early Christian landowners in the south west of
Britain in the fourth century felt it no dishonour to the cross to
represent it on the pavements of their villas. For one of the
most substantial pieces of evidence for the Christian faith and
Christian places of worship in Roman Britain consists of mosaic
floors decorated with medallions containing Christ's portrait

or the Chi Rho monogram, that is, the first two letters of Christ's name in Greek, and with the cross variously employed as a governing factor in the all-over design. At Frampton in Dorset a Romano-British Christian of the fourth century had a floor laid in his villa in a square room opening into an apse. At the entrance to the apse, where presumably the altar stood, the floor was inscribed with the Chi Rho monogram. In the main square portion of the room, surrounded by a band decorated with dolphins issuing from the head of Neptune, was a mosaic sub-

divided into squares, lunettes, and a central medallion, the
lunettes forming the terminals of a large cross, and the medallion its centre. Another narrower rectangular room at Frampton
Villa displayed a central medallion containing the head of
Neptune, and in four other medallions the bust-length portraits
of tritons holding conches [58]. In the interstices between the
medallion heads were four big clearly marked equal armed
crosses. At either end of the floor where the repeat pattern of
crosses was interrupted by the border, the cross lost its final arm,

58 (*opposite*). Frampton Villa mosaic, 4th century

59. Carpet pattern, Lindisfarne Gospels, *c.* 698

being reduced to a T-shaped motif, like the central letter of 'Sator' along the top of the ancient and enigmatic sacred inscription known as the *Sator* square (see p. 220).

In the seventh century the new Christians of the English nation, not just in the south but also in Northumbria, must have known many extant Roman buildings ornamented with great tesserated floors, battered and despoiled but not yet vanished under the weeds and turf. The Christian symbols which some of these floors displayed must have attracted devotion, their admixture of Antique imagery, gods and dolphins and horsemen, must have given them exotic charm, and the splendour of the formal patterns, the geometric compartments, the chequers, and thick meshed strapwork, must have appealed as a grand and coherent decorative language. The influence of the Roman villa floors may perhaps be traced in the Early Christian art of the English, in the luxury Gospel Books produced in eastern England, especially in the northeast, from about the middle of the seventh century. In front of each of the Gospels in these manuscripts, like an inner cover, is a page carrying a rectangular ornamented design or carpet-pattern. The prefatory page to St John's Gospel in the Gospels written by Eadfrith, Bishop of Lindisfarne, uses exactly the motif of the cross which we have seen at Frampton Villa, clearly drawn with equal arms at the centre of the page and cut down to a T-shape on the extremities of the design [59]. Of course there are many ways in which the idea of an all-over pattern of crosses might have been conveyed to the English. In a later chapter we shall come upon textiles and metalwork displaying interlocked or scattered crosses. But the mosaic analogy for the carpet pages in the great insular manuscripts is tempting, and may provide us with our first example of a medieval artist's use of Antique ideas.

As we have seen, the Romano–British mosaics contain figures and figure-scenes from classical mythology. The heads of Neptune and tritons inhabit the cruciform mosaics of Frampton. Perhaps the four tritons with their wind-blown hair and their uplifted conches were interpreted by the Christian owner of the villa as the four angels of the Apocalypse who stand at the four corners of the earth, holding the four winds, 'so that the wind should not blow on the earth or on the sea'. Classical mythological scenes certainly appear to have lost their significance as relics of pagan belief or even of pre-Christian culture, and were evidently being interpreted morally and spiritually in a Christian context, with something of the ingenuity and ingenuousness which Rupert of Deutz displays centuries later in his refined allegorical interpretations of the sensuous *Song of Songs*. At the centre of the great cross on the floor of the square room at Frampton, Bellerophon riding on the winged Pegasus joined contest with the monstrous three-headed Chimera. Another Bellerophon mosaic occurs in a compartment of the famous Hinton St Mary floor, adjacent to the medallion head of Christ. This incident from classical myth was depicted only a few feet from the sites of Christian altars not presumably in any spirit of ill-educated opportunism and compromise but because the theme of spiritual combat, a 'war in heaven', good against evil, could at that particular time be represented allegorically, using the old familiar classical literary repertoire. The Middle Ages proper made little or no use of a system of 'types' drawn from classical mythology, preferring as the classical contribution to the truth of Christianity the patent allusions to the Saviour in Virgil's fourth *Eclogue* and the prophecies of the Sibyl of Tibur. In the tenth-century St Dunstan, Abbot of Glastonbury and afterwards Archbishop of Canterbury, felt only regret for his youthful embroilment with the love poetry of Ovid. The *Ars amandi* could not be frozen into a chaste allegory of Christ's love for his Church, but smouldered fitfully on in the poetry of the Troubadours and Romancers.

When we again meet the theme of Bellerophon and Chimera, in early medieval art, it carries no overtones of an *interpretatio christiana*, that short-lived allegorizing process for which we seem to have evidence at Frampton. The Chimera rushes eagerly towards Bellerophon on a page listing the contents of Genesis in the First Bible of Charles the Bald, and in the upper frame of folio 110 of the Lothair Evangeliary, both of the second quarter of the ninth century [60]. Here the hero and his adversary are reduced to mere marginal decorations. The Carolingian drawing

60. Bellerophon and the Chimera, Tours, *c.* 850

can have no links with any stylistically or iconographically weighty representation of the subject. The illuminator's source of inspiration must simply have been the diminutive engraved design on some finger ring, like that of the onyx ring found at Havering-atte-Bower, Essex, now in the British Museum – the sort of stone which is listed in a medieval catalogue of engraved stones as endowing its owner with swiftness of foot and boldness in war. Classical imagery creeps into the ken of the medieval artist through the narrowest of vents. Here we are very far from that confrontation with Antiquity – the casual meeting of equals – which Benvenuto Cellini experienced when he admired and tinkered with the great bronze Chimera from Arezzo, in the palace of Duke Cosimo de' Medici. No artist of Charlemagne's day would have understood the flattering phrases which Cellini loved to overhear about his work, such as 'far superior to the ancients'. The Chimera in the Carolingian books is employed, along with elephants and lions and centaurs, in the hope of imparting a fashionable classical flavour to the illuminated biblical text. The height of ambition is to emulate Antiquity, not to outdo it, and the sources of visual knowledge which are accessible and comprehensible are at first extremely restricted. The small sprightly Carolingian Chimera has no ferocity, none of the terribleness to which Pollaiuolo and Mantegna were to respond in the Antique. However, the silhouette of the Chimera was not without value as an artistic mentor and model for early medieval draughtsmen. Illustrators called upon to provide pictures for the text of the Book of Revelation were confronted with a strange breed of creatures, Hebrew, not classical, in origin. Many of these, such as the locusts, so oddly described by St John as like mail-clad horses with men's faces and women's hair, posed problems for their portrayers. But the great beast on which the Whore of Babylon rides was a straight-forward enough monster, except for its plethora of heads. In the later Middle Ages it was to be represented with seven equal heads on seven long thin necks, each of which rises independently from its brutish shoulders. But in Carolingian and Ottonian times the beast was painted with a single great neck and head, with six other diminutive heads sticking up in a bristling row along the length of its neck, just as the goat-head projects abruptly from the back of the Chimera [118, 119]. The pictorial traditions of Antiquity are here being picked over in search of shreds and scraps, for re-use in a wholly different intellectual context.

In the fourth decade of the twelfth century, as Abbot Suger brooded over the accumulated splendours of the treasury of St-Denis, his mind inevitably turned with envious longing to Constantinople, the El Dorado of the early medieval world. In his *De administratione*, which is in large measure his personal inventory of and commentary on the St-Denis treasures, Suger wrote: 'From very many truthful men . . . we had heard wonderful and almost incredible reports about the superiority of Hagia Sophia's and other churches' ornaments for the celebration of Mass.' For his own peace of mind as a collector he had tried, as he says, 'to learn from those to whom the treasures of Constantinople and the ornaments of Hagia Sophia had been accessible, whether the things here [at St-Denis] could claim some value in comparison with those there . . .' If Constantinople still in the twelfth century provided a standard of cultural excellence, how much more was it looked up to by the Barbarian nations of western Europe in the early Middle Ages, for whom it represented the unbroken continuity of the Roman Empire. The desire to participate in that glorious Christian classical culture is one of the great motivations of early medieval society in the West. Bede begins his account of the conversion of the English people with the words 'In the year of Our Lord 582, Maurice, the fifty-fourth from Augustus, ascended the throne, and reigned twenty-one years'. Pope Gregory's letter to the newly converted Ethelbert of Kent is dated likewise from the nineteenth regnal year of the Emperor Maurice, that is, the Byzantine Emperor, heir and successor to the treasure-finding Tiberius II. When these terms of reference are employed, Romanism is evidently an active and present force. The wealth and prestige of the Eastern Roman Empire was a useful stimulus to the struggling petty nations of the West. Thus when Chilperic, King of the Franks, received a diplomatic gift from Tiberius II of massive gold medals inscribed on the obverse with the Emperor's image and the sonorous title *Tiberii Constantini Perpetui Augusti*, and on the reverse a four-horse chariot and the words *Gloria Romanorum*, his reaction was positive and mature. He ordered his goldsmiths to make a great gold salver, weighing fifty pounds, studded with gems, which he displayed saying 'This have I made for the glory and ennoblement of the Frankish race.' Political greatness found symbolic expression in shows of material wealth, just as it did in the literally golden days of Rome's prosperity, in the triumphs with which the heroes of the state were honoured.

In a sense even the pagan English Sutton Hoo treasure, although perhaps fairly remote from classical models in style, responds to an Antique ideal of personal and national grandeur. The King of Sutton Hoo was not impervious to Roman standards of symbolic ostentation, since he owned a quantity of Byzantine plate including a vast silver dish bearing the stamp of the Emperor Anastasius, and in his collection of coins, all in mint condition, he acknowledged, even if at second or third hand, the cultural significance of imperial currency. The coins

61A. Coin of St Eligius

61B. Silver denier of Charlemagne, 806–14

61C. Coin of Constantine displaying the labarum, 326 or 327 A.D.

found in the purse in the King's cenotaph at Sutton Hoo are not Byzantine but Frankish, some of them closely resembling coins designed by Eligius when he was in charge of the Palace mint at Paris [61 A]. Frankish coins were directly modelled on past and current Byzantine coins, and are thus a strikingly practical example of the revival of the classical artistic language. The *solidus* issued by Theudebert, grandson of the first Christian king of the Franks, was based on a type of Justinian. In the sixth century also, coins of Justin II and especially of Maurice were copied. The development of the Frankish mints gave substance and meaning to the idea of 'the glory of the Franks', and this process was crowned by the silver *deniers* issued in the later years of the reign of Charlemagne [61 B].

In respect of the high value set upon Roman forms by the Barbarian peoples of the new Europe, we can trace some sort of historical continuity and consistency of attitude among the Scandinavians, the Goths, the Merovingian Franks, and finally the Franks of the Carolingian age. But with the coming of the Carolingians, there was a great intensification of interest. The Carolingians were the first ruling family of post-Roman Europe powerful enough to have scope for Roman pretensions, and the first to indulge in sophisticated self-conscious antiquarianism. Charlemagne's prodigious career was set in motion by his inherited territorial wealth in Frankland and by the established prestige of his family as champions of the Church against Islam on the one hand and German paganism on the other. But the success which he achieved was largely due, like Napoleon's, to his skill in seizing the opportunities presented by a drifting and shifting world situation, and to his genius as a military leader and as an administrator. By the force of his personality he directed and speeded up events, confirmed and realized all kinds of current hopes and theories, and built himself up to embody for the men of his own and later generations the idea of a Roman Emperor [62]. On Christmas Day in the year 800 Charles

Charlemagne's
ne,
nen, *c*. 800

was crowned by Pope Leo III in St Peter's, and hailed by the assembled congregation, drawn from very many European peoples, as 'Charles Augustus, the great and pacific Emperor of the Romans'. Coins struck after his coronation bear the words 'Restoration of the Empire'. It is true that Charlemagne's portrait on his late *denier* shows him with a heavy moustache, almost as incongruous in the visual context as the moustache worn by the figure of Christ adored by the beasts on the Ruthwell Cross [63]. But otherwise the Emperor's broad and flaccid head recalls Nero or Vitellius, and he wears the triumphal wreath about his brow. Round the edge of the coin are the words *Karolus Imp. Aug.*

Imperial imagery and the epigraphy of the Roman world is vigorously brought to life in France and Western Germany in

63. Christ adored
by beasts,
the Ruthwell Cross,
7th century (?)

the early ninth century. Historians no longer dated events by the reigns of the far-off successors of Augustus in the Greek half of the Empire. Caesar was at hand, in the Latin West. Nor was imperial imagery confined to the official products of the royal moneyers. It begins to appear also in Carolingian art. In the Evangeliary of Prüm, on the first page of St Matthew's Gospel, under the great letters of *Liber generationis*, the illuminator depicts two coins or medals, one showing a profile head facing left and inscribed *D[avi]d Imperator Augustus* and the other with a profile head facing right, inscribed *David Rex Imperator*, a calculated blending of the traditions of Rome and Israel [64]. At the court of Charlemagne his inner circle of learned friends constituted themselves as an informal Academy and each adopted the name of some great literary figure of the

64. Beginning of St Matthew's Gospel, Prüm Gospels, 9th century

past, such as Homer and Pindar. Charlemagne himself assumed the pseudonym 'David'. The English scholar Alcuin, who functioned as Charlemagne's Minister for Education, addresses his master in letters as 'King David, illumined with the brightness of all wisdom', 'sweetest King David', 'King David, *victor maximus*'. The biblical David, shepherd of his people, warrior, inspired prophet and poet of the Psalms, represented for medieval men the standard of God-ordained monarchy. In Carolingian eyes he took on the universal sway and authority vested historically in the Roman Emperor. This fantastic political and religious interpretation is vividly summed up in a ninth-century ivory relief at Monza where King David appears in the guise of a Roman consul, as represented on fifth-century consular diptychs, handsomely robed, initiating with a commanding gesture the imperial games. [65].

65. Diptych with figures of King David and Pope Grego the Great, 9th century (?)

The same readiness to render unto God that which is God's, and also unto God that which is Caesar's, is a marked feature of certain early medieval ecclesiastical metalwork. At the centre of the Cross of Eligius at St-Denis [136] was an Antique agate cameo, the head being assumed to be that of a sacred person or a Christian ruler. The beauty and value of Antique portrait gems no doubt sufficiently accounts for their being so frequently found as ornaments of the grand church crosses of the Middle Ages, but recognizably imperial portraits were perhaps specially welcome in this context because the labarum, the original Christian–imperial standard made by Constantine's goldsmiths at his direct orders, bore below the triumphal wreath and monogram of Christ the bust-length figures of the Emperor and his family [61 C]. A large silver-gilt processional cross at Brescia, made probably in the eighth century, of

. Portrait of a
other and
r two children,
century

Lombard or Carolingian manufacture, has a spectacular Late-Antique gold-glass portrait medallion of an aristocratic family group, bust-length, set near the base of the stem [66, 134]. The golden cross of Lothair in the Treasury of Aachen Minster, dating to around the year 1000, was given a strong Antique and imperial connotation – Constantinian in the intention of the goldsmith and his patron – by having a great cameo of Augustus set at its centre [135].

Antique fashions in art made perhaps their most direct and potent appeal to the barbarian nations in the form of engraved gem stones, small portable objects in which art and wealth were merged. They were the currency of diplomacy as much as medals and plate. Charlemagne used a gem cut with the head of Jupiter Serapis as his signet. One of the most noble possessions of the Carolingian Emperors was a superb aquamarine carved with an intaglio portrait of the Roman Emperor Titus's daughter Julia, set face downwards on a foil of gold so that the profile portrait rises as it were in relief within the thickness of the translucent stone. This splendid gem may have come to Charlemagne as a gift from the imperial treasury at Constantinople. It was set

67. The *Escrin* of Charlemagne, 9th century

as the crest of a fantastic many-tiered arcaded relief of jewels and gold known as the *Escrin* of Charlemagne, given by Charles the Bald to the Abbey of St-Denis and preserved there until 1791 [67]. Then because it belonged to the Antique world and not to the despised Middle Ages, the intaglio was preserved as an interesting relic when the *Escrin* itself was demolished at the public mint. One of the gems fixed to the frame of the great intaglio is carved with a Greek monogram identifying the head of Julia as that of the Virgin Mary, a striking example of the Christianization of an Antique portrait, paralleling the Augustus-Constantine conflation on the jewelled crosses. But for the Middle Ages engraved gemstones were steeped in significance beyond any immediate religious function. They were a tangible link with the classical intellectual and literary, as well as artistic, traditions.

The lore of gemstones had been fully set out by Pliny in Book XXXVII of his *Natural History*. In that book the happy owner of stones like the Julia intaglio could read about the varieties and colours of beryls and how best they should be shaped and set. He could read about the marvellous luminosity of emeralds, which alone of gems satisfy without sating the eyes. He would learn the advantages of an engraved sardonyx as a signet, and acquire a connoisseur's appreciation of its colour and banding. He would learn that amethysts are easy to engrave, but that it is false to suppose that they prevent drunkenness or keep off hail or deflect spells. He would discover that amber benefits babies, when worn as an amulet, and that powdered and swallowed in water with mastic, cures affections of the stomach.

Gemstones and their qualities, as defined by Antique authors, held the interest of medieval people on many different levels. The lowest level was that of popular superstition regarding the magical properties of gemstones. In the Middle Ages the loss of iconographic literacy added to the mystique of various gems, since their engraved figures and inscriptions took on magical and incantatory powers. A notable example of this is the magnificent sardonyx cameo, nearly half a foot in length, 'almost too big to hold in one hand', which was presented to the Abbey of St Albans by the Anglo-Saxon King Aethelred II. Matthew Paris in his inventory of the jewels belonging to the Abbey describes it as being engraved with a figure clad in rags holding in one hand a spear on which a serpent is climbing, and on the other a boy with a shield on his shoulder. The main figure has an eagle with outspread wings at his feet. The gem can now be

68. The St Alban's Cameo called *Kaadmau*

recognized even from Paris's drawing [68] as a fourth-century portrait of a Roman emperor, wearing fringed military tunic and kilt, with the attributes of Aesculapius and a Victory in his hands. Such details, however, meant little to its medieval owners. In the early twelfth century Anketil, a monk of St Albans, a goldsmith and formerly moneyer to the King of Denmark, made a gold shrine for the relics of St Alban. His design at first incorporated the great cameo along with other engraved and polished stones. But on further consideration the community of St Albans decided not to fix the cameo on to the shrine but to preserve it detached in the treasury, so that its beneficial powers could still be made available to women in pregnancy or labour. The cameo, known popularly as *Kaadmau*, had a great reputation among expectant mothers, one of whom, after a successful delivery, kept the stone hidden for years in hope of further offspring. *Kaadmau* was solemnly laid between the patient's breasts, with an invocation of St Alban, and then little by little slithered down to the *occiduam corporis partem*, by which process delivery was assured, since the infant awaiting birth fled away from the approaching stone. Of all the uses to which the artistic monuments of Antiquity have been applied by later generations, few can be more bizarre.

It is, however, quite in keeping with the rather narrow approach to the subject of stones, their categories and virtues, exhibited by the twelfth-century German abbess St Hildegarde of Bingen. In the fourth book of her *Natural History* Hildegarde lists twenty-five kinds of precious stone, but she offers no information on the sources and distribution of them, nor any historical or sociological commentary nor visual description, nor does she discuss their uses other than in pseudo-medicine. If a woman is in difficult labour, the sard stone should be held *ad exitum infantis*, and you must say 'Open you, ways and door, in that manner of appearing in which Christ appeared, God and man, and opened the doors of Hell. So too, you infant, come out at that door, without your death and without the death of your mother.' Throughout the book very little first-hand information, either about the practical experiences of doctor and midwife, or about the enthusiasms of the geologist or stone collector, can be discerned. The subject of gemmology is diminished, not enhanced, by Hildegarde's barren catalogue of named but featureless stones and her monotonous list of complaints which they are imagined to allay. The method and principle of her work, the encyclopedic approach to natural phenomena, and the basic belief in the remedial quality of minerals, are classical in origin, but the content is both narrowed and warped in its medieval rehandling.

On the other hand, Marbodus, Bishop of Rennes, teacher and poet, who died at St Aubin's monastery at Angers in the year 1123 at the venerable age of eighty-eight, produced in his *Liber lapidum* a memorably many-sided study of the familiar list of gemstones. For him emeralds conquer all gems and all herbs by their greenness. They are prevalent in uninhabited deserts where, because of the cold, nothing lives except griffins, which symbolize demons who envy men their Christian faith and try to rob them of it. The sardonyx has three colours, red, white and black, signifying those who carry in their hearts the memory of Christ's Passion, who are pure white in mind, but who, without hypocrisy, condemn themselves as being black in sin. Marbodus's poem on stones, in eloquent leonine hexameters, has less medieval elements than his prose moral and allegorical essay. In the poem we have clear echoes of Pliny – the story of Nero's emerald eye-glass, the belief that rock crystal is deeply frozen ice, the facts that amethysts are easy to engrave and that onyx is so called after the human nail with its white band and flush of red beyond. Marbodus elegantly conveys classical lapidary learning to the literate and patron classes of the eleventh and twelfth centuries, the popularity of his poem among lay people being shown by its having been translated into French. His poem forms a link between Pliny's account of the collections of gemstones and the display stands of jewelled vases owned by Pompey the Great and Julius Caesar, and the passionate collecting of gemstones by the English King Henry I, to whose wife, Queen Mathilda, Marbodus addressed one of his shorter poems. Throughout his life King Henry 'amassed in wonderful vessels' a vast array of precious stones, hyacinths, sapphires, rubies, topazes, emeralds. After his death his collection was dispersed by the usurper Stephen of Blois, and, as it chanced, his jewels ultimately passed into the hands of Abbot Suger, who caused them to be set on the reverse face of his great gold cross at St-Denis. As the learned King Henry contemplated his prized stones, it must have pleased him to know not merely their familiar roles in sacred scripture, as the gems on the breast plate of the Jewish High Priest and in the foundations of the heavenly Jerusalem, but also their relations to Crete and India, Pyrrhus and Apollo.

69. The *Coupe des Ptolemées* with medieval mounts

Marbodus's versification of Pliny's critical appraisal of, for example, high-quality sardonyx stones must have influenced his own taste, his conception of the beautiful in material objects. He is a humanist poet, sensitive and strong in expression, very aware of visual beauty. In this context, we can recognize Abbot Suger too as a humanist, when he writes in his *De administratione*, with a fine mixture of didacticism and aesthetic enthusiasm, of the chalice which he procured for the altar of St-Denis, 'made out of one solid sardonyx, which word derives from *sardius* and *onyx*: in which one stone the sard's red hue, by varying its property, so strongly contrasts with the blackness of the onyx, that one property seems to be bent on trespassing upon the other.' Suger's chalice was a fluted Antique bowl, furnished at his orders with a jewelled rim, base, and handles. Just as monastic and cathedral libraries preserved and transmitted classical learning, so also scattered items of Antique art were safely lodged and given an honoured role in the service of the medieval Church. William of Malmesbury, Abbot Suger's contemporary, vividly conjures up for us the now vanished beauty of a great onyx vase, evidently Antique, which was sent as part of a diplomatic gift by Hugh the Great, Duke of the Franks, to King Athelstan in the tenth century, and which Athelstan deposited in Malmesbury Abbey. The vase was 'carved so subtly by the engraver's art that the corn sheaves seemed to stir, the vines to sprout, and the figures of the men to move.' The lost

70. The *Coupe des Ptolemées*, 2nd or 1st century B.C.

Athelstan vase inevitably reminds us of the wonderful sardonyx cup known as the *Coupe des Ptolemées*, which was presented to St-Denis by King Charles the Bald in the ninth century. This is magnificently carved with Bacchic scenes, emblems and animals, the heads of gods and men, and tall vines which spread their branches to shelter ornamented trestles loaded with sacred jars and vases. Suger transformed it, as well as the fluted bowl, into a chalice, and set the donor's name in verses round the base [69]. Happily it still survives, though stripped of its medieval trappings [70].

The appreciation of ancient engraved stones, for the charm of their colour and texture and the skill of the artistry expended upon them, is amply proved by the many portraits of classical intaglios, cut with human figures, slender cranes and quadrupeds, with which the Carolingian illuminators of the Court School ornamented their pages, for example in the arches over the seated figures of the Evangelists. The experience of carefully reproducing the designs of intaglios profoundly influenced their own art of illumination. In a series of mid-ninth-century manuscripts, narrative and figure scenes take on the appearance of intaglios, the figures being seen in silhouette, dark on light or light on dark. In the Bamberg Bible Adam names the beasts – a dark pin man facing a crowd of silhouetted crouching animals and flying birds. In the Sacramentary of Marmoutier great medallions contain busy little scenes of the Nativity, the Baptism and the Last Supper, all designed in silhouette. On another page of the same manuscript, figures of a congregation bowing to receive the benediction, and of Virtues holding giant symbols, are set against dark disks [71]. The appeal of figured gems was not limited merely to pictorial imitations. The great rock-crystal disk of Lothair II, King of Lotharingia, with its eight scenes from the story of Susanna and the Elders, witnesses to the revival of the difficult glyptic art by Carolingian craftsmen. The figures show up dark against a light ground, or light against dark, depending on how the light falls on to the disk [72]. The polished convex crystal is engraved on its flat underside so that the figures appear like relief sculptures in the depths of the stone, exactly the technique used by Euodus, the Antique artist who engraved the Julia intaglio on the *Escrin* of Charlemagne. In its scale and technical brilliance the Lothair Crystal is a product of the strong faith of ninth-century artists and patrons in their own ideal of a revived classical culture. This revival is, however, within very specific limits. The crystal is engraved not with a

71. Abbot Raganaldus blessing the people, the Marmoutier Sacramentary, *c.* 850

72. The Lothair Crystal, Lorraine (?) 855-69

classical theme, but with the imagery of Justice in Hebrew and Christian terms.

Very early in the Middle Ages many northern nations felt the stirrings of artistic ambition in face of the relics of classical monumental sculpture. The challenging and elevating cultural appeal of Roman antiquities was certainly a factor in the development of the Northumbrian Renaissance of the seventh and eighth centuries. The historian Bede's narrative of one of the miracles of St Cuthbert has as its setting the town of Carlisle, formerly an important centre of the British kingdom of Rheged, but by St Cuthbert's time occupied by the English for two generations. Cuthbert was on a sight-seeing tour, when the miracle occurred which it was Bede's purpose to record. 'The next day when the citizens were leading him to see the walls of the town, and the remarkable fountain formerly built by the Romans, suddenly as he was resting on his staff, he was disturbed in spirit, and turning his face sorrowfully to the earth ... he groaned loudly and said in a low voice, "Now then, the conflict is decided ...", that is, he received spiritual warning that Ecgfrith, King of Northumbria, had that moment been killed in battle. When this scene was illustrated early in the

73. St Cuthbert at Carlisle, 12th century

twelfth century by an artist at Durham [73], many details of the narrative, the saint's suddenly entranced pose, his resting on his staff, his hanging of his head, were accurately depicted. The Roman fountain, however, evidently meant nothing to the artist. At Durham in the early twelfth century he had no model available, no stock of visual imagery with which to body out that monument, and so he drew it as a little stone well-head, low to the ground. But in 685, the date of Cuthbert's visit to Carlisle, people had evidently been looking with interest at Roman remains. Roman monuments both public and private with figure sculpture in relief and finely cut inscriptions, were plentiful at the various military stations and townships along Hadrian's Wall from Jarrow at the eastern end to Carlisle at the west, and the influence of such sculptures may be traced in the vigorous portraits of the four Evangelists in the late

Imago aequilae

seventh-century Lindisfarne Gospels. On folio 209*vo* St John
sits frontally on an ornamental bench [74]. He is a squat burly
figure, with a thick neck and broad flat face. The repeated parallel bands of his strongly pleated mantle emphasize his massive
rounded shoulders. The same thick but tightly clinging draperies, the same bandage-like parallel divisions of the mantle and
the same hulking figure with rounded humped shoulders confronts us on the tombstone of a second- or third-century
Romano-British mother and child, from Murrell Hill, Cumber-

74 (*opposite*). Portrait of the Evangelist St John, Lindisfarne Gospels, *c.* 698

75. Tombstone of mother and child, Carlisle, 2nd or 3rd century A.D.

land, now in Carlisle Museum [75]. Just at the time when Benedict Biscop was stimulating his countrymen's minds and eyes with panel-paintings and figured textiles and illuminated books imported from seventh-century Christian Rome, their attention seems to have fixed with a new comprehension and interest on the older stratification of classical art available to them in Northumbria itself. In spite of his brightly coloured, flat, linear qualities, the St John of the Lindisfarne Gospels has also an unmistakable presence and bulk which he owes to his creator's admiration, however shallowly founded, for the naturalistic humanist art of the Mediterranean. Nor was the Northumbrian response confined to painted images. The Ruthwell Cross, erected on the farther shore of the Solway, across from Carlisle, was carved in deep relief in evident formal and technical emulation of Romano-British tomb sculpture. Its figure style is stalwart and sober. Christ blessing St Mary Magdalen stands out in relief against a concave background, like the woman in the Murrell Hill tombstone. Christ's lifted hand throws back a thick long cord of drapery at the edge of his mantle, as do the Roman matron's emerging arms, and he reproduces exactly her broad round shoulders and swathed and banded mantle [140].

Italy and the old provinces of the Roman Empire, notably southern France and Spain, possessed an extensive archive of late classical sculpture of a kind particularly interesting and comprehensible to the Middle Ages. This consisted of the relief carved sarcophagi in which wealthy members of the early Church, and their wealthy pagan contemporaries were buried. Narrative themes from the Old and New Testaments, or symbolic representations of Christ the Good Shepherd or Christ the True Vine of course marked the majority of Early Christian sarcophagi but there were enough exceptions to confuse the issue, and in later centuries the discovery of any large eye-catching sarcophagus, whatever its imagery, was sufficient to ensure the unknown dead within of a fictional sanctity and at least a local veneration. Late classical sarcophagi are one of the basic sources of the idea of the great relic chest of the Middle Ages. The rapidly developing cult of martyrs and confessors made their burial places the focus of religious devotion. St Concordius, a fourth-century Bishop of Arles, was buried in a great marble sarcophagus of regular Early Christian design. On the front Christ occupies the central position, on a raised chair, dispensing the New Law to the twelve Apostles who are seated deliberating in front of a classical arcade, like a company of senators. On the other hand St Lusor, the son of the Gallo-Roman patrician who gave the Christians of Bourges their first church, was buried at St Étienne-de-Deols in Berry in a very pagan-looking sarcophagus, in which vigorous horsemen and their hunting dogs pursue a fierce boar and a fleeing stag. Hunting sarcophagi, sculptured in a 'primitive' decorative manner, continued to be produced in Italy as late as the eighth century, for example the marble tomb of a Lombard duke preserved at

76. Civita Castellana relief, 8th century

Civita Castellana [76], and the same secular theme, handled with great spirit, appears on the tympanum of the church of St-Ursin at Bourges in the twelfth century, presumably copied from an ancient relief such as that on St Lusor's sarcophagus [77]. Gregory of Tours in his *Liber de gloria confessorum* tells of the fifth-century St Germanus of Auxerre worshipping at this tomb, 'wonderfully sculptured in Parian marble'. Gregory also

77. Tympanum of Church of St-Ursin, Bourges, 12th century

mentions the re-use of Antique sarcophagi for later burials. Bishop Felix of Bourges was laid in 'an old sarcophagus of Parian marble'. At Ely in England St Etheldreda, who died in 680, was originally buried in a wooden coffin. But sixteen years later, when the monastic community was considering the translation of her relics into the church, they had the good luck to discover, near the walls of the abandoned Roman settlement of Granchester, an empty Antique white marble sarcophagus, 'most beautifully wrought'. The body of St Etheldreda, and the sarcophagus which seemed to have been miraculously provided for it, were highly venerated at Ely.

Inevitably, stone carvers in Merovingian Gaul were called on to reproduce sarcophagi. The crypts of sixth- and seventh-century church foundations were stocked with big-lidded stone tombs, bearing the Chi Rho monogram and other rather dry designs of stylized looped vines in level relief, and symmetrical plants sprouting fringed leaves. Figures tend to flatten also, and are isolated from one another by vertical pilasters. Deeper relief, and energetic motion, however, are achieved in the ambitious sarcophagus of Agilbert at Jouarre [78]. Agilbert died around 680 as Bishop of Paris, but he had formerly been Bishop

78. Sarcophagus of Bishop Agilbert Jouarre, *c.* 680

of Winchester and had attended the famous Synod of Whitby, where King Oswy, brother of King Oswald, cast his vote for Roman as opposed to Celtic observance, and so officially endorsed Northumbria's growing awareness of Mediterranean culture. Agilbert's sarcophagus displays the image of Christ seated holding a scroll, accompanied on either side by a row of figures. But these companions are not the sober senators of

Concordius's tomb at Arles. They stand, with odd scarf-like
draperies wound about their slim bodies, their broad placid
youthful faces frontal, and their arms flung up in a position of
prayer or ecstasy. The mood of the composition is close to the
cheerful and picturesque St Sever Apocalypse vision of the
Adoration of the Lamb, with its row of palm-bearing martyrs
[137], and may perhaps derive from the same early phase of

Apocalypse illustration. Agilbert's contemporary in Northumbria, St Cuthbert, was buried in 687 in a plain stone sarcophagus, but eleven years later was re-interred in a wooden coffin erected above the floor in the monastic church at Lindisfarne [79]. This coffin bears images of Christ and the Evangelist symbols, the Apostles, the Virgin, and the archangels drawn in thin incisions on the wooden panels. The general effect is of one of the very shallow carved artisan-worked Merovingian stone sarcophagi, although wooden coffins existed in their own right in the early Middle Ages, for example the handsome metal-bound wooden coffin of a seventh-century Lombard nobleman now in the Ferdinandeum Museum at Innsbruck, the cedar-wood coffin at St Paulinus in his church at Trier, and the *capsa tabulis formata ligneis* into which the miracle-working body of Bishop Illidius of Clermont was transferred in the sixth century, for the sake of accessibility to his worshippers.

Close in time to the death and burial of St Cuthbert, as we have seen, stone sculptors capable of working in deep relief and with an understanding of Roman *gravitas* were at work in Northumbria. Thanks to some powerful blending of influences from England and the Continent, the visual idea of the classical sarcophagus was rehandled with vigour and imagination, about a hundred years after the Ruthwell Cross, in the great sandstone sarcophagus at St Andrews, Fife [80]. This object, one of

80. Front of the St Andrews Sarcophagus, *c.* 800

the most fascinating and beautiful monuments of pre-Romanesque art in Europe, was found in 1833 dismembered and buried in the cathedral churchyard. It is the work of an itinerant group of Pictish sculptors of the late eighth or early ninth centuries. At the extreme right of the main rectangular front panel stands David, like a Christ of Ruthwell who has decided after all to fight rather than bless the beasts of the desert. In the First Book of Samuel David tells Saul how a lion came while he kept his father's sheep, and took a lamb out of the flock. 'And I went out after him, and smote him, and delivered it out of his mouth. And when he arose against me, I caught him by his beard, and smote him, and slew him.' On the sarcophagus David grips the jaws of a small lion which rears up showing barred ribs and a narrow waist, a decoratively curled mane and a curled and tufted tail coiled between its hind legs. The lion's elegant trimness increases the apparent bulk and grandeur of David, who easily masters the animal and rends its jaws with his broad strong hands. The man is as richly textured as the lion. His clinging robe and mantle are scored with parallel pleats and edged with deep zig-zags, notably where the drapery swings heavily away from his left wrist. His massive head is crowned with thick round curls. On his thigh he wears a dagger in a rich scabbard. After the grand weighty figure of David, pivoting on one foot towards the right, we follow the movement of men and running animals towards the left. A rider on a long-legged horse lifts his sword to ward off another snarling lion. Beyond the lion, deer and hounds dart into a fine mesh of foliage. The relief of the chase has a delicate, almost romantic mood. We see something of the same lyrical quality in the great silver dish in the Hermitage, bearing the official stamp of the Emperor Justinian and representing a shepherd guarding his goats in a landscape. We have already met the theme of the hunt on St Lusor's sarcophagus, but the fluent mingling of the men, the animals and the trees in the St Andrews Sarcophagus is more reminiscent of the sixth-century Byzantine bronze and silver plaque of a hunting scene in the Louvre. The rider confronted by the lion on the Sarcophagus carries a hawk on his wrist. Directly below him is a fallen pony, sinking down weakly on to the earth, and crawled over by a great winged creature. This is no hawk or eagle. It is a griffin, which clutches the pony's back with its lion's claws as it pecks down fiercely with its eagle's beak [81]. The presence in a northern forest of this exotic beast carries our minds back from the remote headland of Fife to Constantinople, specifically to the huge sixth-century mosaic floor of the Great Palace, where a griffin pounces on a fallen deer. In the St Andrews Sarcophagus we see a Pictish classical *renovatio* conceived in terms ultimately derived from the sixth-century *renovatio* promoted by Justinian and his immediate successors.

81. Griffin and Pony, detail of 80, *c.* 800

The St Andrews Sarcophagus foreshadows the Romanesque style in the monumental quality of the David, the plasticity and sense of surface exhibited in his figure combined with an emphasis on linear pattern and a certain quality of expressive tenseness in the pose. The full maturity of the Romanesque style is seen in the relief of Christ walking on the waters from the church of San Pedro de Roda in Catalonia, dating to about the mid twelfth century [82]. Here the round heads of Christ and his two disciples stand out in full relief from the flat background. The hands with long thin fingers like bamboo-shoots seem to conduct the slow strong composition. The smooth horizontally-laid timbers of the boat contrast with the flat diagonal paddles and the ruffled rippling texture of the sea, on which great scaled fishes are fixed, like fossil fish partly cleared from their limestone matrix. The broad-flanked, huge-headed Christ balances precariously on a little platform of sea. His draperies stream and vibrate, binding his thin arms to his sides, but releasing his large vigorous hands. In the abrupt gestures, the glaring eyes, and sensuous pattern-making, we see medieval qualities of

2. Christ walking on the waters, San Pedro de Roda, *c.* 1150

draughtsmanship and design, but the classical tradition is also strongly apparent, though handled with an habitual grotesquery. Such heads, with the hair framing the large eyes, such stiffly flapping hands, such pliant indented draperies, such sudden changes of proportion, such heaped-up waters, appear in late Antique sarcophagi, for example the tomb of Sextus Probus in the Vatican or the sarcophagus below the pulpit in S. Ambrogio at Milan. Above all, the classical heritage is seen in the technique. The figure of Christ is stabbed over with deep holes which end the flowing grooves of the draperies. These holes prove that the Romanesque sculptor knew the use of the drill, and that he must have studied a model like the *traditio legis* sarcophagus of the late fourth century in the Colonna Chapel at St Peter's. A similar use of sophisticated tools, but a style more authentically Antique in the realism and simplicity of the heads and figures, is to be seen in the reliefs on the west front of the twelfth-century Abbey of St Gilles-du-Gard, near the Mediterranean shore, south of the Roman city of Nîmes.

83. Detail from the scene of St Peter's denial foretold, St-Gilles-du-Gard, c. 1170

The tilted foreshortened head of an apostle in the scene of Christ's foretelling St Peter's denial, with spiral locks of hair, heavy chin, strong deeply moulded features, is handled almost in the bold Hellenistic manner, and certainly reflects direct study of memorials of the great age of the Roman 'Province' [83].

Certain Romanesque sculptures of southern France and northern Spain even seem marked by some faint memory of Greek sculpture of the early classical phase. We may sense this at Jaca Cathedral, in the capitals displaying lithe firmly modelled nude or semi-nude figures, with bland round faces topped by pads of curling hair. In the cloister at Gerona, the heads of the figures in the Genesis reliefs, though the bodies to which they are attached are far from any classical canon of proportions, have an odd resemblance to the Gods and Lapiths of Olympia in the coiled grooved locks of hair, the big smooth oval faces with their look of attentive gravity, calm yet animated in expression, the cleanly chiselled eyes and eye-lids, and the long mouths with full lips [84]. At the corner of the pillar decorated with the

scene of Noah's sons working on the fabric of the Ark at Gerona, the composition is interrupted by a stout feathered Harpy, more to be expected swooping down upon the Argonauts than roosting in the midst of Noah's ship-building yard. Another female-headed Antique monster, the Egyptian sphinx, was a favourite motif of the Roman twelfth-century Vassalletti family of marble sculptors. Sphinxes crouch for example at the base of the mosaic-encrusted paschal candlestick at Anagni. The name Vassalectus was inscribed on the plinth of an Antique statue of Aesculapius, formerly in the Verospi palace in Rome, which suggests that this twelfth-century sculptor actually owned and studied monuments of classical art, just as did a medieval stone-carver whose workshop, uncovered during excavations in Rome in 1886, was found to contain a marble statue of Antinous, evidently set up by the master sculptor as an admired standard of artistry. The head of St John the Evangelist on the Judgement portal on the north transept of the thirteenth-century Cathedral of Reims has been thought to reflect an Antinuous portrait, but the medieval Roman sculptor's appreciation of his full-length statue occurred at an even earlier date, in the twelfth or perhaps the eleventh century. Vassalettus, who owned the Aesculapius statue, flourished around the middle of the twelfth century. We should not, however, exaggerate the practical importance of this evidence for the Roman marblers' taste for Antiquity. The colossal paschal candlestick carved for the church of S. Paolo fuori le Mura by Petrus Vassallettus about 1170, impressive and decorative as, taken as a whole, it undoubtedly is, resembles a series of fairly conventional French or Spanish Romanesque capitals set one above another [85]. It has no specifically 'Roman' flavour, unlike the most distinguished surviving medieval paschal candlestick, the twelve-foot bronze column cast for Bishop Godehard of Hildesheim in the second quarter of the eleventh century. In 1162 the Roman Commune, the popular ruling party which for two decades had been acting out a *Napoleon of Notting Hill* revival of Roman civic greatness, asserted its authority over one of the city's most famous monuments, Trajan's Column, which 'shall remain as it stands, whole and unharmed for the honour of the Roman people, as long as the world endures'. In spite of this contemporary interest in Trajan's Column, it made no formal or iconographic impression on the tall sculptured column designed by Vassallettus for S. Paolo, whereas in Godehard's eleventh-century bronze paschal column the image of Trajan's Column with its ascending spiral of scenes celebrating the Emperor's victorious campaigns, was turned to Christian use, on a miniature scale, being wound round with scenes from Christ's mission ending aptly at the top with the Triumphant Entry into Jerusalem [86]. Godehard's column is clearly conditioned, in part, by the political notions of a renewed Roman Empire fashionable in German government circles late in the tenth century.

The Ruthwell Cross and the St Andrews Sarcophagus summed up for the generations which produced them the ideal of the monumental in art. They are three-dimensional carved

85 (*left*). Paschal candlestick,
S. Paolo fuori le Mura, Rome, *c.* 1170

86 (*above*). Triumphal column, Hildesheim, *c.* 1030

masonry blocks, themselves the focus of attention and devotion, wholly or substantially independent of any architectural setting. The San Pedro de Roda and St Gilles sculptures, on the other hand, have the physical and intellectual context of a grand architectural style. They function as elements in the handling of surfaces in grandiose Romanesque churches. The idea of the monumental in art came to be expressed primarily in architecture. I shall return to this point shortly, but we may meantime bear in mind in evaluating the strongly Antique feeling of the sculptures of St Gilles. It is easy to understand how the great authoritarian institution of Benedictine monasticism, at the height of its power, should call forth a style of figure sculpture large, firm, domineering, vehement – modelled on local Roman antiquities, especially sarcophagi. But the twelfth century offers us an even more exciting revival of Antique values in art, thanks to the dawning curiosity of a few highly educated, gifted, and influential individuals.

The quality of life in late eleventh- and early twelfth-century Europe was considerably enhanced by the large and varied literary output of Bishop Hildebert of Le Mans (*c*. 1055–1133). Hildebert was in correspondence with many of the leading figures of his time, including King Henry I of England and other members of the Anglo–Norman Royal House. He was deeply versed in classical history, mythology, and literature, as well as in Christian scriptures and doctrine. His vocabulary and range of allusions bear the imprint of Virgil, whom he calls 'the most learned of poets', while the constrained and dignified moral tone with which he considers historical and contemporary events show him as the disciple not only of the biblical Ecclesiastes but also of ancient writers like Seneca and the Early Christian Boethius. Bishop Hildebert was an enlightened intellectual who felt deeply the appeal of pagan Rome, while still able to stand aside and judge it from the medieval Christian's point of view. With wise sorrow he looks at the ruined city, 'whose fragments teach the spectator how mighty it was, when whole'. 'Long ages have destroyed your recorded deeds, and the triumphal arches of Caesar and the high temples have fallen to the ground.' He gives an eloquent first-hand picture of Antique Rome as a creative organizing force in warfare and politics, law, and all the arts of civilization. He rises with rare skill and sensibility to an appreciation of the physical beauty of the pagan city and the charm of pagan culture: 'The gods wonder at their own images, and desire to equal their imagined forms. Nature could not create such divine likenesses as man has created in these admired statues. These deities seem alive, yet they are worshipped not on account of their godhead, but because of the mastery of the artists who made them . . .' Hildebert's poem *De Roma*, from which this quotation comes, enjoyed wide fame. It must have helped to form the intellectual background to an important cultural figure of the next generation, Henry of Blois, Bishop of Winchester and Abbot of Glastonbury, brother of King Stephen. In the *Historia pontificalis*, written by the English scholar John of Salisbury, we read an ironical account of how Henry of Blois on a visit to Rome in 1151 purchased a number of *veteres statuas* – 'idols', as the astonished bystanders termed them – in the city market-place. This is our first rumour of the Grand Tour, of the rich Englishman carrying home Antiques, consciously so regarded, from Italy.

It is of course questionable whether this act of discerning patronage of Antique art falls within the scope of this book at all. Has not Henry of Blois quitted the eclectic culture of the early Middle Ages and advanced along the path which leads to High Gothic or alternatively the Early Renaissance? Henry of Blois's ambiguous position in the history of the visual arts, as revealed by his precocious Roman holiday, is paralleled by the bronze statuette of a naked man fighting a lion, now in a private collection in New York [87]. We have already met the theme of man versus lion on the St Andrews Sarcophagus, where the man was David defending his flock. But the nudity of the bronze wrestler suggests that we have here to do with Hercules performing his First Labour, against the Nemaean lion. The sculptor has tackled a classical theme familiar in Antique engraved gems, and found also, in a design close to the bronze, on a sixth-century Byzantine silver platter in the Cabinet des Médailles, Paris, where Hercules similarly grips the great head of the lion under his vice-like arm. The untempered classical theme and the tautness and energy of the design, as the two interlocked bodies shove against each other, represents such a distinguished effort towards a renewal of Antiquity that some scholars have thought that only a very extraordinary cultural milieu could have produced it – the most extraordinary milieu, in fact, of all the Middle Ages, namely the court of the Emperor Frederick II in Apulia, early in the thirteenth century. The bronze has thus been credited to Frederick's proto-Renaissance, as a parallel phenomenon to the Capua Gate and the Barletta bust of the Emperor, as one of the art-works foreshadowing the

87. Hercules strangling the Nemaean lion, 12th century

88. Initial to the Book of Amos, Winchester Bible, 12th century

great Gothic/Renaissance sculptures of Nicola Pisano. But we might not unreasonably argue that the bronze is English Romanesque work, of the age of Henry of Blois. Hercules' thick neck and small skull, with the sloping brow, long nose, and heavy receding chin, are strikingly reminiscent of the heads and faces painted by Anketil, the monk of St Albans, in his great stark illuminations in the St Albans Psalter, before 1123.

Hercules
strangling the
Nemaean lion,
4th century B.C.

Initial to the
prologue of the
Book of Amos,
Lambeth Bible,
1150

In the Winchester Bible the initial to Amos, of the last quarter of the twelfth century, contains a dark-faced, blue-robed, figure of the prophet throwing over his shoulder a huge tawny lion whose muscular limbs, padded feet, and wedge-shaped head closely resemble the bronze lion [88]. In this initial the violent pose of the lion is evidently copied from a classical gem [89]. Even closer is the resemblance of the Amos initial in the Lambeth Bible [90], where a naked man and a lion lean towards each other and meet in a wrestler's clinch, forming the letter A of the prophet's name. The lion grips the man's back with both forepaws, just as he does in the bronze, and the man's rounded buttocks, short thick legs and long feet, are markedly similar. What is missing from the Lambeth initial is the sense of a tough tussle, the slow pressure of the man's arm, the rush and scrape and snarl of the lion, which lifts the New York bronze into the category of a true Renaissance work. Yet something of the same brilliance and boldness of design radiates from the remarkable seal of Richard Basset, recorded in the *Book of Seals* of the seventeenth-century antiquary Sir Christopher Hatton [91]. A knight in full chain mail with a pointed helmet strikes with

91. The Seal of Richard Basset, c. 1129

his sword at a huge rampant griffin, as tall as, and much thicker-bodied than himself, with outspread wings, gripping the naked figure of a man (a human soul?) in its beak. The deed which bears this seal dates to about 1129. The imaginative power shown by the designer of the Basset seal, combined with the design of the Amos initial in the Lambeth Bible, strongly suggests that the New York bronze, with its astonishing Etruscan clarity of outline and its authentically Pollaiuolesque virility and violence, is twelfth-century English work and crowns the long history of early medieval – pre-Carolingian to Romanesque – interpretations of the Antique.

In the New York Hercules we witness the revival of the ability to work, however tentatively, in an Antique idiom. The theme and the manner in which it is handled are properly equated, and the artist, working in an atmosphere evidently literate and liberal, is able to associate himself with the Antique tradition. The loss of association with the classical past, the sense of baffled separateness, was inevitably experienced by the Barbarian occupants of the wrecked Roman Empire in the earliest Middle Ages. They mutilated the great body-politic of the Empire, and themselves suffered from its throes. The 'other-ness' of Roman material culture and the inaccessible scale of Roman endeavour and achievement were fundamental facts in the development of the psychology of the early medieval peoples. This loss of association, of the sense of participation, is dramatically conveyed by the eighth-century Anglo-Saxon poem *The Ruin*, an elegy on a discarded and mouldering city, with huge stone buildings, tiled and arched roofs, and foundations whose blocks are bonded by iron cramps. It is clearly a Roman city, perhaps specifically Bath, the Roman Aquae Sulis, since a hot spring gushing into a great stone reservoir is mentioned. 'Wonderful is thy wall-stone, by fate broken: the city decays, the work of giants moulders.' Another poem, *The Wanderer*, speaks similarly of walls standing in ruins, blown on by the winds. 'The old work of giants stands empty . . .' The writers of these poems lament the loss of a past in which they had no part, and which they think of as remotely distant in time, like the biblical Babel built by the giant Nimrod. This mood, however, had, as we have seen, already given way at Carlisle in the seventh century to healthy curiosity and a proprietary pride. The fountain was pointed out to St Cuthbert as built by the Romans, not as wrought by ancient supermen. The North-umbrians achieved much in the way of seeing themselves in a rational historical context. The Carolingians achieved even more, for they deliberately associated themselves – artificially, sometimes even absurdly, but always positively – with the classical past. They made the act of self-identification with Antiquity, which was the essential basis of a revival of the classical style. Charlemagne's wreathed brows and imperial title stamped on his silver *denier* indicate this association of the Frankish present with the Roman past in clear visual terms [61 B]. Charlemagne's biographer Einhard makes an equally clear association when he describes Charlemagne's physical appearance and character in words borrowed from Suetonius' descriptions of the Caesars. For example, Suetonius wrote of Tiberius, 'corpore fuit amplo atque robusto . . .', so Einhard writes of Charlemagne, 'corpore fuit amplo atque robusto . . .' In the verse preface to his poem in praise of Charlemagne's son Louis the Pious, Ermoldus Nigellus ingeniously contrives to form from the last letter of each line, read vertically, the sentence ERMOLDUS CECINIT HLUDOICI CAESARIS ARMA, coming as close as circumstances allow to the famous opening phrase of the *Aeneid*. Nigellus declares that his theme would prove too lofty for even the combined efforts of 'Maro, Naso, Cato, Flaccus, Lucanus, Homerus, Tullius et Macer, Cicero sive Plato . . .', and the whole poem is strewn with evidence of close reading of classical authors. A self-conscious appreciation of classical literary style is equally displayed by Rabanus Maurus in his commentary on the last figure in his *De Laudibus Sanctae Crucis* [142]. 'My likeness,' he says, 'which I have painted below the cross kneeling at prayer, is inscribed in Asclepiadean metre, the first line consisting of a heroic hexameter, and the second a heroic hemistich.' This pedantry in verse construction and delight in citing and echoing famous writers are a natural corollary to the will to revive accurately the classical language in the visual arts, above all in architecture.

One of the greatest Carolingian manuscripts, the Utrecht Psalter, written and illustrated at Hautevillers near Reims about 830, is marked by a determined effort to coin a classical language of forms, especially architectural. In the Psalter the hopes and fears of the Psalmist are played out against rocky landscapes like those in which Ulysses wanders in the late Antique paintings from the Esquiline, now in the Vatican Library, and amidst a fascinating display of exotic and varied temples, basilicas, turrets and encircling city walls. In the illustration to Psalm 26 a single-storeyed aqueduct conveys water to a splendid

Lion fountain,
cht Psalter,
ns, c. 830

lion fountain, which spouts it into a great cistern [92]. The
shape of a Roman fountain, forgotten by the twelfth-century
Durham illustrator of St Cuthbert's *Life*, is relished by the
Carolingian draughtsman. The pages of the Psalter, with their
vistas of toy architecture, represent a make-believe world which
has captured the imagination of the Carolingian artist and his
patron. This idealistic Romanism, comparable in its nostalgic
artifice to the rusticity of Marie Antoinette's dairy at the Petit
Trianon, may also perhaps be seen in a remarkable object
recorded in a drawing made by a seventeenth-century Jesuit
antiquarian [93]. This drawing shows a maquette of a trium-

Einhard's
mphal Arch
uary and
s base, c. 828

94. Golden altar of S. Ambrogio, Milan, *c.* 850

phal arch of the familiar Antique kind, with a single archway as in the Arch of Titus at Rome. The archway has a magnificent coffered vault, and on the top of the monument is placed a high rectangular plinth, which in Antique triumphal arches would be the site of the victor's chariot. But the maquette does not represent a true Antique edifice for it carries no attached half-columns or sculptured reliefs, but only pictorial ornaments consisting of standing figures of military saints armed with lances and tall oval shields, a group of Christ and the twelve Apostles, portraits of the four evangelists accompanied by the symbolic beasts, and the scene of the Annunciation and St John the Baptist's confession of Christ, taken respectively from St Matthew's and St John's Gospel. The style and iconography of these images links the triumphal arch with the art of the court of Louis the Pious and Charles the Bald. An inscription on a tablet at the front of the arch names Einhard as the author of the monument. Einhard is famous as the biographer of Charlemagne. The inscription makes it plain that the triumphal arch was one of the most elaborate expressions in art of the idea, to which I devote a later chapter, of the cross as the sign of victory. For it was the cross which was to be stationed on the great plinth above the monument. 'Einhard the sinner', reads the inscription, 'laboured to establish and dedicate to God this arch, to support the trophy of eternal victory.' Christ's conquest of Death has drawn to itself the iconography of the Antique triumphal arch.

Einhard's arch was an elaborate toy, similar to Godehard's paschal candlestick, a model free from the practical problems of architectural construction. It has been identified as a reliquary presented by him to the church of St Servatius at Maastricht. We can therefore visualize it in terms of the famous high altar of S.Ambrogio at Milan, a rare example of Carolingian art in Italy and perhaps the finest surviving example of medieval goldsmiths' work, with its gold and gilded plates bearing majestic figures in repoussé, encased in brightly coloured jewelled and enamel frames [8, 94]. Small though it was, Einhard's arch reliquary represents the Carolingians' adoption of the Antique style of architecture, beyond any mere drawn and painted fictions, and provides at least a partial parallel for the outstanding achievement of the architect of the monastery of Lorsch, who at the end of the eighth century built a three-arched freestanding gateway at the entrance to the courtyard in front

95. The Gateway of Lorsch Abbey, c. 800

of the monastic church [95]. The short massive pillars of the gateway are articulated by half-columns with fine Antique-type capitals, while the upper storey carries an arcade of classical pilasters. The handsome ornamental stonework with which the gateway is faced is derived from a famous old tradition of Gallo-Roman mason-craft which had survived into Merovingian times and was so admired by Benedict Biscop that he fetched Gaulish masons to Northumbria to build Monkwearmouth Monastery *iuxta Romanorum morem*. In its function and general composition the Lorsch gateway follows the great propylaeum at the west of the entrance court of Old Peter's. Its dependence on this familiar monument of Early Christian

96. St Cyriakus, Gernrode, begun 961

97. Ground-plan of St Michael's Church, Hildesheim, c. 1000

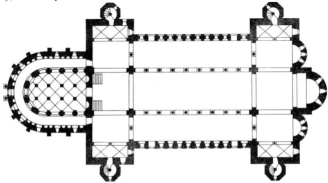

Rome does not, however, account for the consistency of its classical details or for the impressive dignity of its proportions. Its designer, with some faint foreshadowing of Alberti's taste and learning, clearly intended his building to bear the connotation of an Antique triumphal arch.

Contemporary with Lorsch, the architect of the Abbey church of St-Riquier presents an as yet unsolved problem of sources. It seems to derive from a wide range of models, spread all the way from Syria to Yorkshire. Certainly no single classical or Early Christian prototype will answer for St Riquier's many soaring turrets and lanterns, its spiral access stairs, its crypt-like vestibules and superimposed galleried chapels, its strange variety of vistas, above, below, through; its compartmented nave, transept and sanctuary, sectioned off and subdivided by screens and enclosures. This complex design became the standard for cathedrals and abbey churches throughout the Carolingian and Ottonian Empires [96, 97], and in England in the later Anglo-Saxon period. A Latin poem of the early eleventh century on the miracles of St Swithun makes it clear by elaborate description that the Old Minster of Winchester was a building of the St-Riquier type. What is interesting from our present point of view, however, is that the monk Wulfstan, the author of the poem, contrived to find a classical equivalent for the unaccommodating architecture which he celebrates, namely Pliny's account of the Labyrinth built by Daedalus in Crete. In his *Natural History* Pliny writes of the Labyrinth's passages 'that wind, advance, and retreat in a bewilderingly intricate manner' and of its 'doors let into walls at frequent intervals to suggest deceptively the way ahead and to force the visitor to go back upon the very tracks that he has already followed in his wanderings'. So Wulfstan, praising the western entrance to Winchester Old Minster, writes: 'Whoever walks in these courts with unfamiliar tread, cannot tell whence he comes or whither to return, since open doors are seen on every hand, nor does any certain path of a way appear. Standing he turns his wondering gaze hither and thither, and is amazed at the Attic roofs of the Daedalean floor.'

While the Old Minster of Winchester was being perceived by Wulfstan in terms of Pliny's imaginary picture of the Cretan Labyrinth, a new style of architecture was beginning to emerge in Europe, with many practical resemblances to the great public works of the Roman world. The Church Militant, as developed first in Ottonian Germany as the instrument of the state, then emancipated from imperial tutelage in the expansion of reformed Benedictine monasticism, and further as developed by the great Duke of Normandy again as an instrument of the state, found material expression in huge stone buildings, veritable rocks of order, exuding a sense of stability and strength [13, 98]. The Romanesque cathedrals and monasteries, with their walls, gates, towers, expertly hewn stones, great curved vaults, and their quality of being larger than life, bring the fabled 'Ruin' of the eighth-century elegy back to repair and working-order.

98. West front of Jumièges Abbey, 1037–66

Aesthetically Romanesque is a style which emphasizes bulk, thickness, and above all surface – the convex surface of giant columns, the concave surfaces of barrel or groin vaults, the flat surface of horizontal floors and vertical walls [99, 100, 110, 125]. Inevitably Roman analogies for specific eleventh- and twelfth-century buildings spring to mind. In the nave elevation of Southwell Minster we see again the components of a Roman aqueduct, the three huge tiers of pillars, platforms, and arches,

101. Interior of the nave of Southwell Minster, *c.* 1150

as in the Pont du Gard [101]. That is not to say that the designer
of Southwell deliberately took a monument like the Pont du
Gard as his model. The character of the Southwell arcade, the
logic of its construction, stately proportions and fine workmanship inevitably result in a similar visual effect. But in southern
France, where the hulking remains of Roman civilization still
dominate the landscape, twelfth-century architects drew their
inspiration directly from Antiquity. The west front of the Abbey
church of St Gilles, in its architecture as in its sculptures, follows

Roman principles [102]. The façade has a large central portal, under a deep round arch, and two lesser portals and arches, one on either side. Between the central and side portals is a straight entablature and sculptured frieze, supported on freestanding columns with Corinthian capitals. Majestic statues stand with their backs to the wall in the recessed space behind the columns. This huge screen wall, with its vigorously projecting members, its balanced vertical and horizontal rhythms, the cavernous recesses of the arched doorways, the friezes, the figures, and the crouching lions, revives convincingly the image of a Roman theatre, as we see it in ruins at Arles or Mérida, or complete in Palladio's Renaissance version at Vicenza. The Romanesque

102. West front of St-Gilles-du-Gard, c. 1170

adaptation differs from Palladio's reconstruction in that the twelfth-century architect seeks scale and splendour but cares nothing for academic accuracy. The Antique past was not idealized beyond its practical usefulness to the needs of the present. St Gilles represents the supreme confidence of the twelfth century in the values of militant Christendom, and in the role of the international Benedictine Order. Monasticism had begun in a flight from the social and political aspects of decaying classical Rome: but by the eleventh and early twelfth centuries,

103. Interior of Cluny Abbey, ambulatory, c. 1095

as far as material power, social and political organization, and cultural patronage are concerned, monasticism had become Rome's heir and executor.

Around 1100, for a Benedictine monk north of the Alps, Cluny, the great Abbey, mother of a legion of daughter houses, reservoir of discipline, faith and worship, and living exemplar of the beauty of holiness, was the New Rome. The high altar of Cluny was consecrated in 1095 by Urban II, the Pope who on the same visit to France consecrated Marbodus, the poet of stones, as Bishop of Rennes. Cluny was demolished, like the *Escrin* of Charlemagne and a thousand other precious memorials of the Middle Ages, during the French Revolution. Happily its appearance is preserved in a number of drawings. In one, we see the back of the high altar, surrounded by its ring of lofty columns [103]. The vast broad ambulatory stretches away towards the distant transept arms. The outer wall of the ambulatory carries thick fluted pilasters with massive Corinthian capitals, supporting firm round arches, sometimes blank, sometimes opening into chapels beyond. The amplitude and dignity of the design, the vigorous sweep of the tunnel vault overhead, and the clean sharp cutting of the details, are essentially classical. We realize

104. Capriccio, by Robert Adam, 1782

this even more acutely when we put alongside the view of Cluny
a *capriccio* by Robert Adam, representing just such another huge
circular space, with an inner core of masonry (so large that it
encases and dwarfs a cottage) rising to support a colossal over-
hanging vault [104]. Perhaps the eighteenth century's eye for
the grandiose and the dramatic brings the two images artificially close together. But it must be significant enough for the
achievement of the architect of Cluny, that the second drawing,
which so much resembles his great sanctuary and apse, in fact
represents Robert Adam's personal vision of the lost glory of
Antique Rome.

5

Story-telling

In Book II of his *History of the Franks* Gregory of Tours mentions
a church dedicated to St Stephen on the outskirts of Clermont
which was built and endowed in the fifth century by a wealthy
patroness, the wife of St Namatius, Bishop of Clermont. When
the church was finished, says Gregory, 'wishing to adorn it with
colours, she used to hold a book open in front of her, reading
the histories of deeds of long ago [*legens historias actionum anti-
quorum*] and indicating to the painters what they should represent on the walls'. Ideas for a series of descriptive narrative
murals are here taken directly from a book which Gregory of
Tours, writing a century later, evidently did not think of as a
copy of the Holy Scriptures but rather as an historical work of
some kind. It might possibly have been a Universal History
like that of the early fourth-century Bishop of Caesarea,
Eusebius, which St Jerome translated into Latin and brought
up to date, or perhaps Prosper of Aquitaine's further elaboration of the Eusebius-Jerome Chronicle, carried forward to
A.D. 455. This work contains a comparative chronology of
biblical and classical events from which we learn, for example,
that at the time when the Jewish Sanctuary was first established
and Moses's brother Aaron was appointed to minister before
the Lord as High Priest, in Greece at Delphi the famous pagan
Temple of Apollo was being built, and further that the Rape
of Helen and the Trojan War coincided with the career of
Samson. Such a chronological handbook might well have suggested a cycle of scenes from world history, suitable for the
decoration of a church. Alternatively the *Chronica* of Sulpicius
Severus, a recent lively survey of Old Testament history and
the history of the Church might also fit with the impression
which we get that Namatius's wife was reading an historical
compilation. It is not clear from Gregory's account whether
the book contained pictures; but in the seventh century, in
Northumbria, some sort of illustrated chronicle was certainly
known, and perhaps served as a model for local artists. In his
Lives of the Holy Abbots Bede refers to a volume of the 'Cosmographers', of outstanding workmanship, which Benedict Biscop

had bought in Rome and which the learned King Aldfrith of Northumbria obtained from Abbot Ceolfrith in exchange for eight hides of land. This book may have contained a collection of tables for the calculation of Easter, with a world chronicle attached and evidently also some geographical material. The reported grandeur of the book suggests that it contained illustrations.

The presence of a set of pictures of outstanding historical events in Northumbria late in the seventh century might account for the two scenes from Roman history displayed on the back and side of a small carved whalebone box presented to the British Museum by Sir Augustus Franks in 1867, and known by his name. The various scenes, like those on the Ruthwell Cross, are surrounded by explanatory inscriptions, although except for a few words on the back, they are not in Latin, but, like the *Dream of the Rood* fragment on the Ruthwell Cross, are written in Old English and in runic characters. The inscription on the front panel describes the origin of the material from which the box was made: 'This is whale bone. The sea cast up the fish on the rocky shore. The ocean became turbid where he swam aground on the shingle.' In the narrow rectangular composition on the left side of the box two symmetrical pairs of warriors hurry in from the right and left, through a thick wood at whose centre a wolf lies on her back, suckling the straddled inverted figures of the infants Romulus and Remus [105]. 'Far from their native land', reads the inscription,

105. The story of Romulus and Remus, the Franks Casket, *c*. 700

'Romulus and Remus, two brothers: a she-wolf nourished them in Rome city.' Through the wood, among the thick branches and big bud-like leaves, another wolf comes running, its tongue lolling from its open jaw. The mesh of foliated strands penetrated by the figures resembles the design of the animal-filled forest on the great sandstone sarcophagus at St Andrews, of about 800 [80], and the vigorous wolf is like a small simplified version of the Pictish wolf of Ardross [31]. The Roman twins are indeed 'far from their native land', visualized in a thoroughly insular style.

On the front of the box two scenes are represented. On the right half the three magi offer their gifts to the enthroned Virgin and Child, a brief tribute to the inauguration of the Christian era, while on the left half we experience a violent cultural shift with a grim scene from the legend of Weland the Smith [106]. Weland stands in his smithy, above the decapitated body of one of King Niðhad's sons. The head is gripped in the smith's tongs, and he offers a cup formed of the skull of the other son to the King's daughter Beaduhild. At the right of the scene Weland's brother Aegil catches birds, from which he makes magic wings to fly from King Niðhad. On the lid of the box the Weland story is continued in a violent scene of the siege of Aegil in his stronghold by King Niðhad's troops. On the right side of the box a series of mysterious scenes, including at the left a helmeted warrior facing a tall beast-headed figure, and at the centre a large horse, may represent incidents from the

106. The story of Weland the Smith, and the Adoration of the Magi, the Franks Casket, c. 700

story of the hero Sigurd. Three panels on the box therefore give pictorial expression to Teutonic legends, in response to the same taste which created the poem *Beowulf* at roughly the same time. The commissioner and original owner of the box was presumably a layman, someone like King Aldfrith, the purchaser of Ceolfrith's geographers' tract. An illustrated classical history book again leaves its mark on the rear panel of the box, where the war of Titus against the Jews and his seizure of Jerusalem in A.D. 70 is carved in a series of crowded scenes, dominated by a fantastic representation of the Temple, in outline and ornamentation vaguely reminiscent of the Jewish Tabernacle as it appears in early Greek bibles, with its guardian seraphim and animal offerings.

Secular narrative scenes, so lavishly displayed on the Franks Casket, are extremely rare among the surviving monuments of early medieval art and so we cannot now be certain how rapidly or how far pictorial imagery of secular subjects evolved. In the case of the Weland and Sigurd scenes on the Casket, it is doubtful whether the patron described or narrated the incidents which he wished to have represented, or whether a set of illustrations already existed in some other medium, from which the artist could select. Beowulf's adventures, told in the famous Old English poem, lend themselves excellently to the illustrator's art, but no *Beowulf* pictures have come down to us. The nearest thing to illustrations of *Beowulf* which we possess date from the end of the Old English period, in the eleventh century, namely the pictures in a manuscript of the tract known as *The Marvels of the East* written by the scribe responsible for part of the sole surviving copy of *Beowulf* (British Museum, Cotton MS. Vitellius A.xv) and bound up by him alongside the poem, perhaps as a kind of visual aid.

In Scandinavia, Germany and Italy, a quantity of secular pictorial material survives from the seventh century in the form of helmet plaques, plaques from shields, personal ornaments in gold and bronze, and shallow relief sculpture on tomb monuments [107], featuring a horseman armed with a lance. This image of a riding warrior may represent a sacred person from pagan mythology – in the northern examples, Odin on his magical horse Sleipner – but the image remains fixed and self-contained, not participating in anything resembling narrative. The isolated rider is a recurrent theme in medieval sculpture, where he usually represents Constantine (in imitation of the

107. Funerary stele of horseman, Saxony, *c.* 700

celebrated bronze equestrian statue of an emperor preserved at Rome and identified as Constantine in medieval guide-books of the city), or alternatively one of the famous military saints of Christendom, for example the Roman soldier St Martin, or the Apostle St James in the anachronistic context of his Spanish wars. The image of the rider, duplicated in reverse, like two travellers meeting on a lonely road, was used in 1179 to represent SS. Sergius and Bacchus on the lid of their splendid stone shrine now at Verona [108].

108. Sarcophagus of SS. Sergius and Bacchus, Verona, 1179

Close in character and date to the Franks Casket scenes is a relief sculpture on the back of a Pictish cross-slab in the church-yard at Aberlemno, Scotland, where the profile high-stepping horse and lance-bearing knight familiar from his solitary appearances in continental Dark Age monuments is represented five times, as a dynamic element in a magnificent battle scene, waged between cavalry and foot-soldiers, armed with spears, javelins, and convex and round heavily bossed shields [109]. The mounted knights wear helmets with nose-pieces like the helmets worn by Niðhad's and Titus's soldiers on the whale-bone box. At the foot of the composition, beyond two confronted horsemen, a warrior in a mail shirt and helmet lies dead on the battle field, stretched out diagonally across the stone like the figures of Romulus and Remus on the box. His shield has fallen beside him and a bird of prey pecks at his throat. This grand and vigorously handled scene must represent some famous conflict, the kind of battle which was so much the stuff of the heroic literature of the early Middle Ages. A Pict from beyond the Forth was on the side of the Britons in their tragic encounter with the English of Bernicia and Deira at Catterick around A.D. 600, celebrated in the poem *The Gododdin*. The men who went to Catterick 'sowed their spears from the saddle – from the back of a leaping horse'. In 685 the Picts defeated the Northumbrians and killed King Ecgfrith in the notable battle at

109. Battle scene, Aberlemno cross-slab, 8th century

Nechtan's Mere, which caused St Cuthbert to droop his head and lament, while he was viewing the fountain at Carlisle [73]. In this period when one battle could decide the fate of a nation, the battle scene at Aberlemno must have held a powerful significance for the patron who commissioned the sculpture.

Not all the battles, however, which found a place in the remembrance and sentiments of medieval people were of decisive national importance. One battle which captivated popular imagination was a minor skirmish, the confused tail-end of Charlemagne's abortive Spanish campaign of 778, about which no contemporary sources record any picturesque details or hint at any peculiar heroisms. The great King of the Franks, whose prestige and conquests were expanding everywhere in western Europe, was disposed by family traditions to intervene in Moslem Spain, his grandfather Charles Martel having put a stop to Moslem inroads into France by his famous victory at Tours in 732. A political split among the Moslems seemed to offer Charlemagne the chance of establishing himself in Spain as the champion of the Christian minority. He crossed the Pyrenees with an enormous army, but the lack of cooperation of the Spanish Christians and rumours of insurrection in recently subjugated Saxony soon brought his Spanish adventure to an end. In the pass at Roncevaux in the Pyrenees the rearguard of the withdrawing Frankish army was ambushed by Christian Basques and the baggage-train pillaged. Charlemagne's biographer Einhard notes the names of the principal casualties in the attack: 'In the battle that followed the Gascons (Basques) killed their opponents to the last man. Then they seized the baggage and under cover of night scattered with the greatest possible speed in all directions. . . . In this battle Eggihard, the royal seneschal, Anselm, count of the palace, and Hruodland, warden of the Breton frontier, were killed along with very many others.' Colourless as this brief notice of the battle is, the defence, to the death, of Charlemagne's baggage-train at Roncevaux was like the first grain of sand around which the oyster gradually builds its pearl. Three hundred years after the actual event a grand and poignant legend had accumulated about the names of Roland and his comrades, and their courage and prowess were celebrated in a magnificent poem, the *Chanson de Roland*, the most famous of the corpus of Old French poems known as the *chansons de geste*.

An authentic note, a genuine memory of the historical circumstances of the battle, seems to survive in Roland's determination that 'Charles the King of France shall lose nothing with my knowledge. Not the worth of a denier, not a mule that can be mounted, not a beast, not a nag, but is paid by strokes of sword.' But Roland has become the nephew of Charlemagne, and all else is transformed into a military, political and religious fantasy, idealizing King Charles and interpreting the battle at Roncevaux as a brilliant and devoted feat of arms by a picked band of Christian knights faced by an overwhelming force of treacherous Moslems. At the centre of the Christian ranks stands Turpin, Archbishop of Reims. In the battle the Archbishop strikes down a Saracen wizard Signorel, one who the poet says had visited Hell under the auspices of Jupiter. The confrontation of the Archbishop, representative of Christianity, and the pagan sorcerer conforms to a normal hagiographical pattern – St Peter and Simon Magus, St Columba and the magus Broichan – but in the *Chanson de Roland* the Archbishop and the sorcerer do not contend with spells and counterspells but in armed combat, lance to lance. Turpin rides across the field of battle. 'Exceeding swift was his steed, for slender were its legs and its feet well formed. Short of thigh but large of croup, long of side, erect of neck, white of tail, with golden mane, small of ear, with tawny head. Such was the noble beast, and never was its equal seen. The archbishop spurred very valiantly and slacked the golden bridle.' He slices in two a pagan lord, and smashes his wonderful shield, fashioned out of jewels by a devil. 'That was a deed of valour', exclaim the Franks. 'Full well the archbishop knows how to defend the Cross!'

Turpin is one of those great eleventh- and twelfth-century bishops the obverse of whose seals represent them vested and blessing, but whom the reverse shows as territorial magnates riding equipped for war. The battle in which Turpin fights is presented as a Holy War against the Saracens, the enemies of Christ and his saints. The poem does not really reflect the Carolingian situation at all, but the eleventh-century French idea of Crusade. In the eleventh century France was overpopulated with younger sons of the feudal aristocracy, trained in arms but with no possessions. The energies of these young fighting-men were best employed in wars of conquest abroad. In Spain they had the opportunity of extending the boundaries of Christendom at the expense of the Moslems, their efforts being nurtured and blessed by the all-powerful monastic organization centred on Cluny in Burgundy [103], and by Cluny's ally, the Papacy. Reconquered Spanish territory was officially claimed by the popes for the patrimony of St Peter, and Cluniac monasteries were founded as guardians of the redeemed lands. The Spanish wars of the eleventh century form a preliminary to the great eastern Crusade, preached by the former Cluniac monk Pope Urban II at Clermont in 1095. Urban sought to harness the military potentiality of France, to bring again the Golden Age of the Church, of the fifth and sixth centuries, when the Holy Land was still part of united Christendom. But throughout the eleventh century the Spanish wars had been a sure source of spiritual, as well as material, gain for those who fought in them. For example in 1089 Pope Urban announced that all who contributed to the repair of the Spanish frontier

110. Interior of transept Santiago de Compostela, *c.* 1120

post of Tarragona would reap as much benefit as by a pilgrimage to Jerusalem itself.

The focus of Christian enthusiasm and effort in Spain was the shrine of the Apostle James at Compostela in Galicia [110]. The cult of St James in Spain extended back to the ninth century, but was particularly promoted in the eleventh century by monastic houses situated on the major pilgrimage roads leading from various parts of France into Spain. In the cloister of the monastery of Santo Domingo at Silos Christ himself adopts the guise of a pilgrim of St James, wearing the famous cockle-shell badge when he walks with his disciples to Emmaus [111]. The pilgrimages were highly organized and

111. The Journey to Emmaus, Santo Domingo de Silos, *c.* 1100

run as big business. In monasteries and hostelries all along the route, pilgrims were entertained and uplifted by lively narratives about St James and about the brave warriors who fought to free the land of his apostolate from the grip of the heathen. In these stories St James himself became a splendid warrior who manifested himself at moments of crisis, riding on a white horse and leading the armies of the faithful into battle, like the soldier saints represented on horseback in Einhard's triumphal arch reliquary [93]. The deeds of modern soldiers of Christ, such as Duke William of Aquitaine who captured Barbastro in 1064, were likewise celebrated in and made the subject of the rapidly growing number of *chansons de geste*. The hero Roland, burning with Christian zeal and martial courage, hurling himself amongst the scattering ranks of the Moslems, reflects the notion of St James, the 'Moor-slayer'. Archbishop Turpin assures the Frankish knights that if they should die in the ensuing battle they will be holy martyrs and will take their seats with the saints in heaven. This is the psychic source of the valour and resolve of the Frankish troops as their numbers lessen in face of appalling odds. 'Wrong is with the heathen', they say, 'but right is with the Christians.' This blank absolute certainty, and the expression of Christian piety in military discipline and action, helps to explain the bastion-like quality of the eleventh- and twelfth-century churches built along the pilgrimage route from St Martin's at Tours at its northern extremity to Santiago at its south-western terminus [110, 112].

112. The east end of St Martin's Church, Tours, 10th, 11th and 13th centuries

The action of the *Chanson de Roland* is played out against a stolid assured religious background. The religious attitudes and objectives of the participants are stated simply and firmly, and do not evolve. As popular entertainment, as narrative, the *Chanson de Roland* consists of a long string of picturesque encounters of knight against knight. The poet defines in vivid visual descriptions the iconography of battle, the long golden pennants of the battle standards, the swords bloody to the hilt, the careering riderless horses, the broken lances, rent hauberks, and the dead soldiers heaped on the ground. 'Some of them are gashed with wounds, some pierced through the body, and some there are whose heads are severed from their bodies.' The keen visuality of the French *chansons* has a parallel in the terse and graphic imagery of the shield of arms adopted by the kings of Aragon in memory of a victory at Huesca in 1096, 'a cross hatched, between four blackamoors' heads couped at the neck'. What binds the long series of furious hand-to-hand fights at Roncevaux into a single organic narrative line is the high sense of honour of Roland, Oliver, Turpin, and their companions, their physical energy and stamina, their justifiable pride in their feats of strength and skill, their mutual courtesy, and their unflinching loyalty to their master Charlemagne. Turpin addresses the Franks: 'Barons of France, here has Charlemagne left us. For our Lord and Sovereign it behoves us to die.' The Franks answer Turpin, pledging their faith: 'Surely we will not dishonour thee, and please God, never shall ill be reported of us. We will combat with the foe as long as breath remains in us. We have only a few men, but we have very great courage.'

Exactly the same hard core of conscious military virtue, that basic Dark Age code of conduct which underlies all the exotic detail and the Courtly High Medieval tone of the *Chanson de Roland*, is movingly exhibited in a famous Old English poem, directly reporting a Roncevaux-like incident, at Maldon, during the Danish wars. Late in the tenth century pagan Danes, quitting their own country because of the forced imposition of Christianity upon them by King Harald Gormsson [48], began sporadic raids on various parts of the English coast line. In 991 a large army of Vikings, demanding tribute, attacked places round the coast of Suffolk, Essex, Kent, and Hampshire, being bought off at last for 22,000 pounds of gold and silver. During their raid on Essex they were resisted by Byrhtnoth, the Ealdorman of Essex, who refused their demands and challenged them to battle. He rashly allowed the pirate warriors to come ashore in good order from Northey Island in the Blackwater Estuary, and battle was joined at Maldon. The story of Byrhtnoth's valour and of the courtesy and loyalty of his thegns is told in the poem *The Battle of Maldon*. 'Then clamour arose, ravens wheeled, the eagle greedy for carrion. . . . Then they let the spears, hard as a file, go from their hands . . . warriors fell on either hand, young men lay low.' Byrhtnoth himself is killed, but his thegns, mindful of past benefits and oaths, stay beside him, avenging his death upon his enemies to the last ounce of their strength. 'I will not go hence', says one retainer. 'I purpose to lie by the side of my lord.' He exhorts his comrades to fight to the death. 'Thought shall be harder, heart the keener, courage the greater, as our might lessens.' The epic stand of Byrhtnoth and the men of his household did not only inspire a poet. It was the subject also of an embroidered hanging, commissioned by Aelfflaed, Byrhtnoth's widow. Byrhtnoth had been a generous patron of Ely Minster and his body was brought here for burial. Along with a gift of manors and of a golden necklace, Aelfflaed presented to Ely a hanging 'woven and figured with the deeds of her husband . . . as a memorial of his virtues'.

The composition of the scene of the Battle of Maldon on this late tenth-century embroidery cannot have been very different from that of the early eighth-century Aberlemno battle relief. Here we have evidently to do with a long-lasting pictorial tradition of which many examples must once have existed, though few survive. That secular narrative art had been practised and refined over a long period of time in England is strongly suggested by the precise and telling visual language employed by the designer of the Bayeux Tapestry, a highly sophisticated and mature work of art. The 'Tapestry' consists of a strip of linen about seventy metres in length and fifty centimetres wide, embroidered in coloured woollen threads. Like the lost Ely hanging it represents the deeds of a famous historical personage and his death in battle. Harold, Ealdorman of Wessex, sets off on a holiday, or a diplomatic mission, and is driven by high winds on to the French coast in the county of Ponthieu, where he is arrested by Count Guy. Duke William of Normandy orders Guy to deliver up Harold to him, and then Harold joins Duke William's expedition against Conan, Duke of Brittany. After a successful campaign to which he has made useful contributions, Harold receives arms, a helmet, corslet, a sword, and an ornamented standard, from his patron [26]. Harold then takes an oath on the Relics of Bayeux to Duke

William, which can only have concerned his willingness to serve William's English ambitions. He returns home immediately, and on King Edward the Confessor's death receives the crown and is enthroned as King of the English. Omens foretell the doom of the perjurer, and an invasion fleet is built in Normandy and launched. The Tapestry ends with a magnificent series of battles between groups of charging cavalry and stout ranks of shield-covered infantrymen [113]. As the organized

113. The Battle of Hastings, the Bayeux Tapestry, *c.* 1077

groups begin to fragment and the actions become more violent and spasmodic, Harold is hewn down by a galloping horseman. The mastery of the designer is shown by the fluency, economy, and clarity of his story line and by subtle and imaginative detail. When a comet has appeared in the sky immediately after Harold's enthronement, and as he inclines his head to hear from a servant the news of the portent, below him, on the border of the Tapestry, the artist shows the uncoloured outline of ships on water. This is not any real view, but the anticipated invasion fleet which will soon become actuality – a picture, therefore, of an idea, a fear in the mind of the king, like the vivid dreams which haunt Charlemagne before the catastrophe of Roncevaux. The artist of the Bayeux Tapestry's view of the open Channel, scattered over by the Norman fleet, the far-away boats smaller than those in the foreground, is sharp and spare in handling, and surprisingly real and lively, like a remembered sight [42]. Throughout the complexities of the story the designer never loses control. He has above all a firm sense of location, and moves his characters from one place to another only by the explicit process of a journey. In order to express the distance between Guy's castle at Beaurain and Duke William's castle, the narrative proceeds for a short sequence in reverse, running from right to left instead of in the natural sequence of events from left to right. The two castles and their two enthroned lords, Guy and William, are thus clearly differentiated and spatially distinct, and the Duke's agents have a journey to make to link the captive Harold with his distant patron. The story-telling technique, among its many other merits, expresses topography.

The literary basis of the picture-story, if there ever was a specific written source as opposed to word-of-mouth instruction by the patron, will have been a straightforward chronological account without intrusive interpretative matter and without a conscious literary style – a chronicler's narrative rather than a poet's. In the penetrating analysis of the narrative technique of the *Chanson de Roland* and of the Old French *Life of St Alexis* in his book *Mimesis*, Erich Auerbach points out the static frag-mented spasmodic quality of the story-line in these two poems. They are characterized by a series of separate scenes, 'individu-ally independent pictures', each with 'a frame of its own', with-out organic relation to one another. Even within individual scenes one spoken phrase, one declared attitude, need not necessarily lead on to the next. Time is not necessarily repre-sented as passing. We may shift backwards and forwards within the same brief sequence of time. The intellectual isolation of the units of the whole narrative is apparent to Auerbach even in the linguistic membrane itself, in the verses or 'laisses' and in the single lines. He likens the individual verses to 'a bundle of independent parts, as though sticks or spears of equal length and with similar points were bundled together'. A peculiar emphasis on individual statements, actions, and reactions, and an epic quality, slow and inexorable, in the unfolding of the total narrative, result from this elaborate formal literary pre-sentation, whose conventions must have been familiar to and admired by the audience of the poems. The Bayeux Tapestry deals in the form of a cycle of selected scenes with a story not unlike that of the *Chanson de Roland*, or at any rate with the same feudal society, with the meetings of kings and nobles, with their alliances and oaths of service, and with a final ferocious hand-to-hand combat of armies and individual soldiers. The world picture created in the Tapestry is as rigid and limited as it is in the *Chanson*. The relations of a few people to one another are the stimulus to great events, and beyond this world, which the actors fill with their stature, literally in the Bayeux Tapestry from top to bottom of the picture-space, there is only the equally fixed and classified supernatural world, out of which the hand of God will occasionally worm its way to threaten or bless.

But there are evident differences between the narrative structure of the Tapestry and the *Chanson*, which are all the more interesting since they prove the range of aesthetic sensibility of the literate upper classes of the Romanesque period. The retrogressions in the picture-story in the Tapestry, in for example the reverse order of the narrative of Harold's arrest by Count Guy, have no connection with the literary devices of retrogressions and repeated resumptions of the same event, whereby the poet of the *Chanson de Roland* probes the psychological situation and brings out its tragic implications. These reverses in the action of the Tapestry are as we have seen entirely explicable in terms of clear coherent story-telling. Individual characters are not explored and enlarged to symbolic proportions. Edward the Confessor is not the tragic figure which Charlemagne is in the *Chanson de Roland*, with a Cassandra-like consciousness of the inevitable disruption of his court. The individual scenes and the clearly signposted characters in the story all participate in a succinct narrative in which time goes by sometimes so quickly that events represented are hardly able to keep up with it. Each scene is closely linked to the next, and it is in the easy economic depiction of consecutive events that the artistry of the designer is shown. The Bayeux Tapestry is essentially unrhetorical in its approach. Its story-line was not conceived like a fully organized literary epic such as the *Chanson de Roland* but agrees better with simple prose saga narratives, like that of the *Völsunga Saga*, which are allied to folk tales in their steady equitable forwards pace, or again with time-smoothened biblical narratives like that of the Book of Tobit or the Book of Joshua, or the stories of Noah, Abraham, or Joseph.

The outstanding pictorial device used in the Bayeux Tapestry is that of continuous narrative, the stream of action spread out before the spectator along the length of the linen hanging, without any use of frames to break up the narrative into isolated incidents. A formal parallel for this continuous narrative technique is to be found in a fragment of relief sculpture of the early eleventh century unearthed in 1964 in the excavation of the eastern crypt of the Anglo-Saxon Old Minster at Winchester

114. Sigurd
and the Wolf (?),
Winchester,
1016-35 (?)

[114]. At the left of the sculpture a soldier, wearing a mail shirt equipped with breeches like those shown in the Bayeux Tapestry but much shorter on the leg and with a long sword at his side, walks away towards the left, his back turned upon the scene beginning in the right portion of the stone, and himself evidently entering or participating in another scene, now lost. Immediately at the soldier's heels is part of the figure of a man, originally stretched out at full length on the ground, but now reduced to only the head, shoulders, and forearms which are raised and manacled. Standing over the man is a wolf, its muzzle pressed up against his face and its tongue thrust into his mouth. These two partially preserved human figures and the head and paws of the wolf imply a long panel of sculpture, over 2·5 metres in length to complete the two scenes, and probably these two scenes were only part of the original whole. It may be presumed that either the exterior or the interior of the Old Minster was decorated with a sculptured continuous narrative, anticipating the Bayeux Tapestry by about fifty years. The frieze is perhaps to be associated with the funerary monument of a king, for example that of Cnut, King of England and Denmark, grandson of King Harald Gormsson. The wolf's

muzzle with bared teeth and thrust-out tongue close to the face of its victim is reminiscent of a much earlier relief from Rosemarkie in Ross [45], but the Winchester relief is already fully Romanesque in the contrast of the textures of the victim's smooth hair, scored with parallel lines, and the alternatively sunk and projecting chequer pattern on the mail shirt and breeches of the soldier. The Winchester relief may represent the horrific story of the slaying of the sons of Völsung and the escape of Sigmund, as narrated in the prose *Völsunga Saga*. The ten sons of Völsung are tethered in a forest on the orders of King Siggeir. One after the other, on consecutive nights, the young men are devoured by a monstrous wolf, until only one is left. The hero Sigmund, last of the brothers, is saved by a ruse of his sister Signy, who smears honey on his face and lips.

And the next night the same she-wolf came as she was wont and thought to bite him to death like his brothers; but now she scented the honey from him, and so she licked all his face with her tongue and thereafter thrust her tongue into his mouth. Sigmund took no fright, but bit hard on the tongue of the wolf. She started and pulled fiercely away, and thrust her feet on the stock so that it clove asunder; but he held so hard that the tongue was torn out of her by the roots, and of this she had her death. And it is the saying of some men that that same wolf was the mother of King Siggeir, who had put on this shape for the purpose of trolldom and sorcery . . .

The Winchester relief is doubly interesting as the representation of an intensely secular heroic tale located in a major ecclesiastical establishment, paralleling the representation of a manifestly non-biblical battle-scene on the reverse of the cross-slab at Aberlemno, and paralleling the probable use of the Bayeux Tapestry as a noted showpiece of Bayeux Cathedral; and further as anticipating the frieze-like lay-out and unframed scenes of the Tapestry.

An obvious analogy for the Tapestry's continuous narrative flow exists in the famous Greek Rotulus of Joshua, of the tenth century, in which Joshua's skirmishes and pitched battles in the course of his conquest of the Holy Land are displayed as an unbroken sequence, spread out across a continuous landscape. It has been suggested that the strip-system of the narrative in the Joshua Roll echoes a relief scupture representing a Roman Emperor's campaigns arranged as a continuous frieze, winding ribbon-like up a triumphal column, as in Trajan's Column at Rome. The Joshua Roll was one of the treasures of the great palace at Constantinople, and was itself certainly not accessible to artists in the Latin West in the eleventh century. However, a cycle of Joshua scenes with certain specific iconographic connections with the Joshua Roll illustrations occurs in an Old English Bible now in the British Museum, Cotton MS. Claudius B. iv, of the second quarter of the eleventh century. Thus it is not impossible that an early Greek, or Latin, illuminated manuscript constituted physically like the Joshua Roll was one of the

115. Jacob going
to meet Esau,
B.M., Cotton MS.
Claudius B. iv,
11th century

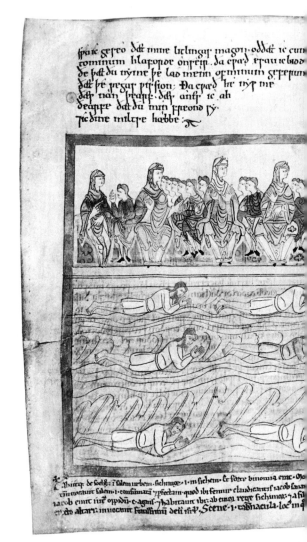

sources of stimulus to the development of continuous narrative in England, although it appears more likely that the early model whose influence we can apparently trace in this country managed to combine a markedly elongated strip-system of narrative with normal book construction in the codex form with bound pages, like a modern book. The artist of Cotton MS. Claudius B. iv,

116. Jacob's meeting with Esau, B.M., Cotton MS. Claudius B. iv

although he uses throughout a system of framed rectangular illustrations, as nearly as possible escapes from the limitations of the separate framed pictures into something very nearly cinematic in its continuity and forward-drive and total visualization of the events described by the text. The story of Abraham's encounter with the three men or angels in Genesis, chapter 18, or of Lot's flight from Sodom in Genesis, chapter 19, for example, are provided with a pictorial equivalent for each incident in the narrative – even the beginning and the end of a conversation is individually represented.

One of the most fascinating sequences of pictures illustrates the later history of Jacob and Esau. In Genesis, chapter 32, Jacob hears with alarm that his estranged brother is approaching with four hundred men. In order to placate him, Jacob orders his servants to advance with lavish gifts of livestock for Esau, the drovers to arrive one after the other with a short space between, first two hundred goats and twenty he-goats, then two hundred ewes and twenty rams, thirty milch camels with their colts, forty kine and ten bulls, twenty she-asses and ten foals. On folio 49 and 49*vo* the artist shows in five separate compartments the herds of goats, sheep, camels, cattle and asses, each being driven from left to right across the page by Jacob's servants. On folio 50*vo* we find an extraordinary picture, which at first sight appears to represent a company of women and children seated on the bank of a river, within whose waters six swimmers are competing [115]. But we have only to glance across at the picture on the opposite page and then at the scriptural text being illustrated, to realize the true significance of the six prone figures on folio 50*vo*. At the top left of the picture on folio 51 a seventh prone figure appears, and immediately beyond him two men meet and embrace [116]. In Genesis, chapter 33 we read the following account of the meeting of Jacob and Esau: 'And Jacob lifted up his eyes, and looked, and behold, Esau came and with him four hundred men.' Jacob organizes his women and children in defensive groups, the most dispensable in front, in case of a sudden attack. 'And he passed over before them and bowed himself to the ground seven times, until he came near to his brother. And Esau ran to meet him, and embraced him and fell on his neck and kissed him . . .' The seven prone figures are all Jacob, casting himself to the ground in his servile approach to his brother. The last prostration is 'near his brother', literally illustrating the text. The whole series of illustrations accurately expresses the time sequence and the location of the meeting, to which all the droves of animals first proceed, and to which Jacob tentatively manoeuvres himself. The meeting place *as* a place is further emphasized by the representation of Esau's cavalry troop, riding forward in two companies from right to left, thus confronting on the opposite page the approach of Jacob, and on previous pages the approaching herds. The meeting place of Jacob and Esau is given, as it were, an actual physical location, journeyed towards from both sides, in just the way that the Castle of Baurain in the Bayeux Tapestry is approached by the arrested Harold from the left and the emissaries of Duke William from the right.

This resemblance of the narrative method of the artist of Cotton MS. Claudius B. iv to that of the Bayeux Tapestry perhaps suggests that the Tapestry was designed in a south English scriptorium, perhaps at Canterbury, where the Old English bible manuscript itself was made sometime before the Norman Conquest. The pictures on folios 50*vo* and 51 are rectangular compositions, separately framed, but they nevertheless have the closest visual relation to one another and form a continuous chain of activity. The fact that the text of Cotton MS. Claudius B. iv is in the vernacular perhaps suggests that the book was required for the exposition of the Scriptures to laymen. The fullness and continuity of the picture cycle might then be explained by its infection by the then familiar standards of secular narrative art, or at any rate by the need to give the layman a clear visual guide to the difficult text, much as the popular illustrated saints' *Lives* in the thirteenth century were designed for upper-class lay people to enjoy while the vernacular text was read aloud to them by their chaplain or secretary. As Matthew Paris says of the history of St Edward the Confessor, in his French verse redaction,

> And for lay people who letters
> Know not, in portraiture
> Have I clearly figured it
> In this present book . . .

But in the case of Cotton MS. Claudius B. iv this is certainly not the whole story. The earliest illustrated bibles or portions of the bible, for example the fifth-century Greek manuscript of Genesis known as the 'Cotton Genesis', are characterized by the remarkable fullness and explicitness of their illustrations, which form a continuous picture-story supplementary to the text, not merely illustrating selected scenes. As I have remarked, the Joshua cycle in Cotton MS. Claudius B. iv has some relation to the cycle of scenes in the celebrated Joshua Roll, and throughout the whole length of the English book, from the first page of Genesis onwards, we find symptoms of dependence on some venerable model or models, in some cases a manuscript belonging to the same family as the 'Cotton Genesis' itself. The pictures often strikingly parallel ancient bible miniatures or paintings in a wide range of places, both in the Latin and Greek worlds. Some of the illustrations in Cotton MS. Claudius B. iv seem to derive from a model or models of extreme antiquity, which has otherwise left no trace in Christian art. On folio 72*vo*, for example, depicting the burial of Joseph, Joseph's corpse is held up by two men. The humped and rounded outline of the shrouded body, its rigidity, and the decorative pattern inscribed all over it are astonishingly like an Ancient Egyptian mummy-

117. The Burial of Joseph B.M., Cotton MS. Claudius B, iv

case [117]. It is impossible that the eleventh-century Anglo-Saxon artist could have known how archaeologically apt such a mode of burial would be for Joseph, 'ruler over all the Land of Egypt'. The Middle Ages had little or no antiquarian consciousness.

Even more puzzling and extraordinary is the representation of the twelve stones set up in the bed of the dried-up River Jordan by Joshua in the picture illustrating Joshua, chapter 4, verse 9. From modern archaeology in the Holy Land we know that the Joshua narrative preserves a memory of the ancient Semite pillar stones, massebas, or menhirs, like those found standing in a row at Gezer. Old Greek bible illustrations such as those in the Joshua Roll and the related Octateuch manuscripts, naturally enough reveal no conception of Joshua's memorial stones as a row of menhirs. The stones are represented as horizontal slabs built up one on top of the other. Yet, somehow, on folio 143 of Cotton MS. Claudius B. iv, the Anglo-Saxon artist shows Joshua completing a row of standing stones, varying in height and girth, just like the irregularly sized menhirs in prehistoric Gezer!

In the seventh century Benedict Biscop brought back to Northumbria from his travels abroad a large quantity of spiritual merchandise, including illuminated books and large-scale panels which he used to decorate the walls of his churches at Wearmouth and Jarrow. In the second half of the seventh century Rome was able to provide a wide range of models, Latin and Greek, and also North African as a result of the flight of artists to Rome after the fall of Alexandria to the Moslems in 641. The north wall of St Peter's at Wearmouth was decorated with subjects from the Book of Revelation, the first cycle of Revelation scenes of which we have record. It seems possible that the content of this insular cycle may be preserved in a late eighth- or early ninth-century Carolingian manuscript of Revelation, at Valenciennes. Later the Valenciennes Apocalypse, or a closely similar book, served as model to the German eleventh-century artist of the Bamberg Apocalypse, for example the picture of St John carried by an angel into the wilderness to view the Whore of Babylon seated on the seven-headed beast in the Bamberg Apocalypse is a careful copy of the Valenciennes Apocalypse's version of the same subject [118, 119]. The revival of the Valenciennes Apocalypse's picture cycle after two hundred years is paralleled by the case of the Utrecht Psalter, a Carolingian manuscript of the early ninth century [92], which after its arrival at Canterbury (given perhaps by a continental ruler or monastery), was made the model for a number of impressive works, notably the Psalter written by the scribe Eadwine in the middle of the twelfth century, now in the Library of Trinity College, Cambridge, and the Canterbury Psalter in Paris, B.N. MS. Lat. 8846, the last great monument of Romanesque illumination in England. Just as the text of the Scriptures and the commentaries of the Fathers and ancient classical texts were revered as the authentic source of wisdom and knowledge and were carefully copied and passed on from generation to generation, so also an old cycle of pictures would be received as authentic and would be copied

118. The Whore of Babylon, Valenciennes Apocalypse, 9th century

as faithfully as the artist's skill and comprehension allowed. The illustrations in the Bamberg Apocalypse of the eleventh century may go back ultimately to painted panels bought in Rome in the seventh century. The illustrations in Cotton MS. Claudius B. iv are like geological strata, layer over layer of diversely aged pictorial material.

At the same time as Cotton MS. Claudius B. iv was being illuminated, an Old English poetic version of Genesis, cast in the epic style of the poem *Beowulf*, was provided with illustrations, perhaps at Canterbury. The book, known as the 'Caedmon' manuscript, is now in the Bodleian Library, Oxford, MS.

119. The Whore of Babylon, Bamberg Apocalypse, 11th century

Junius 11. This move to supply the poem with accompanying pictures parallels the evident intention of the scribe of the *Beowulf* manuscript to associate with the poem text the fantastic monsters depicted in *The Marvels of the East*. The Old English Genesis in the 'Caedmon' manuscript was comparatively easy to illustrate, since much of its narrative follows the sequence of events described in the scriptural Genesis, and the drawings accompanying the poem could be lifted from a conventional bible. Again the 'Caedmon' manuscript was evidently illustrated in a centre possessed of an impressive archive of traditional pictorial material. The main core of the Adam and Eve cycle

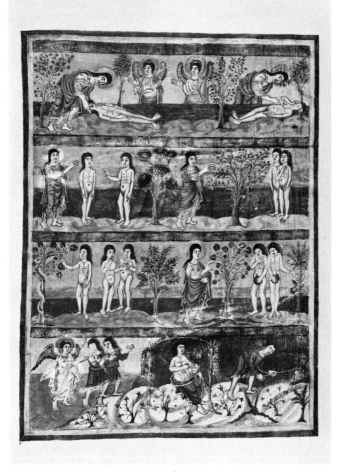

120. The history of Adam and Eve, Moûtiers-Grandval Bible,
Tours, 9th century

has a close relationship to the Genesis illustrations in a group
of magnificent Carolingian manuscripts made in Tours. The
prefatory picture to Genesis in the bible manuscript from Tours,
now in the British Museum and known as the Moûtiers-
Grandval Bible, illustrates the story of mankind from the
Creation of Adam to the Expulsion from Paradise [120]. The
page is divided into four bands, each containing two scenes

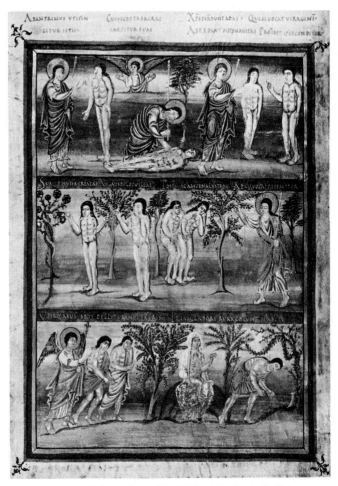

121. The history of Adam and Eve, First Bible of Charles the Bald, Tours, 844–51

played out on a continuous groundline. The short sturdy naked figures of Adam and Eve, the youthful beardless Creator, and the firm detailed description of events link the ninth-century Carolingian illumination to the same early tradition of Christian art, to a work like the 'Cotton Genesis'. Perhaps the eminent English scholar Alcuin, who presided over Charlemagne's Palace School, brought a great fifth-century bible with him to

Tours, when he became Abbot of St Martin's monastery in 796.

The Carolingian copyist responsible for the Moûtiers-Grandval Bible unwittingly recorded part of the process whereby Christian iconography came into being. For at the left of the topmost band of the Genesis picture God stoops over Adam, who lies stiff and inert before him on the ground. God is shaping the man out of the earth. His body is not yet animated by the breath of life. When this scene of the Creation of Adam was first visualized, back in the fifth century or thereabouts, its Early Christian originator was simply applying to a new purpose and a new story a traditional composition familiar to him in another context. A number of late-Antique sarcophagi have survived decorated with reliefs representing the demi-god Prometheus making the first man out of clay, a story told by Ovid. Prometheus is finishing off the lay figure, which lies prone and heavy in front of him. The gods of the Roman pantheon gather behind, to endow the figure with life, just as a pair of angels stand watching the Creator at work in the Moûtiers-Grandval Bible. Thus the Creation of Adam in the Carolingian picture is a relic of Antique art, while the whole sequence of scenes accurately records a grand, naturalistic, and didactic Early Christian original.

The First Bible of Charles the Bald, now in the Bibliothèque Nationale, is similarly a product of Tours, of around the mid-ninth century. Its prefatory picture to Genesis evidently depends on the same model as the Moûtiers-Grandval Bible. We see the same bulky figures of Adam and Eve standing stiffly at attention before God, the same dignified youthful Creator issuing his commands, the same continuous groundline in the horizontal divisions of the page, and the same variegated leafy shrubs [121]. Although these two Tours Genesis pictures look so alike, in fact they differ from one another in content. Each includes an incident which the other omits. While the Moûtiers-Grandval Bible represents God shaping the head of the inert figure of Adam, and thereafter Adam again prone, this time having the rib withdrawn from his side, the Charles the Bald Bible omits the shaping but instead represents God speaking to, or animating with his breath, an upstanding figure of Adam, before in the next scene stooping over the sleeping Adam to withdraw the rib. Here we have clear evidence that the ultimate model of the Genesis pictures in the two Tours Bibles contained more Adam and Eve material than was reproduced by either the artist of the

Moûtiers-Grandval Bible or the artist of the First Bible of Charles the Bald. By adding together the distinct scenes from the two bibles we can reconstruct and visualize their common ancient model. The very elaborate pictorial coverage of the Genesis text in the fifth-century original was broken down, selected and abbreviated, if only slightly, by the ninth-century copyists.

A similar phenomenon, revealing the processes of thought of the medieval book illustrator, engaged in reproducing but also inevitably editing and modifying – sometimes unconsciously – an ancient model, can be studied in two series of English Romanesque illustrations of the history of Moses. These pictures are among the illustrations placed at the front of the last English copy of the Utrecht Psalter, B. N. MS. Lat. 8846, and among the illustrations on one of four pictured leaves which may formerly have prefaced the Eadwine Psalter [122, 123]. The custom of inserting a series of illustrations of bible history before the text of the Psalms seems to have been English in origin, although by the thirteenth century it had spread to the Continent. The earliest English Psalter with preliminary bible pictures is B. M. Cotton MS. Tiberius C. vi, whose first illustration, representing the Creation [131] is based in part on the description of the Creator with the scales and measure in Isaiah, chapter 40, verse 12. At verse 11 of the same chapter we read 'He shall feed his flock like a shepherd; he shall gather the lambs with his arm and carry them in his bosom, and gently lead those that are with young.' This interpretation of God as the Shepherd of his people is easy to associate with the historical personality of David, the author of the Psalms. Scenes from the life of David are a normal part of the iconography of early Psalters, for example the great tenth-century Byzantine Psalter in Paris. Cotton MS. Tiberius C. vi has a series of scenes of the life of David, the first showing David rescuing the lamb from the mouth of the lion, and this scene is immediately preceded by the Creator with the balance, which may have been artificially attracted into the Psalter picture cycle by the conjunction of shepherd imagery and creation imagery in Isaiah, chapter 40, verses 11 and 12. Once a Creation scene is added to a David cycle we have, however cursorily, an Old Testament history cycle proper, and this tendency to preface the Psalms with a history cycle containing Genesis material may well have been encouraged by the summary of Old Testament history, 'the mighty acts of the Lord', given in Psalm 106, mainly dealing

122. Scenes from the Life of Moses, Canterbury Psalter, c. 1200

with the miracles and trials of the Exodus of the Jews from Egypt under Moses, and in Psalm 136, which begins with Creation and then briefly surveys the stories of Moses and Joshua. In a Psalter from St Albans, of before 1123, two Genesis scenes, the Fall and the Expulsion, are inserted in the preliminary history cycle, while in a Psalter of about the middle of the twelfth century, perhaps to be associated with Henry of

123. Scenes from the Life of Moses,
New York, Morgan Library MS. 724, *c.* 1150

Blois, Bishop of Winchester, the history cycle has expanded to
cover the careers of Adam and Eve and their children, Noah,
Abraham, Jacob, Moses and Joseph, before we reach David's
heroic fight with the lion and his successes in war.

In B. N. MS. Lat. 8846, and the detached bible-picture leaves,
we are similarly dealing with an extended bible history, and it
is of interest that these two manuscripts betray their dependence

187

on an older model evidently very elaborate indeed in pictorial content. If we compare certain of the Moses scenes in these two picture cycles, we see many points of agreement which prove the historical relationship of the two versions (for example the naked swimmer rescuing the infant Moses floating in his cradle on the waters of the Nile), but also many differences. At the top right of the detached leaf, now in the Morgan Library, MS. 724, two narrow rectangular pictures represent Moses with the Burning Bush, and Moses before Pharaoh. In the upper scene Moses's rod is miraculously transformed into a serpent, and he flees before it. In the lower scene, Moses and his brother Aaron repeat this miracle before Pharaoh, and when the Egyptian magicians perform the same wonder, the Egyptians' serpent is eaten up by Aaron's serpent. MS. 724 omits all reference to the subsequent miracles of Moses, whereby he brings plagues on the Egyptians. The next two pictures in MS. 724 represent the Children of Israel crossing the Red Sea in safety, led by Moses. They pass along a narrow strip of ground, with water on either side of them. Then as Moses turns and holds out his wand, the sea surges over the place where they have been walking, and drowns the Egyptians.

In MS. 8846 a similar sequence of events is represented. Moses casts down his rod before the Burning Bush, and it begins to turn into a serpent. This picture fills the whole square compartment, and the miracle of the rods before Pharaoh is omitted, so that the artist of MS. Lat. 8846 is abbreviating the cycle as recorded by the earlier artist of Morgan MS. 724. Next Moses and Aaron stand before Pharaoh and his courtiers, and Moses touches water at the foot of the picture with his wand. The picture is inscribed, 'Where Moses and Aaron cross the Red Sea', thus agreeing in subject if not in composition with the actual process of crossing shown in Morgan MS. 724. The next two pictures in MS. Lat. 8846 are the equivalent of the one picture of the destruction of Pharaoh's host in Morgan MS. 724, the later artist making a monumental composition out of this dramatic subject. Now if we look back at the picture described in MS. Lat. 8846 as the Crossing of the Red Sea, we realize that it is nothing of the kind. Moses and Aaron stand before Pharaoh, as they do in the serpent miracle in Morgan MS. 724. Moses strikes a narrow strip of water with his wand. The picture really represents the second miracle of Moses before Pharaoh, when he 'smote the waters that were in the river, in the sight of Pharoah and in the sight of his servants, and all the waters that were in the river were turned to blood'. Was the Romanesque artist perhaps misled by the redness of the river in his model into calling it the Red Sea, or did he perhaps make this redness an excuse for mental and pictorial abbreviation, so that he might press on to the exciting subject of the destruction of the Egyptians? In the cycle of paintings, of Early Christian date, which formerly decorated the Basilica of S. Paolo fuori le Mura at Rome, Moses and Aaron came repeatedly before Pharaoh and his guards, and performed miracle after miracle in his startled but stubborn presence. All the miracles of Moses, the plagues of frogs and locusts and cattle disease, and even a preliminary consultation with God before each plague is summoned, are represented in Cotton MS. Claudius B. iv, another symptom of its dependence on a huge illustrated bible with Early Christian antecedents. The model which lay before the artists of Morgan MS. 724 and B. N. Lat. 8846 was also evidently of this kind, and though these Romanesque artists were typical of their age in seeking monumental and typical compositions rather than repeating scene by scene in blind obedience to their model, they nevertheless leave, by faulty editing, tell-tale traces of the venerable Codex which was their guide and inspiration.

As we have seen, in the fifth century Bishop Namatius's wife at Clermont ordered her painters to represent subjects selected by her from a book. While a secular history may be implied by Gregory of Tours's account, the history of the Jewish people as narrated in the Scriptures themselves would of course be appropriate matter for depiction on the walls of a church, and we might, for example, visualize 'the histories of deeds of long ago' as scenes from the conquest of the Holy Land by Joshua, a Joshua cycle having certainly been created at a very early stage of bible illustration. Alternatively, the Clermont paintings could have dealt with a wider range of biblical history, such as is summarized in Psalms 106 and 136; a similar summary of great deeds done in the past of the Jewish people, mainly emphasizing the career of Moses, is given in the Acts of the Apostles, chapter 7, in the reported affirmation of his faith by St Stephen the Proto-martyr, in whose honour Namatius's wife built the church. Such a summary would perhaps determine the selection of subjects to be represented by the painters. Perhaps Namatius's wife owned an illustrated bible, the earliest surviving examples of which date from her life-time. In that case, the painters' task would have been to reproduce on a grand scale miniatures chosen and explained to them by the patroness. In the late eleventh century the Abbey church of St-Julien at Tours was decorated with monumental wall paintings, illustrating the Old Testament, including a magnificent series of scenes from the history of Moses, now sadly damaged and faded, but known from nineteenth-century water-colour copies [124]. As a model for their mural cycle the Romanesque painters who were employed at St-Julien were directed to a famous

124. The Children of Israel crossing the Red Sea, St-Julien at Tours, 11th century

illustrated codex preserved at that time at Tours, and now in the Bibliothèque Nationale, namely the Ashburnham or Tours Pentateuch, a North African or Spanish work of the seventh century. The Moses scenes in the Pentateuch and those at St-Julien agree strikingly in iconography and composition, and there is no doubt that the wall painters copied their scenes from the miniatures in the four-hundred-years-old manuscript. Thus as in the time of Namatius's wife, so in the late eleventh century, but now with no ambiguity as to the nature and extent of the painters' debt, a book provides the stimulus to a major decorative and descriptive scheme.

The work at St-Julien at Tours has stylistic connections with the greatest surviving monument of Romanesque wall painting, the huge mural scheme at St-Savin-sur-Gartempe, a monastery twenty-five miles east of Poitiers [125]. The vigorous

125. Interior of the Abbey Church of St-Savin, *c.* 1060–1115

126. The Building of the Tower of Babel, St-Savin, 12th century

group of Israelites at St-Julien supporting their baggage on their heads as they march confidently away before the returning waters of the Red Sea is closely paralleled by the group of the builders of the Tower of Babel at St-Savin who carry massive blocks of stone on their shoulders and steady their burdens with their upraised hands [126].

The church of St-Savin was built in the second half of the eleventh century on old foundations, the crypt at the east end and the west tower incorporating walls of a church founded and endowed by Charlemagne and Louis the Pious. The Romanesque Abbey church was, however, designed in a thoroughly up-to-date style, with a grand eastern ambulatory or passage-way from which a number of separate chapels project, a rational and boldly-conceived ground-plan earlier employed at the popular shrine of St Martin at Tours [112], and favoured by other eleventh- and twelfth-century churches of Pilgrimage throughout France and northern Spain, such as Chartres, St-Sernin at Toulouse, and Santiago de Compostela, allowing free motion of crowds to and from the shrines displayed at the eastern extremity of the church while the *opus dei* proceeded undisturbed in the central choir. The columns of the main arcade at St-Savin rise to a great height, and the barrel vault is set immediately above the arches of the main arcade. The close liaison of columns and high vault makes for a direct and simple visual impact, and for an open, airy and bright appearance, since light from the large aisle windows is able to penetrate into the central vessel of the church. The giant columns are painted in imitation of the sumptuous ornamental stones used in the decoration of Santa Sophia in Constantinople, and recall also the splendid striped and banded columns represented in Carolingian canon tables. Originally the entire church was painted with figure scenes, in accordance with Early Christian, Carolingian and German Ottonian practise. The crypt still preserves its cycle of scenes from the Passion of the Gallo-Roman martyrs SS. Savin and Cyprien, the western porch and tower chamber show scenes from the Book of Revelation, and from Christ's Passion, and the barrel vault of the nave, under which the local lay-people congregated and worshipped, displays a vast Old Testament cycle from the Creation to the deeds of Moses.

The style of the paintings in the nave and in other parts of the church has close contemporary parallels in a Sacramentary from the Cathedral of St-Étienne at Limoges and in an illustrated *Life of St Radegonde* made for the monastery of the Holy Cross at Poitiers. The painters employed at St-Savin evidently comprised an itinerant workshop, ready as required to produce small-scale miniatures or monumental wall paintings. The St-Savin style equally clearly descends from a long tradition of pictorial art. The stiff strutting figure of God in the *Building of the Tower of Babel* crosses his legs with a scissors-like action. His mantle is drawn close about his thighs and knees, and his robe, suddenly released from the constriction of the mantle, flares out in a wide fan of flat hard folds. These features can be exactly paralleled in Ottonian painting, for example in the figure of Salome dancing before Herod in the harsh and mannered Gospel Book of Otto III, of about 1000, or the figure of the woman with eagle's wings fleeing from the dragon in the Bamberg Apocalypse [127]. Again, the anatomy of the weight-

127. The Woman in Flight from the Dragon, Bamberg Apocalypse, 11th century

lifting builders of the Tower of Babel, breasts, rib-cage, belly and thighs, is delineated on the surface of their clinging tunics, resulting not only in a grand broad linear pattern but at the same time conveying with masterly ease, from the height of the vault to the eyes of the spectators below, the bulk and motion of the heroic painted figures. Such surface description of the substance of the body beneath the drapery is found in the powerful figures of personified Virtues in the Berne manuscript of the

128. The Fall of Pride, Bern Prudentius, 9th century

Psychomachia of Prudentius, stylistically a late-Carolingian derivative of the Tours school of illumination [128]. Carolingian elements also survive at St-Savin in the purely abstract and decorative motifs, such as the fern pattern painted on the horizontal broad band marking the apex of the nave vault, and the pelta pattern and medallion heads on the painted transverse arch beyond the mighty figure of the giant Nimrod, overseer of the builders at Babel. These motifs are paralleled in the great Carolingian Gospel Books of the Court School of the late eighth and early ninth centuries.

While the style of the paintings at St-Savin is a forceful and almost perfectly integrated amalgam of features derived from three hundred years of Western European painting, the iconographic programme in the nave has its closest analogies in Anglo-Saxon bible illustration. In the 'Caedmon' manuscript, for example, we find a parallel for the unusual portrayal of God actually present in the scene of the building of Babel, speaking to the workmen who turn and gesticulate towards him, and also a very similarly designed Tower, consisting in its lower stage of three short columns supporting round arches. The nave paintings at St-Savin contain a number of very rare subjects and rare visual interpretations, and give a distinct impression of having been selected from a very much longer picture-cycle, of an early type. As in the case of the Moses scenes at St-Julien at Tours, the illustrations in a locally preserved manuscript may have been used by the St-Savin painters. The wall paintings at St-Savin are profoundly interesting in the evidence which they provide that High Romanesque painting style and biblical iconography have roots deep in the past. But the decorative feeling and the swagger and large-scale exposition of the narrative material belong wholly to the Age of the Romanesque, and to the genius of the Master in charge of the St-Savin workshop. The task of painting the nave vault was evidently begun at the west end, and for some distance eastwards is restricted both by architectural divisions of the vault, in the form of transverse arches, and by self-imposed divisions, the pictures being designed as short rectangular compositions like illustrations on the pages of a codex. However, as the work proceeds eastwards on one half of the barrel vault and then returns westwards again in the other half, the narrative method rapidly expands, the space given to the composition increases, and we receive a clear impression of an artist breaking out of the limitations imposed by the fixed rectangular codex page into the freedom and scope of the Roll system. A continuous groundline like a ploughed field runs throughout the various groups of figures, unifying the whole history. The artist's narrative, despite its obvious dependence on older source material, has a new character, a sense of sweep and panorama which is physical, a matter of the scale and the expressive handling, not merely of the wide historical survey which is represented. The artist has awakened to the opportunities for expansive design offered to him by the huge barrel vault, and his personal experience, while working in the nave of St-Savin, can be compared to that of Michelangelo in the Sistine Chapel.

The early twelfth century, the climax of the great age of monastic culture, saw the production of a profusion of grand-scale monuments of figurative art, part decorative, part didactic, part public in their domineering physical presence and immediate visual impact, part private in their complex and learned imagery. The same energy and exuberance which we saw reforming the nature of the St-Savin picture-cycle threw up a magnificent series of sculptured portals in French Romanesque abbeys and cathedrals, in which traditional material was handled with unprecedented power, and iconographic novelties were boldly attempted. At Moissac, about 1115, a great tympanum was erected over the main portal representing the majesty of God, as it was revealed to St John in the Book of Revelation, chapter iv [129]. This theme had been illustrated by Carolingian artists back in the ninth century, for example the dome of the imperial chapel at Aachen bore a mosaic representation of God, nearly four metres high, enthroned in heaven, while the much smaller figures of the elders of the Apocalypse acknowledged his sovereignty by rising from their thrones and holding up their golden crowns. The vehemence which very occasionally breaks through the mellow and classical tone of Carolingian art [138] and which was fixed upon and made the standard mode of expression in the grandiose, hieratic, yet intense art of the Ottonians [119, 127], was pushed to its logical extreme by the Romanesque sculptor of the Moissac tympanum. The colossal figure of God has the physical glamour, vivid strained features, even the broad sharp shoulders, of an Archaic Greek statue like the Acropolis calf-bearer or the marble enthroned Goddess from Taranto or the bronze charioteer at Delphi. The clean stiff edges of his draperies laid out in hard flat zig-zag folds look as though they could cut the hand. Forming an endless figure-of-eight movement around God are the four beasts of the Apocalypse, stretching their necks and turning their heads to gaze in a compulsive rapture at the Author of their being, whom they cease not to praise day and night. Two rigid tall seraphim terminate the large central composition, the rest of the tympanum being filled up by the spasmodically twitching agitated figures of the elders, enthroned among the clouds, increasing by their diminutiveness the terrible majesty of their enthroned Emperor, to whom the world is a footstool and the stars a canopy.

A style very like that of the Moissac tympanum is displayed in the tympanum of the church at Souillac, about 1125 [130]. Here the hieratic grand manner is applied with extraordinary effect to a narrative relief, a series of scenes from the story of the apostate Theophilus, who was to the medieval world what Dr Faustus was to the Renaissance. Theophilus, a sixth-century priest of the church of Adana in Cilicia in Asia Minor, having

29. Apocalypse tympanum, Moissac, *c.* 1115

been slandered and wrongly dismissed from his offices of treasurer and archdeacon, has recourse to Satan, to whom he signs away his soul in exchange for a restored reputation and re-instatement. Then, overcome by revulsion, he prays to the Virgin for forty nights, and at last she agrees to save him, show-ing her potency as a patroness of repentant sinners and of all who implore her intercession before Christ. Chronological narrative holds no interest for the Souillac sculptor. Allowed remarkable freedom from convention in his choice of subject for a major

130. Theophilus tympanum, Souillac, *c.* 1125

portal tympanum, he relies, in the true High Romanesque man-ner, upon form to convey the core and substance of the story to the spectator. The visual language is both expressionist and abstract. The narrative composition is locked between the two seated figures of St Benedict and St Peter, respectively leader of the monastic order and leader of the whole Christian Church, just as the Moissac tympanum is bounded and constrained by the two thin vertical seraphim. St Benedict is smooth and placid, St Peter rigid and sinewy, with stiff fluttering draperies. A tension between the surface treatment of these two guarding figures disturbs the eye and mind, and prepares us for the melodramatic theme of the compact with Satan, twice represented, as if Satan once invoked would keep company with his rash postulant for ever. The two formidable figures of Satan are different from one another. In the first he has feet shaped like a bear's paws, while in the second he has one foot like a griffin's claw and the other like a bull's hoof. His head changes too, so that even while he clutches Theophilus's hand, Satan, unreliable, inconstant, treacherous and deadly, shifts from shape to shape, Proteus-like. In the central zone of the tympanum, above the heads of Theophilus and Satan, the penitent lies prostrate before the church and altar of the Virgin, and above him again, plunging vertically from the wildly stirring clouds, the Virgin comes with her bodyguard of angels, bringing the bond of compact which she had forced Satan to relinquish. The flourish of the banked clouds across the triple arch which encloses the whole relief, gives promise, even when Theophilus swears his allegiance to his false god, that the forces of heaven are in turmoil on his behalf. The narrative is expounded upwards, not sideways, and is radically reduced to three basic scenes, the bond-giving, the oath-taking, and the rescue. All the qualities which we admired in the Bayeux Tapestry, and which stem from old and impressive traditions of narrative, the lucidity and fullness of the handling, the consciousness of the passage of time and the traversing of space as elements in the story-telling, are utterly neglected here. At Souillac Romanesque narrative art makes its way towards a wholly original kind of visual description, concentrated, oblique, poetic, sensuous, personal, formally entering on a 'Baroque' phase at the very moment when psychologically it begins to show affinities with the Mannerists.

131. The Creation, B.M., Cotton MS. Tiberius C. vi, *c.* 1050

6

De Laudibus Sanctae Crucis

The illustration on the opposite page, an eleventh-century English artist's interpretation of the Creation, has the strange grandeur of a William Blake design, though with none of Blake's Regency voluptuousness of form [131]. This Ancient of Days is reduced like Count Ugolino to an emaciated spectre, and his world is still a mere diagram, a spiritual fabrication. God's head, breathing the divine inflatus down two thin tubes, and his hand, elegantly manipulating the apparatus of creation, stick up over the rim of the Universe. 'By the word of the Lord', says the Psalmist, 'were the heavens made, and all the host of them by the breath of his mouth.' In representing a pair of scales dangling from God's little finger the artist evidently had in mind the Prophet Isaiah's description of the Almighty – he 'who hath measured the waters in the hollow of his hand and meted out heaven with a span and comprehended the dust of the earth in a measure and weighed the mountains in scales and the hills in a balance'. The dividers held between God's thumb and middle finger are derived from the famous self-apostrophe of Holy Wisdom in Proverbs 8, 'when he prepared the heavens, I was there: when he set a compass upon the face of the depth . . . then I was by him, as one brought up with him.' These phrases were echoed by Dante in *Paradiso* XIX, with his 'Colui che volse il sesto all' estremo del mondo', and Milton, for whom the scriptural account may have been reinforced by familiarity with Old English drawings like that illustrated here, also describes the great Geometer's work with his 'golden compasses':

> One foot he centred, and the other turned
> Round through the vast profundity . . .

In 1102 a pilgrim named Saewulf saw an inscription, based on Isaiah's text about the measuring of heaven and earth, outside the Church of the Holy Sepulchre in Jerusalem, marking the spot called 'compas', and then regarded as the centre of the world. Pilgrims to Jerusalem were able to contemplate the very place where God's compasses had stood and turned as he described the circumference of the world. Saewulf says that Christ had assigned and marked out the spot 'with his own hand', and as proof he quotes from Psalm 73 (Vulgate), 'God our King before the ages wrought his salvation in the midst of the earth'. These words were regarded, from the early years of the Church, as literally true. The mid-point of the earth had a special role in God's plan for the regeneration of mankind. For the Fathers of the Church, such as St Jerome, and for Christian tourists in the golden age of the pilgrimage to the Holy Land, from the fourth to the sixth century, the mid-point of the earth was located a few paces to the west of the spot where the twelfth-century pilgrim Saewulf was to see it. It was located on a naked spur of rock, surrounded by a colonnaded atrium or cloister, built between the great Basilica of the Passion, called the *Martyrium*, and the rotunda called the *Anastasis*, the church of Christ's burial and resurrection. This spur of rock had witnessed many significant events in the world's history. Here, after the Flood, the bones or at least the skull of Adam found a final resting-place. Here Abraham received from the priest-king Melchisedek the mystical offerings of bread and wine. Here Abraham later built an altar and prepared to sacrifice his son Isaac, in allegorical anticipation of the Passion. At last, up the eight steps cut in the rock, Christ himself climbed to his crucifixion, for this place, ordained from the beginning of the world, was Golgotha. The rock was scored with deep fissures where Christ's blood had drenched and split it.

Celebrating this focal point of the Christian faith, a fourth-century poet wrote 'This is the middle of the earth, this is the sign of victory'. From apostolic times the cross of Christ was, of course, a symbol of redemption and everlasting life, the hard-won fruits of Christ's victory over sin and death. The conversion of the Emperor Constantine, and the ultimate adoption of Christianity as the religion of the Roman state, inevitably underlined the cross's militant connotation. Describing the great political and religious crisis of his life, Constantine told his biographer Eusebius how he had seen, with his own eyes, about midday when the sun was just beginning to decline, 'the trophy of a cross of light in the heavens, above the sun, bearing the inscription "Conquer by this" ' [132]. The cross now emerged as the official standard of embattled Christendom, a stimulus to valour and sacrifice in this world and an assurance of triumph in the next. This sign of victory was physically

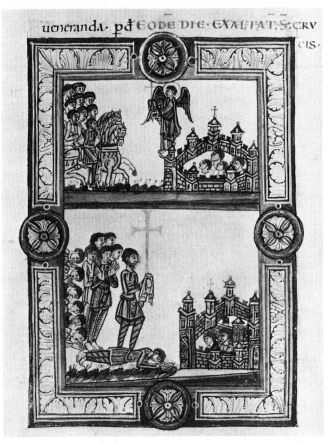

ueneranda· p̄ᚦ eode die · exalṫaṫ· s̄·crv cis·

132. The Exaltation of the Cross,
New York, Morgan Library MS. 641, c. 1050-65

present at the top of Golgotha. After the reputed Golgotha and Sepulchre areas had been sumptuously laid out by Constantine's orders and equipped with churches worthy of the state cult, a commemorative cross was erected where Christ's wooden cross had stood. This cross was the goal of a procession from Gethsemane at dawn on Good Friday, led by the Bishop of Jerusalem, and later that day it was the site of a three-hour vigil when the Bishop sat in a chair placed in front of the cross, and the Gospel narratives of the Passion together with interpretative passages from the Old Testament and the Epistles were read to the assembled faithful. A fifth-century mosaic in the apse of the Basilica of S. Pudenziana at Rome helps us to visualize this Easter vigil in the open air before the cross [133]. The crowd in the mosaic consists of the Apostles: their leader, seated holding an open book, is Christ himself. Behind his throne we see the tiled roof of the covered walk around the cloister and over this rises the rock of Golgotha, surmounted by the cross of gold, set with jewels and bordered with pearls, the extremities of the cross spreading a little by the placing of oval pearls on each corner. The cross gleams against the sky, in which float, huge and mysterious, the animal symbols of the Evangelists,

133. Apse mo[
S. Pudenziana
Rome, 401-1[

investing the cross with a heavenly as well as an earthly splendour.

This glorified cross, linking earth and heaven, clothed in precious metal and beautified with precious stones, symbol of Christ dead and again living, ascended on high and reigning for ever, is the prototype of innumerable masterpieces of goldsmiths' work with which every well-endowed ecclesiastical establishment in Christendom decked its altars [134, 135]. In the late tenth century the famous monastery of Reichenau in Lake Constance was lavishly furnished by Abbot Witigowo with altars and with crosses of gold and silver upon which were fastened precious necklaces, 'marvellous webs of gems'. Similarly, a 'most noble necklace' of seventh-century work-

204

manship was used to enrich the huge cross of Charlemagne, one of the many crosses possessed by the monastery of St-Denis near Paris. These crosses are described by the English diarist John Evelyn who visited St-Denis in 1643: 'The Treasury is kept in the Sacristy above, where were shew'd us greate Presses full of Sacred Reliques; especialy that greate Crosse of Gold inchas'd & studded with precious stones: also another full of pearles & gold, another of massy Gold 3 foote high, set with Saphyres, Rubies and greate oriental Pearles: Another given by Charles the greate, having a noble oriental Amethist in the middle of it, stones & pearles of inestimable value.' The relics and art treasures of St-Denis were looted in the French revol-

Processional
s, Brescia,
r 8th century

ution, but a view of the interior of the church as it was in the fifteenth century is recorded in a Flemish painting in the National Gallery, London [136]. In the painting silk brocades conceal much of the sumptuous ornamental figure work with which the high altar was encased from the twelfth century

onwards, but a high relief gold and jewelled panel presented to St-Denis in the ninth century by Charlemagne's grandson Charles the Bald is exhibited as a retable, and above and behind this rises the 'greate Crosse of Gold', the work of Eligius, the seventh-century *aurifex peritissimus*. This cross had a long stem and stood six feet high. In design and technique it was typical

of the ornamental metalwork of its time, the ground-work of the cross being made up of thin walled gold cells or cloisons into which glass mosaic, shaped plaques of semi-precious stones and mother of pearl were laid, the all-over pattern consisting of interlocked shallow-armed crosses. Large jewels were set at intervals on the arms and shaft of the cross, and the whole bordered by pearls.

The representation of the cross as something stately, noble in proportions and glittering and precious in its materials, reveals an interesting process of idealization, an Apollean transformation of the crude gibbet on which Christ died. The Emperor Julian, the last defender of the Antique pagan pantheon, took no pains to gloss over the true nature of the Christians' cult object. He spoke bluntly of their worshipping the 'vile wood' of a criminal's cross. But the attractiveness of Christianity lay in its many sidedness. As a corollary, not a contrast, to its grand scale and elaborate conception of the invisible and supernatural world, it firmly emphasized the human and material basis of its faith. Although for obvious reasons the cross came to be visualized in a gracious and beautiful form, it was as a symbol of deity seldom permitted to become detached from the historical reality of Christ's crucifixion. In St John's Gospel the words 'Now is the Son of Man glorified' are introduced not in the resurrection narrative but right at the beginning of the story of the Passion, when Judas has betrayed Christ, thus presenting the whole process of Christ's death as honourable and glorious. The Easter ceremonies at Jerusalem were not solely concentrated upon the ornate commemorative cross erected on the rock of Golgotha, but were essentially bound up with the actual cross, located and identified by Constantine's mother Helena as the necessary preliminary to the Emperor's great building programme at Jerusalem. The wood from the cross and the board inscribed by Pilate with Christ's titles were preserved in a silver-gilt casket and were exposed for veneration after the dawn procession on Good Friday and before the vigil by the commemorative cross, in a small chapel built behind Golgotha. The faithful entering by one door and coming out by another were scrutinized with the vigilance which we popularly associate with the departure of gangs of diamond workers after their day's work. The wood from the cross and the title board were placed on a table, but gripped by the bishop and guarded by attendant deacons, so that while the pilgrims filed by and each in turn bowed over the cross and kissed it, no pious thief might unobserved nip off a fragment with his teeth.

With the capture of Jerusalem by the Persians early in the seventh century, Constantinople, the capital city of the Roman Empire, became the chief repository of relics of the cross. In the cathedral church of Santa Sophia three portions of the cross were preserved in a wooden chest. On three consecutive days each year, Maundy Thursday, Good Friday, and Holy Saturday the chest was placed open on a golden altar. The cross was adored and kissed on the first day by the male population of the city led by the Emperor, on the second day by the matrons and virgins led by the Empress, and on the third day by the clerical order, led by the Patriarch. The whole church was filled with a wonderful perfume while the relics remained on view, and they also emitted a miraculous curative oil. Two western Latin accounts of this magnificent ceremonial have survived, one written down by Adomnan, Abbot of Iona, from the description narrated personally to him by the pilgrim Arculf, and the other written by the great English historian Bede in his *Book on the Holy Places*, on the basis of what Adomnan had told him of Arculf's reports. In the tiny stone churches set in the bleak wastes of eighth-century Northumbria and even more in the remote western island of Iona, this news of a ritual solemnized by vast crowds before the authentic cross in the metropolis of the Christian world must have seemed marvellous indeed, a convincing evocation upon earth of the glories of heaven.

St John in the Book of Revelation had described the worship accorded to Christ the sacrificial lamb, by his armies of angels, patriarchs, martyrs and confessors. In Revelation chapter 5, St John sees the Almighty on his throne, holding a book, closed and sealed. No one in earth or heaven is found worthy to open the book. The nature of God is as it were closed to men. St John weeps, and is comforted by one of the twenty-four elders who attend on God: 'Behold, the Root of David will break the seals and open the book.' A Lamb 'as it had been slain' appears at the throne and takes the book from the hand of the Almighty. With singing and harps and with 'golden vials full of odours, which are the prayers of the saints', the Lamb is worshipped by the inhabitants of heaven. 'And I beheld, and I heard the voice of many angels round about the throne, and the beasts and the elders, and the number of them was ten thousand times ten thousand, and thousands of thousands, saying with a loud voice "Worthy is the Lamb that was slain to receive power

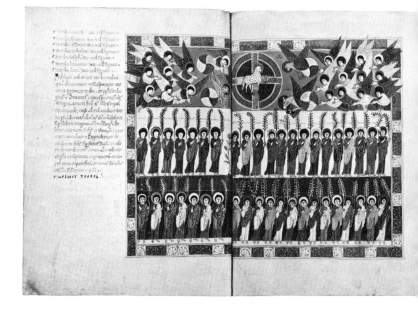

and riches and wisdom and strength and honour and glory and blessing".' To this first version of the acclamation of the Lamb the author of Revelation adds another, in chapter 7, where a great multitude, whom no man could number, of all nations, and kindreds, and peoples, and tongues, stood before the throne and before the Lamb, clothed in white robes, with palms in their hands – all those who have washed their robes and made them white in the blood of the Lamb. In the great mid-eleventh-century Apocalypse manuscript from the monastery of St Sever in western France this vision is impressively represented with its row-upon-row of cheerfully beaming palm-bearers. The angels and the evangelist beasts fly rapidly to prostrate themselves before the sacrificial Lamb who stands holding the book at the centre of a grand cross-medallion [137]. This kind of image of the Church triumphant adoring the sacrificial Lamb underlies the ceremonies of the Church militant centred on the cross, its fragments and its replicas. It underlies also, of course, the efforts of Christians to design a new God-centred society, specifically a communal and ascetic way of life. One of the pioneers of western monasticism, St Paulinus of Nola, writes of 'the glorious thousands of the saints who raise to the sublime stars their winged feet freed from earth's fetters. Borne by the light clouds, they pass through the constellations in the airy spaces, to pay homage to the King of Heaven, and to join their bright ranks to the adored Christ.'

Although, as we have seen, precautions were taken to prevent the diminution by theft of the relics at Jerusalem, partitions, official and unofficial, frequently took place. Cyril of Alexandria writing in the mid-fourth century says that portions of the cross had already been scattered throughout the world. St Paulinus received a fragment of the cross from his kinswoman St Melania on her return from the Holy Land. He in turn sent it, or part of it, to his friend Sulpicius Severus in 402, on the occasion of the dedication of the great church built by Sulpicius at his villa of Primuliacum in Aquitaine near the Pyrenees. 'Accept', wrote Paulinus, 'in a small thing a great gift, and take to yourself in this minute fragment of a fragment a defence in this present life and a pledge of eternal salvation.' St Paulinus credited the authentic cross with the power of multiplying itself like the loaves and fishes, but in explaining the number of relics of the cross which spread through Christendom we have also to take into account the principle of sanctification by contact with an authentic relic. Holy wood of this secondary quality, rapidly indistinguishable from its great original, and other materials, textiles and easily portable unguents, were widely distributed. A notable example of the transference of the accumulated merit of the True Cross to something which had touched it is vouched for by St Gregory of Tours in the sixth century, in his *Book of Miracles*. He received from the hands of a traveller and deposited in an oratory at Tours, an old silk textile which had formerly been used at Jerusalem to wrap the relics of the cross. The textile miraculously cured the blind, the deaf, and the paralysed. The poet Venantius Fortunatus in his verses praising Gregory's

138. The Lamb unsealing the Book, Bible of S. Paolo fuori le Mura, between 870 and 875

oratory, describes it as white and purple and ornamented with woven crosses – just such a textile as is symbolically drawn aside by Joshua in a miniature in the ninth-century Moûtiers-Grandval Bible showing the establishment of the Jewish Law by Moses, and such as clothes the heavenly altar in a representation of the Lamb unsealing the book in the St Paul's Bible made for Charles the Bald [138].

Devout enthusiasm for relics of the cross finds its classic expression in another poem by Fortunatus, written on the occasion of the reception into Poitiers in 569 of a fragment of the True Cross. Queen Radegonde, one of the more dispensable consorts of the lascivious thug Chlotar I, King of Soissons, was permitted to retire from court and to establish by means of her private fortune and her state pension a monastery at Poitiers dedicated to the Holy Cross. Through the good offices of Chlotar's son and successor Sigibert, Radegonde was able to send ambassadors to the Emperor Justin II in Constantinople, requesting a portion of the cross from the imperial treasury. The relic, consisting of a number of small pieces of wood, themselves built into the shape of a cross with the title board as an extra transverse bar at the upper part of the stem, was duly despatched to Radegonde and is still preserved at Poitiers, together with the Queen's heavy wooden reading desk, carved with crosses in many different shapes flanking the sacrificial Lamb of the Apocalypse [139]. Radegonde and her clerical

139. Reading desk of St Radegonde, Poitiers, before 587

friends arranged a splendid procession to welcome and to convey their new Palladium to the church which was to be its
shrine. The famous hymn *Vexilla regis prodeunt* was first sung
as the relic was borne into Poitiers:

> The battle standards of the King advance.
> The mystery of the Holy Cross illumines the world,
> By which Life patiently endured death
> And brought a greater life out of death.

Fortunatus links the wood of the cross with the ideas of regality
and triumph, and writes of the beautiful radiant tree arrayed in
royal purple, which bore on its branches the body of Christ. An
echo of this mystical solemn tone, as well as of the many interlocked ideas which the *Vexilla* hymn contains, is found in the
greatest Old English poem, *The Dream of the Rood*, in which a
Northumbrian poet narrates his midnight vision of a cross,
raised on high, ablaze with light and glittering with gold and
jewels. The cross tells its history, how it grew as a tree, was cut
down, shaped into a gallows, and drenched with the blood of
the dying Saviour. Flung away into a ditch in obscurity and
shame, the cross is afterwards raised up as a source of gladness
and healing to all men who honour and bow to the sign of
Christ's victory. 'Now I tower under heaven, in glory attired.'

The intrusion of these ideas into the English tongue and into
the English heroic tradition, as reflected both in the vernacular
poetry and in the Latin historical narrative of Bede, began in
597 when St Augustine at the command of Pope Gregory the
Great carried the banners of Christendom across the Channel
and preached the Gospel to the heathen English of Kent. The
missionaries were received by King Ethelbert in the open air,
since he was afraid to confront such powerful magicians in an
enclosed space. The Christian clergy came in procession chanting the litany and carrying a picture of Christ painted on a
board and a silver cross as their 'vexillum'. One of their audience, the Frankish Princess Bertha, wife of the pagan king and
great-niece to Queen Radegonde, must have understood the
symbolism of the cross as the Christian standard and trophy in
continental terms. But the king may have had associations of
his own by which to interpret the tall metal pole with the transverse bar that these strangers bore towards him. The kings of
the English in the seventh century evidently made use of
various traditional emblems of authority, including banners
and standards. The historian Bede writes of King Edwin of

Northumbria (died 632) that 'his dignity was so great throughout his dominions that his standards were not only borne before him into battle, but even in time of peace, when he rode about his cities, towns, and provinces with his officers, the standard bearer (*signifer*) was accustomed to go before him. Also when he walked along the streets, that sort of standard which the Romans call *Tufa* and the English *thuuf* was likewise carried before him.' Edwin, a prince of one of two rival Northumbrian royal families, spent part of his adventurous youth in exile at the court of Raedwald, the powerful ruler of East Anglia, and may there have encountered for the first time the military and sacral iconography of a royal standard. At Thanet, when spiritual battle was joined between declining paganism and the Gospel, the *thuuf* of Ethelbert may have stood planted at his feet as a sign of his preeminence among the kings of the English, the Bretwaldadom to which first Raedwald of East Anglia, then Edwin of Deira, and afterwards Oswald of Bernicia succeeded him.

The official communications of the Church with English rulers in the period of the conversion, for example Pope Boniface IV's letter to King Edwin, have an elevated tone of high diplomacy and higher theology. The pope greets the illustrious king of the English and then proceeds to define the nature of Almighty God, who with the co-eternal Son planned and disposed all things at the beginning of time, and disposed the heights of empire and the powers of the earth. The Pope speaks of the Creator 'now kindling by the Holy Spirit, to a knowledge of Himself, the cold hearts of the nations seated at the extremities of the earth', a cosmic picture well realized in the eleventh-century drawing with which I began this chapter [131]. Pope Boniface invites Edwin to draw near to the God who breathed the breath of life into him, and summons him to take upon himself the 'sign of the Holy Cross'. As well as on this bland official plane, so also down among the practical politics, personalities, and dark intrigues of the age of the conversion, the image of the cross plays a potent part. Early seventh-century England was the meeting place of strong cultural influences, oddly juxtaposed rather than blended. We have the shocked report of Bede that Raedwald toyed with Christianity in the midst of his idol worship, erecting an altar to Christ alongside the altar to his gods. Edwin in exile at Raedwald's court, amidst this vacillating intellectual atmosphere and beset by well-grounded fears for his life, was visited in the night by a mysterious messenger, who promised him victory over his enemies and a glorious reign, in return for spiritual obedience. Between the prince and his unknown well-wisher a sign, a manual gesture, was employed as a secret pledge, which, when oral tradition hardened into written narrative, was interpreted as the sign of the cross. Edwin's midnight visitor is obscurely described as being 'crowned with the cross of Christ'. The whole incident as we have it recorded is coloured by the story of the apparition of the cross in Eusebius's *History of Constantine*. Eusebius's *History* in a Latin translation by Rufinus was certainly known in England in the Early Christian period. A stone cross-slab from the seventh-century monastery of Jarrow in Northumbria is carved alongside the cross stem with an inscription *In hoc singulari signo vita redditur mundo*, the first four words being taken from Rufinus's account of the inscription set beneath a statue of Constantine in Rome, which held in its hand 'the vexillum of Our Lord's cross'.

The same story-pattern, but with a powerful pro-Celtic slant, is found in the preface to the *Life of Columba* by Adomnan, Abbot of Iona. Here King Oswald, of the rival Northumbrian royal house, who regained power after Edwin's death, is the recipient of divine encouragement. In the night, before a crucial battle against the British King Cadwallon, Oswald had a vision of St Columba, 'radiant in angelic form', standing in the midst of the English camp, his head touching the clouds. The saint promises him victory and a happy reign. Adomnan writes that having defeated and killed Cadwallon, 'the victor, returning from battle, was afterwards ordained by God as emperor of the whole of Britain'. In Adomnan's story Oswald and his twelve attendants alone were Christians, having been converted at the Celtic monastery on Iona, and the first fruit of his victory was that his heathen army, convinced by his account of his vision, accepted baptism. Bede, although he must have heard this story from Adomnan, says nothing about a vision of St Columba, and depicts Oswald's army as Christian to a man. The focal point of Bede's narrative is a cross raised on the battlefield by Oswald as his standard. 'The place is shown to this day where Oswald, being about to engage, erected the sign of the Holy Cross. . . . The cross being made in haste, and the hole dug in which it was to be fixed, the King himself, full of faith, laid hold of it and held it with both his hands, till it was set fast by throwing in the earth.' Although Bede later reports that Oswald's *vexillum*, made with gold and purple, was placed above the King's tomb at Bardney in Lindsey, the fact that a wooden cross was thrust into the ground before the battle at Hefenfelth would suggest that at that moment of crisis, at least, the Old English royal standard or *thuuf* had yielded its place to the sign of the cross itself, wrought of rough timber. It is unknown whether Edwin discarded or modified his *thuuf* after his baptism in 627. He donated a 'large gold cross' to the church founded at York by St Paulinus, and after Edwin's death and the temporary disruption of the church in Northumbria, this cross was brought for safety to Canterbury. Strictly contemporary with the great cross at St-Denis, it is probable that Edwin's cross, judging from the extant remains of seventh-century English goldsmiths' work [28], could have rivalled that of Eligius in beauty and technical bravura.

Bede claims that the wooden cross at Hefenfelth was the first outward sign of Christianity to make its appearance in Bernicia, that is in the area between the Tyne and the Forth. The battlefield was 'near the wall with which the Romans formerly enclosed the island from sea to sea'. Nothing now survives of Oswald's cross, but its contemporary fame and sanctity make it the probable immediate prototype of the gigantic stone crosses which still stand in close proximity to the Roman wall, at Bewcastle and Ruthwell. The Ruthwell Cross, towering eighteen feet, with its tall stem and short arms, must in its former open-air site near the shores of the Solway have recalled the silhouette of the golden memorial cross on the mound at Golgotha [140]. The specific function of this kind of monumental stone cross is illuminated by a passage in the eighth-century *Hodoeporicon* or *Guide Book* taken down from the verbal narrative of St Willibald, the English missionary to Germany who died in 785 as Bishop of Eichstadt. Willibald recalls that in his infancy he fell sick with what was feared to be a mortal illness.

While his parents, in great anxiety of mind, were held in suspense as to the death of their son, they made an offering of him before the great cross of our Lord and Saviour. For it is the custom of the Saxon race that on many of the estates of nobles and of good men they are wont to have, not a church, but the standard of the Holy Cross dedicated to Our Lord and reverenced with great honour, lifted up on high so as to be convenient for the frequency of daily prayer. They laid him there before the cross and begged Our Lord God, the maker of all things, to console them and save their son's life . . . and then they promised that if the health of the child were restored they would at once offer him to receive the tonsure . . .

Here we have a vivid picture of the cross as a meeting place for prayer and intercession, while its associated meaning as a fount of healing and a battle standard are assumed in the miraculous restoration of the child's health and his parents' subsequent gift of him 'to the heavenly King as his soldier'.

The Ruthwell Cross has figure reliefs, copied probably from carved ivory panels and illuminated Gospel Books, on its broad front and back, and on its sides it has meander patterns of vine branches, symbolizing Christ the True Vine. It may originally have borne the image of Christ, the sacrificial Lamb, at its apex, set amidst the four beasts of the Apocalypse. On its narrow flanks it bears a long runic inscription in the Northumbrian dialect of Old English, consisting of the account of the crucifixion from *The Dream of the Rood*, when the cross suffers with Christ, is pierced by nails and stands all wet with blood. 'Those warriors left me standing, covered with blood. I was all wounded with arrows.' The sacramental connotation of the cross emblem, its identification with Christ himself, has perhaps never been more dramatically stressed than here.

According to the legend of the discovery of the cross by St Helena, the True Cross was singled out from the other crosses buried with it in a ditch in Jerusalem by its miraculous curative properties, demonstrated upon the sick who touched it. We have seen that the fragments of holy wood, oil and cloth distributed throughout Christendom were regarded not merely as sources of spiritual benefit but as remedies against all kinds of physical debilities. This decline of the sacred treasure or emblem into a *nostrum* for the vulgar rapidly overtook King Oswald's wooden cross at Hefenfelth. Bede, commenting on the victory of Oswald over Cadwallon, writes: 'In that place of prayer very many miraculous cures are known to have been performed, as a token and memorial of the King's faith. For even to this day many are wont to cut off small chips from the wood of the Holy Cross, which being put into water, men or cattle drinking thereof, or sprinkled with that water, are immediately restored to health.' In the tight little system of medieval cosmography the solemn service of the Exaltation of the Cross at Constantinople or Rome and a recipe for mending the sprained leg of a horse were inevitably not very far apart in the intellectual scale. In early medieval leechcraft the cross is invoked and inscribed in charms against elf-shot, snake bites, rats and mice, rheumatism, typhoid fever, theft, and the swarming of bees, as well as in ceremonies to improve the fertility of the land. Corpus Christi College MS. 41, a book given to Exeter Cathedral by Bishop Leofric (1046–72), contains alongside Bede's *History* and various other tracts a collection of spells and recipes in Old English and Latin. One charm against loss of cattle invokes St Helena who found the True Cross when it was concealed in the earth. 'I thought of St Helena, and I thought of Christ hanging on the cross. So I think that I shall find these cattle and they shall not go far away.' Another charm against theft reads, 'May the Cross bring it back again. The Cross was lost, and then found. May Abraham close up to you the roads, mountains, woods, lanes, streams, and passage-ways. May Isaac bring darkness over you. May the Cross bring you to judgement. The Jews crucified Christ and were not able to conceal that deed. So this theft is unable to be hidden.' A charm for easy child-birth invokes the Creator and sanctifier, with the Son and the Holy Ghost, and has as its core the words *sator. arepo. tenet. opera. rotas.* These words written one below the other form a square and a palindrome,

```
S A T O R
A R E P O
T E N E T
O P E R A
R O T A S
```

The Sator formula has been found scratched on the plaster of a column at Pompeii, inscribed four times at the famous Early Christian site at Doura Europas, and again on Roman plaster at Cirencester. It may be tentatively translated, 'The sower (creator) holds with labour (or 'might') the wheels (rotation?) of the plough (?). 'Arepo' is perhaps a Celtic word for plough, but being only looking-glass writing for 'opera', 'arepo' may itself be meaningless. Within the limitation of a palindrome, the word-square gets as near to sense as it can, and seems in fact a fair approximation to the idea of God at the beginning of his great work of Creation, revolving the compasses. But the word-square itself guards and conceals the specific sense and arrangement of the letters, which as E. Grossner pointed out in 1926 are the opening words of the Lord's Prayer in Latin, 'PATER NOSTER', written twice to form an equal armed cross, converging on the single central letter N, and with the Apocalyptic titles of God, A (Alpha) and O (Omega) suspended above and below the horizontal arms of the cross. With perfect theological aptness the beneficent Father and the suffering Son are integrated visually. In the later Middle Ages the most frequently employed iconography of the First and Second Persons of the Trinity shows the Father supporting in his hands the cross on which the Son is hanging. That evolved pictorial imagery was unknown in the Pre-Carolingian, Carolingian, and Romanesque periods, but its essential meaning is expressed by the spare and elegant device of the crossed strands of letters unscrambled from the Sator formula. Even in its disguised form as a word-square, the cross dominates the design in the horizontal and

141. God enthroned with the symbols of the four Evangelists, Prüm Gospels, 9th century

vertical word 'tenet', and so provides a satisfying image of the penetration of Creation by the cross, an idea to which I have already referred.

Thus the Sator formula was a portmanteau packed with meaning, and its popular use as a curative charm, on a level with, say, the sonorous names of the Seven Sleepers of Ephesus, or half-comprehended fragments of Hebrew and Greek, was inevitable. Such credulous and banal leechcraft invocations of the cross exaggerate but do not basically modify universally accepted ideas and attitudes. We have already witnessed Bede's sudden lapse from heroic narrative to a cattle-cure. The assumed veracity of the Scriptures on the central facts of the relation of God and Man, and on all subsidiary subjects such as history and natural science drove scholarly inquiry in upon itself, like the *ourobouros* serpent of the alchemists devouring its own tail. The best minds of the Early Middle Ages derived keen pleasure from the kind of verbal by-play found in the Sator formula. Verbal parallels, anagrams, acrostics, were regarded as a valid and significant part of theological exposition. In a Gospel Book from the church of Prüm in Germany, dating to the second quarter of the ninth century, God is depicted seated with his feet on a rainbow [141]. The three arms of his cross-nimbus are inscribed *Rex, Lex,* and *Lux*, the form as well as the sense of these words having appealed to the artist or his instructor.

The supreme examples of this type of verbal manipulation are found in the treatise *De Laudibus Sanctae Crucis* by Rabanus Maurus, Abbot of Fulda and Archbishop of Mainz (780–856). Rabanus's incantatory eloquence is so calculated as to throw up, as if inevitably, pictures and diagrams. He excels in acrostics and palindromes. A cross inscribed horizontally and vertically (and in both directions) with the words *oro te ramus aram ara sumar et oro* emerges from the text of a poem in which the author praises God as 'dux', 'via', 'lux', 'vita'. Without causing a break in the general drift or tenor of the lines of the poem, a picture of Rabanus is superimposed on the text and inscribed with a prayer which he personally addresses to Christ [142]. With similar ingenuity other poems in the treatise body forth a portrait of Charlemagne's son Louis the Pious, sacred letters and numbers, the sacrificial Lamb with the four evangelical symbols and the cross in various decorative forms. Rabanus's masterpiece is perhaps *Figura I*, in which he literally draws with his verses the image of Christ crucified, hanging with outstretched arms. This liking for combining a representation of

2. Portrait of Rabanus Maurus at the foot of the Cross, Fulda, *c.* 840

the cross with an inscribed commentary or devotional formulae is highly significant. The cross, the central visual image of the Early Middle Ages, has an encyclopedic role. It is regarded as growing more potent, the more expository material is added to it. So Latin and Old English inscriptions are crammed into every clear space on the Ruthwell Cross. The pictorial representation and the inscription are exactly on a par. In designing the monuments under discussion here, there is no question of the painting or sculptured image being created as the books of the unlettered. We are dealing with an esoteric and allusive art, the product of the narrowly learned monastic culture of the period. Literacy had a special mystique, which is clearly reflected in the visual arts produced and appreciated. The great phrase from the beginning of St John's Gospel, *Deus erat verbum*, is deeply impressed upon early medieval art.

Perhaps the supreme surviving example of the blending of recondite words and images in devout recollection of the Passion is the walrus-tusk ivory cross, of about the middle of the twelfth century, now in the Cloisters Collection at the Metropolitan Museum, New York [143]. Before ever we have read its inscriptions or identified its imagery, this object has stamped itself on the memory by the dense matted texture of its figure-scenes and the austere elegance of its long thin upright stem and transverse bar. The principal inscription, boldly cut in large noble letters down the full length of the stem, celebrates in short sonorous phrases the overthrow of the Jewish Synagogue and Christ's victory over death. The two descending columns of the inscription form a border to the thrusting vertical of a simulated rough timber cross-stem, and the transverse arm of the cross is similarly treated, with regularly lopped branches giving a jagged outline. This type of cross was particularly favoured by English artists of the eleventh century, for example by the draughtsman whose Creator with the compasses is reproduced at the beginning of this chapter. In the Cloisters ivory cross the ancient idea of the cross as formed from a series of magically potent words or letters is most happily combined with the equally ancient iconography of the cross as a great tree, destined from the beginning of the world to bear the burden of the body of Christ. To these two basic visual interpretations of the cross are added a host of others. At the foot of the cross stem, and clinging to its very root, is the reclining figure of Adam, awakened, with Eve, from his long death by the revivifying blood of Christ. Below Adam the square base terminal contains the scene of Christ suffering the buffets of the servants of the High Priest. The right arm terminal contains Christ's death and burial, the left terminal the angel seated on the tomb announcing the Resurrection, and the top terminal represents Christ ascending already half lost to sight among the clouds. On the back of the cross the terminals contain the symbolic beasts of the Book of Revelation, and at the intersection of the arms and stem is a great boss, swathed in inscribed scrolls, containing at its centre the apocalyptic Lamb. The breast of the Lamb is pierced by a lance, held not by the centurion Longinus but symbolically by the Jewish Synagogue. St John weeps alongside the Lamb, as if he was stationed beside the cross, but he sheds his tears in another context, in illustration of Revelation, chapter 5, for he is comforted by the angel with a scroll bearing the command 'Do not weep', and in addition the words shouted in heaven by the multitudes of angels, 'Worthy is the Lamb who was slain to receive power and riches.' Under the Lamb's feet is Jeremiah, holding a scroll inscribed with his own prophetic words, 'I was like a lamb brought to the slaughter'. The stem and arm of the cross carry the effigies of eighteen other Old Testament prophets, each holding a scroll inscribed with a phrase or sentence from their writings in which the revelation of God in Christ is foreshadowed. Here, where the didactic and scholarly content of his art is at its most weighty, the designer rises to his greatest aesthetic heights. Along the left arm of the cross three scrolls held by three prophets curve upwards from right to left. On the right arm, the first scroll rises, as we would expect for purposes of symmetry, from left to right. But the other two, with a sudden dramatic reversal of great effectiveness, sweep from left to right downwards. The design seems to burst into spontaneous life, to pulsate with the skill and intelligence of its creator. The boss on the front of the cross continues the interpretation of Christ's Passion in terms of Old Testament prophecies. The central figure of Moses is encased by a band of figures in perpetual fluid motion, like the archivolt figures suspended in lines about the head of Christ on the central portal of Chartres. Moses strides forward in the foreground of the scene, and above him stands his brazen serpent drooping over a cleft stick, raised up as a restorative to to the people (Numbers, chapter 21), an allegory of the crucifixion, as pointed out in St John's Gospel, chapter 3, where Christ expounds to Nicodemus the Pharisee the need for regeneration and says 'And as Moses lifted up the serpent in the wilderness, even so must the Son of Man be lifted up.' On the cloisters Cross no less than five inscribed scrolls, like banners streaming in the wind, are displayed in loving analysis of the layers of meaning perceived by the twelfth-century theologian-designer in this one scene.

For early medieval writers one of the most compulsive exercises was to probe into the Old Testament in search of veiled allusions to Christ's life and redemptive death. St Luke's account of the Journey to Emmaus and St Peter's sermons as reported in the Acts of the Apostles show that this process was already well underway by the time that the books of the New Testament were composed. As we have noted, the reading of Old Testament prophecies of the Passion was a feature of the Easter vigil at the memorial cross at Jerusalem in the early centuries of the Church. The emergence of liturgical use of parallel or analagous passages from the Old and New Testaments gradually gave rise to their equivalents in pictorial form. In the famous doors of the fifth century basilica of S. Sabina on the Aventine Hill in Rome, for example, Elijah's departure into heaven in a fiery chariot is represented as a type of Christ's ascension. Bede records the presence of an elaborate picture series of 'types and antitypes' in Northumbria in the seventh century. The church of the monastery of St Paul at Jarrow was adorned with panel paintings brought by Benedict Biscop from Italy, 'ably describing the connexion of the Old and New Testament; as for instance Isaac bearing the wood for his own sacrifice, and Christ carrying the cross on which he was about to suffer, were placed side by side. Again, the serpent raised up by Moses in the desert was illustrated by the Son of Man elevated on the cross.' These panels, which represented the first illustrations of the Old Testament recorded in the history of English art, have vanished long ago. The solitary survivor of this early phase of Old Testament allegorical imagery is the half-length figure of an archer, about to discharge an arrow, carved on the lower arm of the cross-head of the Ruthwell Cross [140]. This archer is no secular motif, strayed in from the everyday world, but is the deliberate foil to the image of the sacrificial Lamb formerly placed in the middle of the cross-head on the other side from the archer. St Augustine in *The City of God* writes of Abraham's two sons, Ishmael the child of Hagar the bondswoman and Isaac the child of Sarah, as symbols of the Old Covenant of the Jews and the New Jerusalem of the Christians, that is of Synagogue and Church. Ishmael the persecutor of Isaac is rejected and cast out into the Wilderness of Paran. There according to Genesis, chapter 21, 'he grew . . . and became an archer'. At Ruthwell Ishmael is not contrasted with Isaac, but directly with Christ, the Lamb offered in sacrifice, of whom Isaac was the most distinguished 'type'. Ishmael again appears on the front of an ivory reliquary made in southern England in the eleventh century. This reliquary is in the shape of a cross [144], and Ishmael crouches in the central

144. English reliquary cross, 11th or 12th century

medallion, amidst a thick tangle of fleshy foliage, and aims his arrow at a bird perched in the upper arm of the cross. On the back of the cross the Holy Lamb stands, surrounded by the four Evangelist symbols on the cross terminals. Here the Old and New Covenants are each represented by a single image, and the emphasis is on antithesis rather than concordance. But large pictorial schemes of concordance, such as had been available to Benedict Biscop in Rome in the seventh century, came into special vogue towards the end of our period, due in part to the deep interest taken in types and antitypes by Rupert of Deutz (*c*. 1075–*c*. 1127), a native of Liège and Abbot of Deutz on the Rhine beside Cologne. His tirelessly allegorical exegesis influenced design in the local goldsmiths' workshops in the Rhine and Meuse valleys.

In the first half of the twelfth century the Mosan metalworkers were the special exponents of types and antitypes in art. At St-Denis in the 1140s a group of some half dozen of these skilled craftsmen was given one of the most ambitious commissions in the history of medieval art, to make a spectacular figured cross-base and cross, the whole rising to more than twenty feet

145. The Crucifixion, enamel plaque, Mosan, 1140–50

in height. The base consisted of a pedestal supporting a square pillar eight feet tall, decorated on each of its four sides with seventeen enamel plaques displaying as Abbot Suger records 'The history of the Saviour, along with the testimonies of the allegories from the Old Testament' – a didactic cycle worked out in elaborate detail in sixty-eight scenes. Suger's cross was lost in the sixteenth-century French Wars of Religion, but a number of plaques surviving in various museums, bold and shimmering in colour and monumental in composition despite their individual four-inch span, may come from it and certainly represent the style and quality of workmanship which it displayed [145]. In the technique of champlevé enamel on gilt copper, and in the solemn calm figure scenes, we have moved far from Eligius's cross at St-Denis with its fretwork of cells filled with stones and paste, and its formal patterned surface design.

Around the pedestal of Suger's cross sat figures of the four evangelists, accompanied by their symbols, as we see them on a contemporary cross-base from the monastery of St Bertin, now at St Omer [146], which evidently reproduces the St-Denis cross-base on a much reduced scale. Like Rabanus before his strange cross of letters, Suger was represented kneeling at the foot of his great cross, interceding to Christ in verses which were inscribed beside his figure. Other verses displayed on the cross began with the words *Terra tremit*, words also inscribed, in celebration of the world shaking event of the crucifixion, on the shaft of the Cloisters' altar corss a decade or so later. The upper part of the pillar of the St-Denis cross, like the miniature reproductions at St Omer, bore figures of the four elements, earth and water, air and fire, looking up and lamenting over the sufferings of their maker. The cross itself was erected on top of the pillar. Suger speaks of it in Constantinian terms as 'the life-giving cross, the health-bringing *vexillum* of the eternal victory of the Saviour', and specifically as 'the sign of the Son of Man, appearing in the sky at the moment of utmost danger'. The splendour and potency of Constantine's visionary cross was to be evoked by the lavish use of gold and gems. The back of the cross was encrusted with a vast treasure of topazes, emeralds, rubies and sapphires. Unlike Eligius's cross, Suger's cross was a crucifix, that is, it bore on its front an effigy of Christ, suffering still in remembrance of the Passion. This life-size image was the focal point for the priest saying mass before the cross.

16. Pedestal of the St-Berlin Cross, Mosan, c. 1180

In the early centuries of the Church the cross as an object of veneration was represented in its glorified form only, as the sign and banner of victory, but in the context of Gospel narrative illustration, from the fifth century onwards, the historical depiction of Christ hanging on the cross became familiar to the faithful. A vigorous heavily-built figure of Christ, naked except for the loin-cloth, is represented on his cross between the two thieves on the wooden doors at S. Sabina. Outwith history painting the image of the crucified Christ, as an evocation of the Passion and redemption, was slow to make itself felt against the symbolic sacrificial Lamb of the Apocalypse, and indeed the devotion of the Western Latin church to the image of Christ the Lamb increased rather than weakened with the passing of the centuries, in part due to the criticism and repudiation of the Lamb image by the Eastern Greek church at the end of the seventh century. At the beginning of the eighth century Pope Sergius I gave peculiar emphasis and drama to the image of the Lamb by his introduction into the Latin Mass, at the moment when the host is broken by the priest, of the singing of the words '*Agnus Dei qui tollis peccata mundi, misere nobis*'. Pilgrims to Rome in Bede's day could have seen a great mosaic of the Holy Lamb and the Evangelist symbols on the gable of the west façade of St Peter's Basilica. But by then other solemn devotional images recalling the sacrifice of Christ were making headway in Western churches. In Rome, both in St Peter's and S. Maria Antiqua the pilgrim could have seen mosaics and wall paintings showing Christ hanging on the cross, his nakedness decorously veiled in a long sleeveless robe, called the *collobium*, and though the context of these images was still historical or narrative, a sculptured figure of the crucified Christ, wearing a long straight robe with heavy loose sleeves, was perhaps already by the eighth century attracting special devotion at Lucca [147]. The Volto Santo as this figure was called became a cult object revered throughout Europe and was many times reproduced, for example at Bury St Edmunds shortly before the Norman Conquest, and often in Germany. Early in the eighth century, also in S. Maria Antiqua, the pilgrim could have admired a huge new fresco, nearly twenty feet high, painted on the triumphal arch of the church by command of Pope John VII, showing the apocalyptic elders and the host of heaven bowing in reverence not to the Lamb, but to a colossal figure of Christ stretched on the cross, naked but for the loin cloth as at S.

147. The Volto Santo of Lucca, 13th century?

Sabina, but now indubitably rising out of historical illustration into formal devotional imagery, displaying his victory over death in the very act of his sacrifice.

By the ninth century in northern Europe the depiction of Christ on the cross was the principal preoccupation of artists in every medium. A powerful figure of Christ, black bearded, raw fleshed, his thighs wrapped in golden draperies, hangs in a relaxed expansive pose, bleeding from hands and feet and side on the great blue and gold capital letter T of *Te igitur* in the Coronation Sacramentary of Charles the Bald [148]. Here at the very beginning of the canon of the Mass, the image of the redemptive

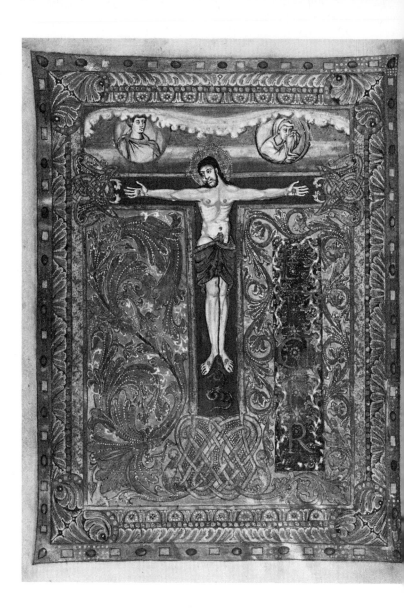

148 (*above*). Crucifixion, Sacramentary of Charles the Bald, *c.* 870

149 (*opposite*). Book cover with Crucifixion, Liège, 11th century

death of Christ is brought before the eyes of the worshipper. On an eleventh-century ivory in the treasury of the church of Tongres, made perhaps at Liège, Christ on the cross hangs in a more drooping pose, his long arms not horizontal but lifted at an angle, and his knees tilted a little to the side [149]. The cross is decorated on its borders with a diaper pattern, perhaps in recollection of some ornamented metalwork cross. The sweet dignified St John and the Virgin, with big heads and slim wistful figures, stand on the left and right of the cross looking towards Christ and raising a hand to their faces in a gesture of commiseration and grief. Between St John and Christ a slender draped figure, grasping a thin withered palm, moves away from the cross and looks back at it, turning her back and partly-concealed profile to the spectator. She is Synagogue, the rejected handmaid of God, whose shadowy lore is no longer needful to men. Advancing towards the cross from beside the mourning Virgin and like an *alter ego* of the Virgin herself, is the Bride, the Church, bearing her banner fixed to a lance, and holding a flourishing branch. Thus the Passion is being revealed historically and symbolically. The triumph of Christ as well as his sufferings are celebrated where the cross rises into the sky and where it plunges into the earth. The personified sun and moon mourn for Christ, half-hidden in massive coils of cloud as in the Sacramentary illustration. But alongside, directed by the hand of God, two angels bring a crown for the head of Christ, whose locks of hair, segmented and bunched on his brow and flowing back down his neck, already resemble an imperial wreath. Restored to life by Christ's death, three figures spring from their several graves and eagerly stretch up their arms to their Saviour. In either corner, at the base of the ivory, two further personifications, the Sea, identified by his huge crab's claw horns and the vase emptying undulating waters beside him, and Earth holding a pair of earth-born creatures, a tree and a serpent, look up in sympathy at Christ, already in the early eleventh century displaying the rich allegorical imagery and something of the firm yet expressive and spontaneous figure-design characteristic of twelfth-century work from the same part of Europe.

The scale of the figures in the Tongres ivory varies widely, but Christ is twice the size of the largest of the other actors. The simple broad handling of his figure makes it easy to visualize the lost large-scale sculptures of the Carolingian age, in stone, stucco, wood and metal. In the tenth and eleventh centuries, with the steady development of an austere yet massive powerfully plastic architectural style, the altars of the Holy Cross in monasteries and cathedrals of both the insular and the continental Saxons were signposted by the image of Christ on the cross. Among the examples which have survived there is great range in iconography and feeling, but perhaps the most impressive are those in which a new darker and more melancholy mood prevails. The wooden life-sized figure of the crucified Christ in Cologne Cathedral, dating from the time of Archbishop Gero (*c.* 970), is peculiarly identified with the suffering

5. Crucifix of Archbishop Gero, Cologne, 969–76

Saviour since the back of the head is hollowed out to form a receptacle for the consecrated host. The kind of solid chunky description of the body employed by the painter of the Sacramentary of Charles the Bald has been interpreted by the sculptor of the Gero crucifix in a remarkably individual and expressive way [150]. Christ's torso here has a Rembrandtesque lack of idealization, with its corpulent sagging breasts and belly, and the long leathery pleats of muscle drawn tense across the chest and along the arms, denoting the overwhelming burden which the nailed hands support. The head is tilted, the chin sunk into the chest. The face is haggard and grim, the mouth set in a deep straight line and the eyes closed. The hair rises in a high oval crown, and over the shoulders spreads far out in magnificent thick hanks, like the hair of Samson. Across the thighs the draperies make strong patterns like the locks of hair, corded and interwoven. The theological interpretation offered by this sculpture lies in its own sombre dignity. Christ here hangs bleakly alone, stripped of the consoling and harmonious iconography of the allegorical exegetes, and powerfully evoking the language of the crucifixion Psalm: 'I am poured out like water and all my bones are out of joint. My heart is like wax; it is melted into the midst of my bowels. My strength is dried up like a potsherd, and my tongue cleaveth to my jaws; and thou hast brought me unto the dust of death . . .' But the Gero Cross also provides a direct visual equivalent to the grandeur and pathos of the dead Christ described long before, but not attempted in the contemporary visual arts, in the Old English heroic poem *The Dream of the Rood*. The last two lines inscribed on the Ruthwell Cross read: 'And for a time he rested there, weary after the long struggle.' The society which could give visual expression to this tragic interpretation of the crucifixion, as an image less overtly of victory as of defeat, had unshakeable confidence in its own value and values, and in its foundations both religious and political. It was a society in which the Sword of Peter was wielded in firm alliance with that of the Empire, and in which the Church, disciplined and monastic in character, saw itself as rightly participating in the material and the spiritual worlds at once: 'For the Kingdom is the Lord's, and He is the Governor among the Nations.'

Catalogue of Illustrations

1. PORTABLE ALTAR AND RELIQUARY OF ST ANDREW. Made for Archbishop Egbert of Trier, 977–93. Gold, gold cloisonné, filigree, ivory, enamel, pearls, almandines and other precious stones. Length 44·7 cm. Width 22 cm. In front of the golden foot is an altar slab in millefiori glass. At the heel end of the casket is inserted a fibula containing a *solidus* of the Emperor Justinian (527–65). Trier, Cathedral Treasury. (Photograph: Bildarchiv Foto Marburg.)

    Lit: N. Irsch, *Die Kunstdenkmäler der Rheinprovinz,* XIII, *Dom zu Trier,* 1931, 329ff; F. Rademacher, 'Der Trierer Egbertschrein', *Trierer Zeitschrift,* XI, 1936, 146ff.

2. HEAD OF THE EMPEROR HADRIAN (?). Second quarter of the second century (?). Bronze. Height 11·4 cm. From Worlington, Cambridgeshire. Cambridge, Museum of Archaeology and Ethnology. (Photograph: Museum.)

    Compare the Bacchus Aquamanile, twelfth-century Mosan work in Aachen Minster, for which see H. Swarzenski, *Monuments of Romanesque Art,* 2nd ed., 1967, Pl. 163, fig. 358.

    Lit: J. Liversidge, 'A Hoard of Romano-British Ironwork from Worlington', *Proceedings of the Cambridge Antiquarian Society,* XLIX, 1955, 89; J. M. C. Toynbee, *Art in Roman Britain,* London, 1962, No. 2, 124.

3. HEAD OF ST LUKE. Early eighth century. Illumination on vellum, page size 29·2 × 22·3 cm. The Lichfield Gospels, p. 218. Lichfield, Cathedral Library. (Photograph: reproduced by courtesy of the Dean and Chapter.)

    Notes in Welsh in the manuscript show that it was in the monastery of Llandaff by the late eighth century, and at Lichfield from the tenth.

    Lit: E. H. Zimmermann, *Vorkarolingische Miniaturen,* Berlin, 1916, 116f, 269f; E. A. Lowe, *Codices Latini antiquiores,* II, Oxford, 1935, No. 159, 12; G. L. Micheli, *L'Enluminure du haut moyen âge et les influences irlandaises,* Brussels, 1939, 18 f.; F. Henry, 'The Lindisfarne Gospels', review of *Evangeliorum quattuor codex Lindisfarnensis, Antiquity,* XXXVII, 1963, 100 ff; F. Henry, *Irish Art in the Early Christian Period (to 800 A.D.),* revised ed., London, 1965, 183 ff.

4. MONUMENT TO ABBOT CLEMENT, *c.* 1160. Purbeck marble. Breadth of enclosing arch 40 cm. Sherborne, Abbey Church, N. aisle of Presbytery. (Photograph: Crown copyright: National Monuments Record.)

    For Abbot Clement's seal, featuring St Benedict adored by monks, see W. de G. Birch, *Catalogue of Seals in the Department of Manuscripts in the British Museum,* I, 1887, No. 4010, 740.

    Lit: *The Victoria History of the County of Dorset,* ed. W. Page, II, London, 1908, 64, 69; *Royal Commission on Historical Monuments: West Dorset,* 1952, 206 f.

5. GROPINA PULPIT. Twelfth century. Pieve di S. Pietro, Gropina, Tuscany. (Photograph: Mansell collection.)

    For the siren, compare A. Venturi, *Storia dell'arte italiana,* III, *L'Arte romanica,* Milan, 1904, Figs. 101, 103; for the knot on the columns, compare the portrait of the Church of the Holy Apostles at Constantinople in the Ascension miniature in the twelfth century MS. of the Homilies of James of Kokkinobaphos, Paris, B. N. Gr. MS. 1208, folio 3*vo*, for which see *The Dark Ages*, ed. D. Talbot Rice, London, 1965, 123.

Lit: W. Biehl, *Toskanische Plastik des frühen und hohen Mittelalters*, Leipzig, 1926, 29; M. Salmi, *La Scultura romanica in Toscana*, Florence, 1928, 39.

6. INTERIOR OF PALATINE CHAPEL, AACHEN, 792–805. (Photograph: Bildarchiv Foto Marburg.)

Lit: P. Clemen, *Die Kunstdenkmäler der Rheinprovinz*, x, *Die Kunstdenkmäler der Stadt Aachen*, I, Düsseldorf, 1916; F. Kreusch, *Über Pfalzkapelle und Atrium zur Zeit Karls des Grossen*, Aachener Beiträge zur Baugeschichte, IV, 1958; K. J. Conant, *Carolingian and Romanesque Architecture, 800 to 1200*, Harmondsworth, 1959, 14 f; F. Kreusch, 'Kirche, Atrium und Portikus der Aachener Pfalz', *Karl der Grosse, Lebenswerk und Nachleben*, ed. W. Braunfels, Düsseldorf, 1965–68, III, 463 ff.

7. SITULA OF ARCHBISHOP GOTFREDUS, 974/5–80. Given to the Church of S. Ambrogio, Milan, in connection with the reception of the Emperor Otto II at Milan in 980. Ivory. Height 18·5 cm. Milan, Cathedral. (Photograph: Bildarchiv Foto Marburg.)

Lit: A. Goldschmidt, *Die Elfenbeinskulpturen aus der Zeit der karolingischen und sächsischen Kaiser*, Berlin, 1914–26, 11, No. 1; G. de Francovich, 'Arte carolingia ed ottonia in Lombardia', *Römisches Jahrbuch für Kunstgeschichte*, VI, 1942–4, 148 ff; P. E. Schramm and F. Mütherich, *Denkmale der deutschen Könige und Kaiser*, Munich, 1962, No. 76, 145.

8. ARCHBISHOP ANGILBERT PRESENTING THE GOLDEN ALTAR TO ST AMBROSE, detail of the Golden Altar of S. Ambrogio, Milan, *c.* 850. Gold, silver, silver gilt, filigree, enamels, precious stones. Length of the altar 219·8 cm. Height 86 cm. Width 121·9 cm. Milan, Church of S. Ambrogio. (Photograph: Bildarchiv Foto Marburg.)

The Altar was donated by Archbishop Angilbert II (824–859) and made by 'Wolvinius magister phaber' and his workshop. On the front is represented God in majesty, and twenty scenes from the Life of Christ. On the back is the history of St Ambrose, together with the portraits of the donor and the chief artist. On the sides are jewelled and enamelled crosses and figures of angels, with bust-length saints in medallions. The form of the Altar relates it to saints' shrines and to sarcophagi. See also illustration 94.

Lit: N. Tarchiani, 'L'Altare d'oro di Sant' Ambrogio di Milano', *Dedalo*, 11, 1921, 5 ff; G. B. Tatum, 'The Paliotto of Sant' Ambrogio at Milan', *Art Bulletin*, XXVI, 1944, 25 ff; V. H. Elbern, *Der karolingische Goldenaltar von Mailand*, Bonn, 1952, Bonner Beiträge zur Kunstwissenschaft, 11; V. H. Elbern, 'Der Ambrosiuszyklus am karolingischen Goldaltar zu Mailand', *Mitteilungen des kunsthistorischen Institutes in Florenz*, VII, 1953, 1 ff; V. H. Elbern, 'Liturgisches Gerät in edlen Materialien zur Zeit Karls des Grossen', *Karl der Grosse, Lebenswerk und Nachleben*, ed. W. Braunfels, Düsseldorf, 1965–8, III, 119 f.

9. WEST FRONT OF ABBEY CHURCH OF S. MARIA DE RIPOLL, *c.* 1150. (Photograph: Foto Mas.)

Lit: A. K. Porter, *Romanesque Sculptures of the Pilgrimage Roads*, Boston, 1923, I, 255 ff.

10. DETAIL OF PULPIT, S. AMBROGIO, MILAN. Early twelfth century. (Photograph: Alinari.)

Lit: A. Venturi, *Storia dell'arte italiana*, III, *L'arte romanica*, Milan, 1904, 201; A. K. Porter, *Romanesque Sculptures of the Pilgrimage Roads*, Boston, 1923, I, 67 f.;

R. Jullian, *L'Éveil de la sculpture italienne,* Paris, 1945, 22 ff.

11. DURHAM CARYATID, *c.* 1140. One of a group that formerly carried the vaulting ribs in the chapter house, Durham Cathedral. Durham, Cathedral Library. (Photograph: Warburg Institute.)

  Lit: G. Zarnecki, *Later English Romanesque Sculpture 1140–1210,* London, 1953, 16 f.

12. GOLDEN ALTAR FRONTAL OF BASLE, given by the Emperor Henry II for the dedication of Basle Minster in 1019. Embossed and stencilled gold, pearls, and precious stones. Length 177·5 cm. Height 120 cm. Paris, Musée de Cluny. (Photograph: Service photographique des Musées nationaux.)

  The inscription refers also to the traditional function of the archangels Gabriel, Raphael, and Michael, who are represented alongside St Benedict and Christ.

  Lit: R. F. Burckhardt, *Basler Münsterschatz,* 1933, 29 ff; W. Otto, 'Reichenauer Goldtreibarbeiten', *Zeitschrift für Kunstgeschichte,* XIII, 1950, 57 ff; T. Buddensieg, 'Die Basler Altartafel Heinrichs II', *Wallraf-Richartz Jahrbuch,* XIX, 1957, 133 ff; H. Swarzenski, *Monuments of Romanesque Art,* 2nd ed., London, 1967, figs. 92–5, 99, 101; P. E. Schramm and F. Mütherich, *Denkmale der deutschen Könige und Kaiser,* No. 138, 166.

13. INTERIOR OF NAVE, DURHAM CATHEDRAL. First quarter of the twelfth century. (Photograph: Courtauld Institute.)

  Lit: J. Bilson, 'Durham Cathedral: The Chronology of its Vaults', *Archaeological Journal,* LXXIX, 1922, 101 ff; T. S. R. Boase, *English Art 1100–1216,* Oxford, 1953, 13 ff; N. Pevsner, *County Durham* (The Buildings of England), Harmondsworth, 1953, 78 ff.

14. MIRACLE AT THE TOMB OF ST CUTHBERT, *c.* 1200. Illumination on vellum. 13·7 × 9·9 cm. London, British Museum, Add. MS. 39943, p. 83. (Photograph: by permission of the Trustees of the British Museum.)

  The sick man who was restored to health by 'an accession of strength' coming from the incorruptible body of the saint was a priest of St Willibrord, from Frisia, visiting Lindisfarne on business.

  Lit: F. Wormald, 'Some Illustrated Manuscripts of the Lives of the Saints', *Bulletin of the John Rylands Library,* XXXV, 1952–3, 259 f; T. S. R. Boase, *English Art 1100–1216,* Oxford, 1953, 287. See also B. Colgrave, 'The Earliest Saints' Lives Written in England', *Proceedings of the British Academy,* XLIV, 1958, 35 ff.

15. MEDALLION OF THE EMPEROR GRATIAN (367–383) IN GOTHIC MOUNT, *c.* 400. From Szilágy-Somlyó in Transylvania. Gold, total diameter 6.4 cm. Vienna, Kunsthistorisches Museum (Photograph: Kunsthistorisches Museum, Vienna.) The reverse carries the inscription *Gloria Romanorum.* See text, p. 103.

  Lit: A. Odobesco, *Le Trésor de Pétrossa,* Paris, 1889–1900, 195 ff; A. Alföldi, *Numismatikai Közlöny,* XXVIII–XXIX, 1929–30, Budapest, 1933, 3 ff.

16. GERETE BRACTEATE. Sixth century. Gold, filigree, diameter 9·5 cm. From Fardhem parish in Gotland. The geometrical border contains a row of human heads, moulded and soldered on. Stockholm, Statens Historiska Museum. (Photograph: Antikvarisk-Topografiska Arkivet, Stockholm.)

  Lit: B. Salin, 'De nordiska guldbrakteaterna', *Antiqvarisk tidskrift för Sverige,* XIV, 1899; M. Mackesprang, *De nordiske Guldbrakteater,* Århus, 1952; J. Brøndsted, *Danmarks Oldtid,* III, *Jernalderen,* Gyldendal, 1960, 316 ff.

17. WEST FRONT OF CHURCH AT ÉCHILLAIS. Charente-inférieure, *c.* 1135. (Photograph: Jean Roubier, Paris.)

  Lit: R. de Lasteyrie, *L'Architecture religieuse en France à l'époque romane,* 2nd ed., Paris, 1929, 460.

18. TWELVE-SIDED GOTHIC VESSEL FROM PETROSSA. Fourth century. Gold, openwork inlaid with garnets and glass pastes. Handles shaped like leopards, gold, with pearl and carbuncle spots. Diameter 17·8 cm. Height 12·1 cm. Illustration from A. Odobesco, *Le Trésor de Pétrossa,* Paris, 1889–1900, opp. p. 94.

The Petrossa Treasure of gold vessels and jewellery was hidden *c.* 375 at the foot of Mount Istrita in the Carpathian Mountains, and was discovered in 1837. Subsequent thefts have diminished the original twenty-two items to twelve. The Treasure is now in the National Museum of Antiquities, Bucharest.

Lit: A. Odobesco, *Le Trésor de Pétrossa,* Part II, 91 ff; E. Dunàreanu-Vulpe, *Le Trésor de Pietroasa,* Bucharest, 1967; E. Dunàreanu-Vulpe, *Tezaurele antici,* Studii asupra Tezaurului restituit de USSR, Editura Academiei Republicii populare Romine, 40 ff; Catalogue, *Treasures from Romania,* The British Museum 1971, 81 ff.

19. EAGLE FIBULA, *c.* 500. Gold cloisonné and almandines. Height 12·1 cm. Found at Domagnano, Italy. The companion piece to this fibula is in the collection of the Marquis de Ganay, Paris. Nürnberg, Germanisches Nationalmuseum. (Photograph: Germanisches Nationalmuseum, Nürnberg.)

Lit: *The British Museum Quarterly,* VIII, 1933–4, 45 and Pl. XIII; W. Holmqvist, *Germanic Art during the First Millenium A.D.,* Stockholm, 1955, 29; W. F. Volbach, 'Sculpture and Applied Arts', *Europe in the Dark Ages,* London, 1969, 222. See also N. Åberg, *Die Goten und Langobarden in Italien,* Uppsala, 1923; G. Thiry, *Die Vogelfibeln der germanischen Völkerwanderungszeit,* Bonn, 1939; W. A. von Jenny, *Die Kunst der Germanen im frühen Mittelalter,* Berlin, 1940; and G. Annibaldi and J. Werner, 'Ostgotische Grabfunde aus Acquasanta (Provinz Ascoli Piceno)', *Germania,* XLI, 1963, 356 ff.

20. RING GOLD AND INGOTS. Sixth century. Coils of gold wire made into openended rings of various sizes. Total weight 7 kg. Found in 1904 at Timboholm, Västergötland, Sweden. Stockholm, Statens Historiska Museum. (Photograph: A.-T.A, Stockholm.)

Lit: O. Janse, *Le Travail de l'or en Suède à l'époque mérovingienne,* Orléans, 1922; M. Stenberger, *Sweden,* Ancient Peoples and Places, London, 1962, 134.

21. PICTISH CHAIN AND OTHER ORNAMENTS, *c.* 600–700. Silver. Weight of chain 1·7 kg. Length of plaques 8·9 cm. Breadth of brooch 7·7 cm. The chain found at Whitecleuch, Lanarkshire; the plaques from Norries Law, Largo, Fife; brooch from Tummel Bridge, Perthshire. Edinburgh, National Museum of Antiquities. (Photograph: National Museum of Antiquities, Edinburgh.)

The most massive of the Pictish chains, consisting of sixteen pairs of rings plus one single ring and weighing 2·6 kg. was found in 1809 during the digging of the Caledonian Canal near Inverness.

Lit: R. B. K. Stevenson, 'Pictish Chain, Roman Silver and Bauxite Beads', *Proceedings of the Society of Antiquaries of Scotland,* LXXXVIII, 1954–6, 228 f; I. Henderson, *The Picts,* Ancient Peoples and Places, London, 1967, 108, 115, 212 ff; Exhibition Catalogue, *Early Celtic Art,* Arts Council of Great Britain, 1970, No. 173, 33.

22. ÅLLEBERG GOLD COLLAR. Fifth century. Gold tubes and gold wire. Spaces between the three gold tubes are filled with masks and animal figures. Diameter of collar 20·5 cm. Stockholm, Statens Historiska Museum. (Photograph: A.-T.A, Stockholm.)

Lit: S. Lindqvist, *Vendelkulturens ålder och ursprung,* Stockholm, 1926, 55 ff; W. Holmqvist, *Germanic Art during the First Millenium A.D.,* Stockholm, 1955, 22 f; M. Stenberger, *Sweden,* London, 1962, 135.

23. PORTAL OF RICCALL CHURCH, Yorkshire. Twelfth century. (Photograph: Kenneth-Richardson Assoc. Ltd.)

Lit: F. Henry and G. Zarnecki, 'Romanesque Arches Decorated with Human and Animal Heads', *The Journal of the British Archaeological Association*, 3rd series, XX–XXI, 1957–8, 33 and Pl. XIII(4).

24. PORTAL OF KILPECK CHURCH, Herefordshire, *c.* 1140. (Photograph: Crown copyright: National Monuments Record.)

Lit: G. Zarnecki, *Later English Romanesque Sculpture 1140–1210*, London, 1953 10 f; L. Stone, *Sculpture in Britain: The Middle Ages*, Harmondsworth, 1955, 68 f; D. M. Wilson and O. Klindt-Jensen, *Viking Art*, London, 1966, 160.

25. THE TREASURE OF KING CHILDERIC. Fifth century. Sword hilt, gold and almandines; gold coins; cicadas, gold and almandines; gold signet ring; crystal ball. The Treasure buried at Tournai at the King's death, 482, found 1653, part stolen 1831. Paris, Cabinet des médailles, Bibliothéque Nationale. Plaster-cast of (lost) gold signet ring, Oxford, Ashmolean Museum. (Photograph: photomontage reproduced by courtesy of Thames & Hudson.)

Lit: J. J. Chifflet, *Anastasis Childerici I, Francorum Regis; sive thesaurus sepulchralis Tornaci Nerviorum effosus, et commentario illustratus*, Antwerp, 1655; Abbé J. B. D. Cochet, *Le Tombeau de Childéric 1er roi des Francs*, Paris, 1859; see also J. Werner, 'Frankish Royal Tombs in the Cathedrals of Cologne and Saint-Denis', *Antiquity*, XXXVIII, 1964, 201 ff. For the background of polychrome style jewellery, see K. Böhner, 'Das Langschwert des Frankenkönigs Childerich', *Bonner Jahrbücher*, 1948, 218 ff.

26. THE BAYEUX TAPESTRY, EARL HAROLD RECEIVING ARMS FROM DUKE WILLIAM, *c.* 1077. Woollen embroidery on linen. 70·34 m. long. 50 cm. wide. Bayeux, former Bishop's Palace. (Photograph from *The Bayeux Tapestry* by Frank Stenton, published by Phaidon Press.)

See also a soldier (the Psalmist) wearing chain mail and helmet, armed by God with a sword and a shield, in the Utrecht Psalter, Psalm 144 (Vulgate 143), 'Blessed be the Lord my strength, which teacheth my hands to war, and my fingers to fight . . .' reproduced in E. T. De Wald, *The Illustrations of the Utrecht Psalter*, Princeton, 1933.

Lit: *The Bayeux Tapestry*, ed. Sir F. Stenton, London, 1957; 2nd. ed. revised and enlarged, 1965.

27. THE SUTTON HOO HELMET. First half of the seventh century. Iron with small bronze, silver, tin, gold and garnet ornaments, and partly embossed with figural designs. London, British Museum. (Photgraph: by permission of the Trustees of the British Museum.)

The visor carries a gilt-bronze nose, mouth and upper lip, the latter equipped with a moustache, like the image of Christ on the Ruthwell Cross, illustration 63, and Charlemagne on his late silver denier, illustration 61B. For the plaques with figural designs, compare illustration 55.

Lit: R. L. S. Bruce-Mitford, *The Sutton Hoo Ship-Burial: A Handbook*, British Museum, 1968. For additional material on aspects of the Sutton Hoo find, see R. and M. Bruce-Mitford, 'The Sutton Hoo Lyre', *Antiquity*, XLIV, 1970, 7 ff; P. Grierson, 'The Purpose of the Sutton Hoo Coins', ibid., 14 ff.

28. THE SUTTON HOO SWORD MOUNTS. First half of the seventh century. Gold cloisonné, curved and angled garnets, gold filigree, millefiore glass. Over-all length of sword 85·1 cm. Blade 71·2 cm. (Photograph: by permission of the Trustees of the British Museum.)

The scabbard bosses are decorated with a cross at the centre of a petal design.

The cutting of the garnets, notably in the unique pyramid-shaped objects, exhibits almost miraculous skill.

29. THE EAGLE SYMBOL, THE BOOK OF DURROW. Third quarter of the seventh century. Illumination on vellum 24·4 × 15·6 cm. Dublin, Trinity College Library, MS. 57 (A.IV.5), folio 84*vo*. (Photograph: by courtesy of the Board of Trinity College, Dublin.)

It is the peculiarity of the Book of Durrow, as opposed to the other Insular Luxury Gospel Books of the seventh–eighth century, that the Eagle symbol prefaces St Mark's Gospel, not that of St John, and that St John's Gospel is prefaced by the Lion symbol. Contrast the Evangelist symbols in illustrations 74 and 141.

While the Durrow eagle's head is designed like cloisonné work, the appearance of the breast and upper wing-feathers is reminiscent of Roman body armour of brass scales, *lorica squamata*.

Lit: E. A. Lowe, *Codices Latini antiquiores*, II, No. 273, 43; A. A. Luce, *Evangeliorum quattuor codex Durmachensis*, Olten, 1960. For a short but balanced and useful discussion of the Book of Durrow, see K. Hughes. *The Church in Early Irish Society*, London, 1966, 99 f.

30. THE CALF SYMBOL, THE ECHTERNACH GOSPELS. Last quarter of the seventh century. Illumination on vellum. 33·7 × 25·5 cm. Paris, Bibliothèque Nationale, MS. Lat. 9389, folio 115*vo*. (Photograph: Bibliothèque Nationale, Paris.)

This manuscript was deposited by the Northumbrian-born St Willibrord (died 739) in the library of his monastery at Echternach. Contrast the calf symbol in the Lichfield Gospels, which agrees in the turned position of its head with the calf in both the Lindisfarne Gospels and the Coffin of St Cuthbert, for which see illustration 79.

Lit: E. H. Zimmermann, *Vorkarolingische Miniaturen*, Berlin, 1916, 123 f and 276 f; E. A. Lowe, *Codices Latini antiquiores*, V, Oxford, 1950, No. 578, 18; I. Henderson, *The Picts*, London, 1967, 124 ff and Pls. 32–8.

31. THE ARDROSS WOLF, *c.* 600. Incised sculpture on sandstone. Length 50·4 cm. From Ardross, Ross, Scotland. Inverness, Museum. (Photograph: George Farquharson, Inverness.)

Lit: J. Romilly Allen, *The Early Christian Monuments of Scotland*, Edinburgh, 1903, Part III, 55 f; C. L. Curle, 'The Chronology of the Early Christian Monuments of Scotland', *Proceedings of the Society of Antiquaries of Scotland*, LXXIV, 1939–40, 64.

32. BEGINNING OF ST MATTHEW'S GOSPEL, LINDISFARNE GOSPELS, *c.* 698. Illumination on vellum. 34·1 × 24·5 cm. London, British Museum, Cotton MS. Nero D. iv, folio 27. (Photograph: by permission of the Trustees of the British Museum.)

The manuscript contains a tenth-century note stating that the Gospel Book was written by Eadfrith (Bishop of Lindisfarne 698–721) in honour of St Cuthbert and of all the saints who (i.e. whose relics, for example the severed head of St Oswald) were on the Island (of Lindisfarne).

Lit: T. D. Kendrick, T. J. Brown, R. L. S. Bruce-Mitford, *Evangeliorum quattuor codex Lindisfarnensis*, Olten, 1956–60.

33. NIGG CROSS-SLAB, *c.* 800. Sandstone. Height 221 cm. Breadth 104·2 cm. Ross, Scotland. (Photograph: National Museum of Antiquities, Edinburgh.)

Lit: J. Romilly Allen, *The Early Christian Monuments of Scotland*, Part III, 75 ff; C. L. Mowbray, 'Eastern Influences on Carvings at St Andrews and Nigg, Scotland', *Antiquity*, X, 1936, 428 ff; R. B. K. Stevenson, 'The Chronology and Relationships of Some Irish and Scottish Crosses', *Journal of the Royal Society of*

Antiquaries of Ireland, LXXXVI, 1956, 84 ff; I. Henderson, *The Picts*, London, 1967, 128, 133, 148 f, 152 ff.

34. BEGINNING OF ST MATTHEW'S GOSPEL, Court School of Charlemagne, *c.* 800. Illumination on vellum. 37·1 × 24·8 cm. London, British Museum, Harley MS. 2788, folio 14. (Photograph: by permission of the Trustees of the British Museum.)

   Lit: W. Koehler, *Die karolingischen Miniaturen*, II, *Die Hofschule Karls des Grossen*, Berlin, 1953, 56 ff.

35. INTERLACE ORNAMENT ON CAPITALS, Tours, 844–51. Illumination on vellum. 49·5 × 37·5 cm. From canon table in the First Bible of Charles the Bald, Paris, Bibliothèque Nationale MS. Lat. 1, folio 328*vo*. (Photograph: Bibliothèque Nationale, Paris.)

   Lit: W. Koehler, *Die karolingischen Miniaturen*, I, 1, *Die Schule von Tours*, Berlin, 1930, reprinted 1963, 250 ff; I, 2, Berlin, 1933, reprinted 1963, 27 ff.

36. INITIAL IN MONTE CASSINO HOMILIES. Eleventh century. Illumination on vellum from Homilies written by the Monk Leo, Montecassino MS. H. H. 99. Montecassino Abbey Library (Photograph: Bildarchiv Foto Marburg.)

   Lit: E. Bertaux, *L'Art dans l'Italie méridionale*, Paris, 1904, 193 ff. A. Caravita, *I codici e le arti a Montecassino*, Monte Cassino, 1869–70; P. Baldass, 'Disegni della scuola cassinese del tempo di Desiderio', *Bollettino d'arte del Ministero della pubblica Istruzione*, 1952, 102 ff.

37. PORTAL OF URNES CHURCH. Late eleventh century. Carved wooden panels on the north portal of the stave-church at Urnes, province of Sogn, Norway (Photograph: Universitetets Oldsaksamling, Oslo.)

   Lit: D. M. Wilson and O. Klindt-Jensen, *Viking Art*, London, 1966, 147 ff.

38a, b DETAILS OF FIGURE OF CHRIST, VÉZELAY, *c.* 1130. Stone sculpture from tympanum of the church of Ste- Madeleine, Vézelay. (Photographs: by courtesy of R. G. Phélipeaux-Zodiaque).

   Lit: C. Porée, *L'Abbaye de Vézelay*, Petites monographies des grands édifices, Paris, 1909. See also illustration 39.

39. PENTECOST TYMPANUM, VÉZELAY, *c.* 1130. (Photograph: by courtesy of R. C. Phélipeaux-Zodiaque.)

   Lit: A. Katzenellenbogen, 'The Central Tympanum at Vézelay', *The Art Bulletin*, XXVI, 1944, 141 ff.

40. MAMRES AT THE MOUTH OF HELL, *c.* 1025. Illumination on vellum. Picture size 16·5 × 15 cm. *Marvels of the East*, London, British Museum, Cotton MS. Tiberius B.v, folio 87*vo*. (Photograph: by permission of the Trustees of the British Museum.)

   Lit: M. R. James, *Marvels of the East*, Roxburghe Club, 1929; R. Wittkower, 'Marvels of the East. A Study in the History of Monsters', *Journal of the Warburg and Courtauld Institutes*, v, 1942, 159 ff; D. Talbot Rice, *English Art 871–1100*, Oxford, 1952, 224.

41. THE SNARTEMO SWORD HILT, Norway. Late sixth century. Gold and silver. Oslo, Universitetets Oldsaksamling. (Photograph: Universitetets Oldsamling, Oslo.)

   Lit: B. Hougen, *Snartemofunnene*, Norske Oldfunn VII, Oslo, 1935; W. Holmqvist, *Germanic Art during the First Millenium A.D.*, Stockholm, 1955, 19 f; E. Oxenstierna, *Die Nordgermanen*, Stuttgart, 1957, 87, 257.

42. THE NORMAN INVASION FLEET, THE BAYEUX TAPESTRY. (Photograph from *The Bayeux Tapestry* by Frank Stenton, published by Phaidon Press.)

   On the right is Duke William's flagship with signal lantern fixed to the masthead.

43. SIGURD KILLING FAFNIR. Eleventh century. Incised sculpture with runes. Ramsund, Södermanland. (Photograph: Harald Faith, A.-T. A, Stockholm.)

The hero kills the dragon and roasts its heart, with his thumb in his mouth. Two birds in a tree speak to Sigurd and warn him against the treacherous Smith, the dragon's brother. The Smith is shown beheaded. The hero's horse is laden with the treasure.

Lit: E. I. Seaver, 'Some Examples of Viking Figure Representation in Scandinavia and the British Isles', *Medieval Studies in Memory of A. Kingsley Porter,* ed. W. Koehler, Harvard, 1939, 589 ff; D. M. Wilson and O. Klindt-Jensen, *Viking Art,* London, 1966, 139; H. R. Ellis Davidson, *Pagan Scandinavia,* Ancient Peoples and Places, London, 1967, 126 f.

44. GRÖNBY FIBULA. Sixth century. Silver, with filigree and inset stones. Length 11 cm. Grönby, Schonen, Sweden, now Lund, Universitets Historiska Museum. (Photograph: Lunds Universitets Historika Museum.)

Lit: B. Alenstam, 'Zwei Reliefspangen aus Grönby, Skåne', *Meddelelser från Lunds Universitets Historiska Museum,* 1949, 183 ff; E. Oxenstierna, *Die Nordgermanen,* Stuttgart, 1957, 91.

45. FRAGMENT OF A RELIEF SCULPTURE. Eighth century. Sandstone. Length 29·2 cm. Height 22·8 cm. Rosemarkie, Ross, Scotland, now Edinburgh, National Museum of Antiquities. (Photograph: National Museum of Antiquities.)

Lit: J. Romilly Allen, *The Early Christian Monuments of Scotland,* Part III, 86 f.

46. BRONZE PLAQUE, Pictish or Irish. Eighth century. Provenance and purpose uncertain. Saint-Germain-en-Laye, Musée des Antiquités nationales. (Photographs: Musée des Antiquités nationales.)

Lit: F. Henry, Deux objets de bronze irlandais au Musée des antiquités nationales. *Prèhistoire,* VI, 1938, 65 ff. See also J. Petersen, British Antiquities of the Viking Period found in Norway, *Viking Antiquities in Great Britain and Ireland.* ed. H. Shetelig, Part V, Oslo, 1940, No. 84, 61 and Fig. 67a, b, 62; No. 94, 68 f and Fig. 76, 69.

47. DETAIL FROM THE OSEBERG CART, *c.* 850. Found with four richly carved wooden sledges in the Oseberg ship burial, containing two female corpses, one perhaps a queen. Oslo, Universitetets Oldsaksamling (Photograph: Universitetets Oldsaksamling, Oslo.)

Lit: H. Shetelig, *Osebergfundet,* III, Kristiania, 1920; S. Lindqvist, 'Osebergmästarna', *Tor,* I, 1948, 9 ff; D. M. Wilson and O. Klindt-Jensen, *Viking Art,* London, 1966, 48 ff.

48. RUNE STONE AT JELLING, Jutland, 965-85. Granite. Height 244 cm. (Photograph: reproduced by permission of the National Museum, Copenhagen.)

Harald Bluetooth, King of Denmark, became a Christian in 965 and died in 985.

Lit: H. Christiansson, 'Jellingestenens bildvärld', *Kuml,* 1953, 72 ff; J. Brøndsted, *Danmarks Oldtid,* III, *Jernalderen,* 335 ff.

49. CRUCIFIXION IN ST GALL GOSPELS, *c.* 750. Illumination on vellum. 29·3 × 22·1 cm. St Gallen, Stiftsbibliothek MS. 51 folio 266 (Photograph: Stiftsbibliothek, St Gallen.)

Compare the Crucifixion in the Gospel fragment in Durham Cathedral Library, MS. A.II.17, folio 38₃vo, for which see R. A. B. Mynors, *Durham Cathedral Manuscripts to the End of the Twelfth Century,* Oxford, 1939, No. 4, 15 f and Pl. 3; also O. K. Werckmeister, 'Three Problems of Tradition in Pre-Carolingian Figure-Style', *Proceedings of the Royal Irish Academy,* LXIII, Section C, No. 5, 1963, 185 ff; L. Gougaud, 'The Earliest Irish Representation of the Crucifixion', *Journal of the Royal Society of Antiquaries of Ireland,* L, 1920, 128 ff;

M. MacDermott, 'An Openwork Crucifixion Plaque from Clonmacnoise', *Journal of the Royal Society of Antiquaries of Ireland*, LXXXIV, 1954, 36 ff.

Lit: E. H. Zimmermann, *Vorkarolingische Miniaturen*, Berlin, 1916, 99 f and 240 f; G. L. Micheli, *L'Enluminure du haut moyen âge et les influences irlandaises*, II, note 6, and 20.

50. THE HARROWING OF HELL. From a Psalter, *c.* 1050. Pen drawings on vellum. The Manuscript has shrunk unevenly as the result of the fire in the Cotton Library in Ashburnham House, Westminster, 1731. Written space 21·6 × 12·4 cm. London, British Museum, Cotton MS. Tiberius C.vi, folio 14. (Photograph: by permission of the Trustees of the British Museum.)

Lit: F. Wormald, 'An English Eleventh-Century Psalter with Pictures, British Museum, Cotton MS. Tiberius C.vi', *The Walpole Society*, XXXVIII, 1960–62, 1 ff. and Pls. 1–30.

51. CAPITAL WITH MAN AND MONSTER. Twelfth century. St Pierre, Chauvigny, Vienne. (Photograph: Jean Roubier, Paris.)

Lit: D. McDougall, 'The Choir Capitals of S. Pierre-en-haute, Chauvigny, Poitou', *Burlington Magazine*, XXXVI, 1920, 11 ff; R. de Lasteyrie, *L'Architecture religieuse en France à l'époque romane*, 2nd ed., Paris, 1929, 456 f, 464; *Poitan roman,* introd. R. Crozet, Zodiaque, La nuit des temps, 2nd ed. 1962, 96 ff.

52. CAPITAL WITH MISER'S DEATH. Twelfth century, St-André, Besse-en-Chandesse, Puy-de-Dôme. (Photograph: Jean Roubier, Paris.)

Lit: *Congrès archéologique de Clermont-Ferrand*, 1924, 251 ff; P. Deschamps, *French Sculpture of the Romanesque Period*, Florence and Paris, 1930, 51.

53. FRANKISH BELT BUCKLE. Seventh century. Bronze, Height 14·5 cm. Found at Criel-sur-mer. Musée des antiquités, Rouen. (Photograph: by courtesy of the Musées départementaux de la Seine-maritime.)

Lit: W. F. Volbach, 'Sculpture and Applied Arts', *Europe in the Dark Ages*, Part III, 278. For general background, see W. Holmqvist, *Kunstprobleme der Merowingerzeit*, Stockholm, 1939.

54. SCULPTURES ON WEST INNER WALL OF THE PORCH OF MOISSAC, *c.* 1125. (Photograph: Bildarchiv Foto Marburg.)

These sculptures date from the period of Abbot Roger (1115–31)

Lit: M. Schapiro, 'The Romanesque Sculpture of Moissac', *Art Bulletin*, XIII, 1931, Part I(1), 249 ff; Part I(2), 464 ff.

55. MAN LEADING A BEAR, *c.* 600. Bronze. 6 × 5 cm. From Torslunda, Öland, Sweden. Stockholm, Statens Historiska Museum. (Photograph A-TA, Stockholm.)

One of a group of moulds used in the production of embossed metal plaques on helmets. Such plaques occur on the helmet from Sutton Hoo, see illustration 27.

Lit: W. Holmqvist, *Germanic Art during the First Millenium A.D.*, Stockholm, 1955, 50.

56. A DEMON AND A PERSONIFICATION OF LUST, Moissac, *c.* 1125. (Photograph: Bildarchiv Foto Marburg.)

Lit: A. Schapiro, 'The Romanesque Sculpture of Moissac', *Art Bulletin,* XIII, 1931, 508.

57. TRUMEAU AT SOUILLAC, *c.* 1125 (Photograph: Bildarchiv Foto Marburg.) Compare the naked man gripped by the griffin's beak with illustration 91.

Lit: M. Schapiro, 'The Sculptures of Souillac', *Medieval Studies in Memory of A. Kingsley Porter*, Harvard, 1939, 359 ff.

58. FRAMPTON VILLA MOSAIC, fourth century A.D. 679·7 × 386·3 cm. Discovered in the years 1794-6. *In situ,* covered over (?). From S. Lysons, *Reliquiae Britannico-*

Romanae, I, London, 1813, Part III, 'Figures of mosaic pavements, discovered near Frampton, in Dorsetshire', 1808, Plate VII. The dimensions are given in the general plan of the Frampton mosaics, Plate III. (Photograph: by courtesy of the Signet Library, Edinburgh.)

59. CARPET PATTERN, LINDISFARNE GOSPELS, *c.* 698. Illumination on vellum. 34·1 × 24·5 cm. London, British Museum, Cotton MS. Nero D.iv, folio 210*vo*. (Photograph: by permission of the Trustees of the British Museum.)

Lit: see note on illustration 32.

60. BELLEROPHON AND THE CHIMERA, Tours, *c.* 850. Illumination on vellum. 32·2 × 25 cm. The Lothair Evangeliary, Paris, Bibliothèque Nationale, MS. Lat. 266, folio 110. (Photograph: Bibliothèque Nationale, Paris.)

Compare Bellerophon and the Chimera in a fifth-century ivory in the British Museum, for which see O. M. Dalton, *Catalogue of the Ivory Carvings of the Christian Era*, London, British Museum, 1909, No. 6, 4 f; also W. F. Volbach, *Elfenbeinarbeiten der Spätantike und des frühen Mittelalters*, Mainz, 1952, No. 67, 44. For a finger ring with Bellerophon and the Chimera in the British Museum, see F. H. Marshall, *Catalogue of Finger Rings, Greek, Etruscan, and Roman*, London, British Museum, 1907, No. 571.

Lit: W. Koehler, *Die karolingischen Miniaturen*, I, 1, *Die Schule von Tours*, 260 ff.

61A. COIN OF ST ELIGIUS. Obverse bears likeness of Clovis II, 638–57.

(Photograph: Bibliothèque Nationale, Paris.)

Lit: See *Revue numismatique*, 1836, 94; 1847, 20; 1858, 394. Also G. de Ponton d'Amécourt, *Annales de la société française de numismatique*, 1882, 79.

61B. SILVER DENIER OF CHARLEMAGNE, 806–14.

(Photograph: Staatliche Museen, Berlin.)

Lit: A. Blanchet and A. Dieudonné, *Manuel de numismatique française*, Paris, 1912, 339, 369; P. Grierson, 'Money and Coinage under Charlemagne', in *Karl der Grosse, Lebenswerk und Nachleben*, ed. W. Braunfels, Düsseldorf 1965–8, I, 501 ff.

61C. COIN OF CONSTANTINE DISPLAYING THE LABARUM, 326 or 327 A.D.

(Photograph: by permission of the Trustees of the British Museum.)

Lit: J. Lafaurie, 'Médaillon constantinien', *Revue numismatique*, 5th series, XVII, 1955, 236 f and note 22, 248.

62. CHARLEMAGNE'S THRONE, AACHEN, *c.* 800. Marble. Height 242 cm. Aachen Minster. (Photograph: Bildarchiv Foto Marburg.)

Lit: P. E. Schramm and F. Mütherich, *Denkmale der deutschen Könige und Kaiser*, No. 1, 114; H. Beumann, 'Grab und Thron Karls des Grossen zu Aachen', in *Karl der Grosse, Lebenswerk und Nachleben*, ed., W. Braunfels, Düsseldorf, 1965–8, IV, 9 ff.

63. CHRIST ADORED BY BEASTS THE RUTHWELL CROSS. Last quarter of the seventh century (?) Sandstone. Height of shaft 528·7 cm. Height of cross head 94 cm. Shaft tapers from 53·3 cm. to 33 cm. at front and back. (Photograph: Crown copyright: Ministry of the Environment, Edinburgh).

This is the central relief on the back of the cross. See also illustration 140.

Lit: *County of Dumfries*, Royal Commission on the Ancient and Historical Monuments of Scotland, 1920, Appendix, 219 ff; F. Saxl, 'The Ruthwell Cross', *Journal of the Warburg and Courtauld Institutes*, VI, 1943, 1 ff; M. Schapiro, 'The Religious Meaning of the Ruthwell Cross', *Art Bulletin*, XXVI, 1944, 232 ff; R. Cramp, 'The Anglican Sculptured Crosses of Dumfriesshire', *Dumfries and Galloway Archaeological Society Transactions*, XXXVII, 1959-60, 9 ff; E. Mercer, 'The Ruthwell and Bewcastle Crosses', *Antiquity*, XXXVIII, 1964, 268 ff; R. Cramp, 'Early Northumbrian Sculpture', Jarrow Lecture, 1965.

64. BEGINNING OF ST MATTHEW'S GOSPEL, PRÜM GOSPELS. Second quarter of the ninth century. Illumination on vellum. 29·4 × 23·3 cm. Berlin, theol. lat. fol. 733, folio 23*vo* (Photograph: Staatsbibliothek Preussischer Kulturbesitz Handschriftenabteilung.)

The initial letters continue the classicizing process begun in Charlemagne's Court School Gospel Books. Compare illustrations 32 and 34.

Lit: W. Koehler, *Die karolingischen Miniaturen*, I, 1, *Die Schule von Tours*, 256 ff and 403 f; P. E. Schramm and F. Mütherich, *Denkmale der deutschen Könige und Kaiser*, No. 29, 125.

65. DIPTYCH WITH FIGURES OF KING DAVID AND POPE GREGORY THE GREAT. Ninth century (?) Ivory. Height 16·5 cm. Monza, Cathedral Treasury. (Photograph: by courtesy of Professor David Talbot Rice.)

Lit: J. Beckwith, *Early Medieval Art*, London, 1964, 34.

66. PORTRAIT OF A MOTHER AND HER TWO CHILDREN. Fourth century. Gold leaf, stippled on glass. Diameter of medallion 6 cm. On later silver processional cross, for which see illustration 134. Brescia, Museo civico. (Photo: Alinari.)

Lit: H. Leclercq, *Manuel d'archéologie chrétienne*, Paris, 1907, II, 496, fig. 332; C. R. Morey, *Early Christian Art*, 2nd ed., Princeton, 1953, 127.

67. THE ESCRIN OF CHARLEMAGNE. Third quarter of the ninth century, destroyed in the French Revolution. Engraving from M. Felibien, *Histoire de l'abbaye royale de Saint-Denys en France*, Paris, 1706, Pl. IV, 542.

Three superimposed arcades like a church façade, made of gold or silver gilt bands set with pearls and precious stones, standing on a shallow reliquary casket; compare the design of the altar frontal of Charles the Bald at St-Denis of repoussé gold and precious stones, in illustration 136. The engraving illustrated here records the contents of one of the show-cases in the Treasury of St-Denis. See note on illustration 70.

Lit: Sir M. Conway, 'The Abbey of Saint-Denis and its Ancient Treasures', *Archaeologia*, LXVI, 1914–15, 128 f, and Pl. X opp. p. 128; J. Hubert, 'L'Escrain dite de Charlemagne', *Cahiers archéologiques*, IV, 1949, 71 ff; P. E. Schramm and F. Mutherich, *Denkmale der deutschen Könige und Kaiser*, No. 47, 152.

68. THE ST ALBANS CAMEO CALLED KAADMAU. Drawing on vellum by Matthew Paris, 1257. *Liber additamentorum*, London, British Museum, Cotton MS. Nero D.i. folio 146*vo*. The cameo was about 15 cm. long, set in a silver mount engraved in niello with the name of the donor, King Aethelred. (Photograph: by permission of the Trustees of the British Museum.)

Examples of mis- or re-interpretation of antique gems are found in the seals of English monasteries, e.g. the bust of Jupiter Serapis used by the Chapter of Durham as a seal inscribed *caput sancti oswaldi regis,* and the head of the Emperor Honorius used by Selby Abbey and inscribed *caput nostrum Cristus est*, for which see. W. de G. Birch, *Catalogue of Seals in the Department of Manuscripts in the British Museum*, I, Nos. 2511 and 3981.

For other examples of misinterpretation, see the notes on the Cameo of Chartres and the great Cameo of France in E. Babelon, *Catalogue des camées antiques et modernes de la Bibliothèque Nationale*, Paris, 1897, No. 1, 1 ff and No. 264, 120 ff. Also G. Bruns, 'Der grosse Kameo von Frankreich', *Mitteilungen des deutschen archäologischen Instituts*, VI, 1953, 86 f.

For medieval use of gems, see 'Gemmes' in F. Cabrol and H. Leclercq, *Dictionnaire d'archéologie chrétienne et de liturgie*, VI, Paris, 1927, 794 ff.

Lit: *Mathaei Parisiensis chronica majora*, ed. H. R. Luard, Rolls Series, 1882, VI, 387 f; C. C. Oman, 'The Jewels of St Albans Abbey', *Burlington Magazine*, LVII, 1930, 81 f.

69. THE COUPE DES PTOLEMÉES with its now destroyed medieval mounts. Engraving from M. Felibien, *Histoire de l'abbaye royale de Saint-Denys en France,* Pl. VI, 545.

Lit: Sir M. Conway, 'The Abbey of Saint-Denis and its Ancient Treasures', *Archaeologia,* LXVI, 1914-15, 119 f; E. Panofsky, *Abbot Suger on the Abbey Church of St-Denis,* Princeton, 1948, 202 ff.

70. THE COUPE DES PTOLEMÉES. Alexandrian, second or first century B.C. Sardonyx. Height 12 cm. Paris, Bibliothèque Nationale, Cabinet des médailles. (Photograph: Bibliothèque Nationale, Paris.)

The English poet Thomas Gray responded memorably to this beautiful vase when he visited St-Denis in 1739: 'Stopt at St Denis', he wrote in a letter to his friend Richard West, 'saw all the beautiful monuments of the Kings of France, and the vast treasures of the abbey, rubies and emeralds as big as small eggs, crucifixes and vows, crowns and reliques of inestimable value. But of all their curiosities the thing the most to our tastes, and which they indeed do the justice to esteem the glory of their collection, was a vase of an entire onyx, measuring at least five inches over, three deep, and of great thickness. It is at least two thousand years old, the beauty of the stone and sculpture upon it (representing the mysteries of Bacchus) beyond expression admirable. We have dreamed of it ever since . . .'

Lit: E. Babelon, *Catalogue des camées antiques et modernes de la Bibliothèque Nationale,* No. 368, 201 ff; P. E. Schramm and F. Mütherich, *Denkmale der deutschen Könige und Kaiser,* No. 50, 133.

71. ABBOT RAGANALDUS BLESSING THE PEOPLE, THE MARMOUTIER SACRAMENTARY. Written at Tours for Abbot Raganaldus (Rainaud) of Marmoutier, *c.* 850. Illumination on vellum. 33·3 × 24·1 cm. Autun, Bibliothèque municipale, MS. 19 bis, folio 173vo (Photograph: G. Varlez, Autun.)

Prudence, Fortitude, Temperance and Justice occupy the subsidiary corner medallions. The figures are in gold on a green ground. As well as the rock crystal carving in illustration 72, compare the gold glass medallion in illustration 66. The stooping gold figures on the green ground are also reminiscent of the gold dolphins swimming across the round green porphyry paten, one of the early treasures of St-Denis, for which see Sir M. Conway, *Archaeologia,* LXVI, Pl. VIII, fig. 1, opp. p. 124.

Lit: W. Koehler, *Die karolingischen Miniaturen,* I, 2, *Die Schule von Tours,* 96 ff.

72. THE LOTHAIR CRYSTAL. Lorraine (?), commissioned by King Lothair, probably Lothair II, 855-69. Engraved rock crystal, in fifteenth-century bronze mount. Diameter of crystal 10·5 cm., with setting, 18 cm. London, British Museum. (Photograph: by permission of the Trustees of the British Museum.)

The Crystal is engraved with eight scenes from the history of Susanna and Daniel's just judgement. It was preserved at Waulsort Abbey, Belgium, from the tenth century down to the French Revolution.

Lit: O. M. Dalton, 'The Crystal of Lothair', *Archaeologia,* LIX, 1904, 25 ff; O. M. Dalton, *Catalogue of the Engraved Gems of the Post-Classical Period in the British Museum,* London, 1915, No. 559, 77; P. E. Schramm and F. Mütherich, *Denkmale der deutschen Könige und Kaiser,* No. 31, 125 f.

73. ST CUTHBERT AT CARLISLE. Early twelfth century. Drawing on vellum. 19·4 × 11·9 cm. Oxford, University College MS. 165, page 79. (Photograph: by courtesy of the Master and Fellows of University College, Oxford.)

Lit: T. S. R. Boase, *English Art 1100-1216,* Oxford, 1953, 28; M. Rickert, *Painting in Britain: The Middle Ages,* 2nd ed., Harmondsworth, 1965, 63.

74. PORTRAIT OF THE EVANGELIST ST JOHN, LINDISFARNE GOSPELS, *c.* 698. Illumination on vellum. 34·1 × 24·5 cm. London, British Museum, Cotton

MS. Nero D.iv, folio 209*vo*. (Photograph: by permission of the Trustees of the British Museum.)

The triangular opening where the trumpet-shaped pleat reaches the hem above St John's right foot, and the continuous band along the hem of his mantle, as well as the flat incised parallel folds, are found in a relief sculpture of a seated mother-goddess from Bewcastle near the Roman Wall, for which see F. Haverfield, *Catalogue of the Roman Inscribed and Sculptured Stones in the Carlisle Museum, Tullie House*, 1922, No. 132.

75. TOMBSTONE OF MOTHER AND CHILD. Second or third century A.D. Stone. Height 129·5 cm. Breadth 91·4 cm. From Murrell Hill, Cumberland. Carlisle Museum, Tullie House. (Photograph: Warburg Institute.)

Lit: F. Haverfield, *Catalogue of the Roman Inscribed and Sculptured Stones in the Carlisle Museum, Tullie House,* 1922, No. 103.

76. CIVITA-CASTELLANA RELIEF. Eighth century. Marble. Portion of a sarcophagus (?) with hunting scenes. Civita Castellana, Cathedral. (Photograph: Mansell Collection.)

Lit: A. Haseloff, *Pre-Romanesque Sculpture in Italy*, Florence and Paris, 1930, 56.

77. TYMPANUM OF CHURCH OF ST-URSIN, BOURGES. Twelfth century. (Photograph: Jean Roubier, Paris.)

Lit: Abbé de Roffignac, 'Le Tympan de la porte de Saint-Ursin de Bourges, son caractère religieux', *Mémoires de la société des antiquaires du centre*, XXXVI, 1913, 47 ff; P. Deschamps, *French Sculpture of the Romanesque Period, Eleventh and Twelfth Centuries*, Florence and Paris, 1930, 60 f.

78. SARCOPHAGUS OF BISHOP AGILBERT. North crypt of Jouarre Abbey, *c*. 680. Limestone. (Photograph: Archives photographiques.)

Agilbert became Bishop of Paris in 668 and died *c*. 680.

Lit: J. Hubert, *L'Art pré-roman*, Paris, 1938, 156 f; J. Hubert, 'Architecture and Decorative Carving', *Europe in the Dark Ages*, London, 1967, 72 ff.

79. ST CUTHBERT'S COFFIN, 698. Wood. Length 168·9 cm. Width 41·3 cm. Height 46·4 cm. Oblong box, disinterred in 1827, carved at one end with the images of the Virgin and child, and at the other end with figures of two archangels; on the two long sides five bust-length archangels and the twelve apostles, and on the lid the majesty with the four evangelist symbols. Durham Cathedral Library. (Photograph: by permission of the Dean and Chapter of Durham.)

Lit: E. Kitzinger, 'The Coffin-Reliquary', in *The Relics of St Cuthbert*, ed. C. F. Battiscombe, Durham, 1956, 202 ff.

80. FRONT OF THE ST ANDREWS SARCOPHAGUS, *c*. 800. Sandstone, made of a number of panels, grooved and slotted together. Length of entire sarcophagus 175·3 cm. Height 71·2 cm. Width 88·9 cm. St Andrews Cathedral Museum. (Photograph: copyright Dr Isabel Henderson.)

The sarcophagus was discovered in 1833 in the burial ground adjoining the Cathedral either 'a little west of St Regulus' Tower' or 'about thirteen yards north from the Tower of St Regulus' Chapel', containing a 'miscellaneous accumulation of human bones'. Portions of the structure were lost immediately after its discovery.

Lit: J. Romilly Allen, *The Early Christian Monuments of Scotland*, Part III, 351 f; D. H. Fleming, *St Andrews Cathedral Museum,* Edinburgh, 1931, 3 ff; C. L. Mowbray 'Eastern Influence on Carvings at St Andrews and Nigg, Scotland', *Antiquity*, X, 1936, 428 ff; H. M. Roe, 'The "David Cycle" in Early Irish Art', *Journal of the Royal Society of Antiquaries of Ireland*, LXXIX, 1949, 39 ff; I. Henderson, *The Picts,* London, 1967, 88, 149 ff.

81. GRIFFIN AND PONY, detail of the front of the St Andrews Sarcophagus, *c.* 800. (Photograph: copyright Dr Isabel Henderson.)

82. CHRIST WALKING ON THE WATER, *c.* 1150. Marble relief from the church of the Monastery of San Pedro de Roda. Barcelona, Museo Marés. (Photograph: Foto Mas.)

   The same mannered treatment of the hands occurs in this sculptor's marble tympanum at Cabestany, Rosellon, for which see J. Gudiol Ricart and J. A. Gaya Nuno, *Ars Hispaniae,* v, *Arquitectura y escultura románicas,* Madrid, 1948, 63, Fig. 99.

   Lit: J. Gudiol Ricart and J. A. Gaya Nuno, *Ars Hispaniae,* v, 57, 64.

83. DETAIL FROM THE SCENE OF ST PETER'S DENIAL FORETOLD, ST-GILLES-DU-GARD, *c.* 1170. West Front of St-Gilles-du-Gard. (Photograph: James Austin, Cambridge.)

   Lit: R. Hamann, *Die Abteikirche von St Gilles und ihre künstlerische Nachfolge,* Berlin, 1955.

84. THE BUILDING OF THE ARK, CLOISTER OF GERONA CATHEDRAL, *c.* 1170. Relief on the east face of the south-west pillar of the cloister. (Photograph: Foto Mas.)

   Lit: J. Puig y Cadafalch, *L'Arquitectura romanica a Catalunya,* Barcelona, Institut d'estudis catalans, 1909, 241 f; C. Cid Priego, 'La Iconografia del claustro de la Catedral de Gerona', *Anales del Instituto de estudios Gerundenses,* VI, Gerona, 1951, 5 ff.

85. PASCHAL CANDLESTICK. By Nicolaus de Angilo and Petrus Vassallettus, *c.* 1170. Marble. Height 600 cm. Rome, S. Paolo fuori le Mura. (Photograph: Mansell Collection.)

   Lit: A. Venturi, *Storia dell'arte italiana,* III, 771 f; E. Hutton, *The Cosmati,* London, 1950, 19 f.

86. TRIUMPHAL COLUMN, HILDESHEIM, *c.* 1030. Made for Bishop Godehard (1022–38), successor of Bishop Bernward. Bronze. Height of whole column 379 cm. From St Michael's, Hildesheim, now in Hildesheim Cathedral. (Photograph: Bildarchiv Foto Marburg.)

   Lit: A. Fink, *Zeitschrift für Kunstwissenschaft,* 1948, 1 ff; F. J. Tschan, *St Bernward of Hildesheim,* University of Notre Dame, II, 1951, 251 ff; R. Wesenberg, *Bernwardinische Plastik,* Berlin, 1955, 117 ff; H. Swarzenski, *Monuments of Romanesque Art,* No. 52/3, 47.

87. HERCULES STRANGLING THE NEMAEAN LION. Second half of the twelfth century (?). Bronze. Height 13·3 cm. New York, Irwin Untermyer Collection. (Photograph: Metropolitan Museum, New York.)

   For a close Antique parallel, see the bronze Herakles, probably from a candelabrum, Etruscan, *c.* 430 B.C., British Museum, No. 672, Payne Knight Bequest.

   For medieval Italian analogies, see the Hercules as Strength on the south portal of the Duomo, Borgo San Donnino, in A. Venturi, *Storia dell'arte italiana,* III, Fig. 320, and the cameos discussed by H. Wentzel, 'Mittelalterliche Gemmen in den Sammlungen Italiens', *Mitteilungen des kunsthistorischen Institutes in Florenz,* VII, Part IV, 1956, 244 f, 259 f.

   Lit: W. Oakeshott, *Classical Inspiration in Medieval Art,* London, 1959, 95, 143; Y. Hackenbroch, *The Irwin Untermyer Collection,* v, New York, 1962, ix, 5, pls. 2, 3; H. Swarzenski, *Monuments of Romanesque Art,* No. 217, Fig. 510, and 81; C. Gómez-Moreno, Catalogue of Exhibition, *Medieval Art from Private Collections,* The Metropolitan Museum of Art, 1968, No. 96.

88. INITIAL TO THE BOOK OF AMOS, WINCHESTER BIBLE. Illumination on vellum. Last quarter of the twelfth century, over a drawing of *c.* 1150. Whole

page size 58·2 × 39·5 cm. Winchester Cathedral Library. (Photograph: by courtesy of the Dean and Chapter.)

Lit: W. Oakeshott, *The Artists of the Winchester Bible*, London, 1945.

89. HERCULES STRANGLING THE NEMAEAN LION. Etruscan, late fifth to fourth century B.C. Agate scarab. 1·7 cm. New York, Metropolitan Museum of Art, Rogers Fund, 1911. (Photograph: Metropolitan Museum, New York.)

Lit: G. M. A. Richter, *Catalogue of Engraved Gems: Greek, Etruscan, and Roman, Metropolitan Museum of Art, New York,* Rome, 1956, No. 173, 46.

90. INITIAL TO THE PROLOGUE OF THE BOOK OF AMOS, LAMBETH BIBLE, *c.* 1150. Illumination on vellum. Whole page 52 × 34·3 cm. Lambeth Palace Library, MS. 3, folio 301*vo.* (Photograph: by permission of the Archbishop of Canterbury and the Trustees of Lambeth Palace Library.)

A man wrestles with a beast also in the initial to the Prologue to Ruth on folio 130 of the Lambeth Bible, and in an initial in another Canterbury manuscript, Cambridge, Trinity College MS. B.3.11, reproduced in T. S. R. Boase, *English Art 1100–1216*, Oxford, 1953, Pl. 67a. Compare also the naked wrestler with the lion on a capital in the crypt of the choir of Canterbury Cathedral, reproduced in E. S. Prior and A. Gardner, *An Account of Medieval Figure-Sculpture in England*, Cambridge, 1912, 164, fig. 142.

A group similar to the Amos initial in the Lambeth Bible, though with the man a head taller than the lion, was on an antique engraved gem used as his privy seal by Prior Hugh (?), of the Austin Priory or Hospital of St Gregory, Canterbury, 1263, for which see W. de G. Birch, *Catalogue of Seals in the Department of Manuscripts in the British Museum*, I, No. 2858, 490.

Lit: C. R. Dodwell, *The Great Lambeth Bible*, Faber Library of Illuminated Manuscripts, 1959.

91. THE SEAL OF RICHARD BASSET, *c.* 1129. Diameter 8 cm. Seventeenth-century drawing on vellum from Sir Christopher Hatton's Book of Seals, in the custody of the Northamptonshire Record Society. (Photograph: reproduced by courtesy of the Trustees of the Earl of Winchelsea.)

This seal is attached to a charter of William (Basset) Abbot and the monks of St Benet of Holme, granting the Manor of Heigham next Norwich to Richard Basset, British Museum Harleian Charter 44 E. 19. Of the original seal only the indistinct central portion survives.

Richard Basset (died 1144?) and his father Ralph are described by their contemporary, the historian Henry of Huntingdon, as *viros clarissimos . . . justitiarios totius Angliae*. Sir Simonds D'Ewes (died 1650) speculated that the imagery of the seal was an allegory of Justice. The Basset seal foreshadows the seal of Roger de Quincy of about one hundred years later, in which, perhaps infected by Romance imagery, the knight is in combat with a lion. For this see W. de G. Birch, *Catalogue of Seals in the Department of Manuscripts in the British Museum*, II, 1892, No. 6346, 342; H. Laing, *Descriptive Catalogue of Impressions from Ancient Scottish Seals*, Edinburgh, The Maitland Club, 1850, Pl. XI, fig. 2. For Richard Basset, see J. H. Round's entry in the *Dictionary of National Biography*, I, 1305 f; also W. T. Reedy, 'The First Two Bassets of Weldon – *Novi Barones* of the Early and Mid-Twelfth Century', *Northamptonshire Past and Present: Journal of the Northamptonshire Record Society*, IV, 1969–70, No. 4, 241 ff; 1970–71, No. 5, 295 ff.

For the lore of griffins, see Marbodus of Rennes, *Liber de gemmis*, in Migne, *Patrologia Latina*, CLXXI, col. 1773; also Sir Thomas Browne, 'Of Griffins', *Pseudodoxia Epidemica*, Bk. 3, chapter XI, in *The Works of Sir Thomas Browne*, ed. Sir G. Keynes, 1964, II, 190 f.

Lit: For the Charter and seal see *Sir Christopher Hatton's Book of Seals*, ed. L. C. Loyd and D. M. Stenton, Oxford, 1950, No. 407, 276 f. For a lively description and discussion of the 'great orbiculate seal' when in a good state of preservation in 1632, see *The Autobiography and Correspondence of Sir Simonds D'Ewes, Bart., During the Reigns of James I. and Charles I.,* ed. J. O. Halliwell, London, 1845, 73 ff.

92. LION FOUNTAIN, UTRECHT PSALTER, Reims, *c.* 830. Pen and ink on vellum. 32·7 × 25·1 cm. Utrecht University Library, MS. 32, folio 14*vo*, Psalm xxv (Iudica me Domine), verse 6, 'Lavabo inter innocentes manus meas'. (Photograph: University Library, Utrecht.)

Lit: E. T. DeWald, *The Illustrations of the Utrecht Psalter*, Princeton, 1933; D. Tselos, 'New Light on the Origin of the Utrecht Psalter', *Art Bulletin*, XIII, 1931, 13 ff; D. Panofsky, 'The Textual Basis of the Utrecht Psalter', *Art Bulletin*, XXV, 1943, 50 ff; F. Wormald, *The Utrecht Psalter*, Utrecht, 1953; D. Tselos, 'The Influence of the Utrecht Psalter on Carolingian Art', *Art Bulletin*, XXXIX, 1957, 87 ff.

93. EINHARD'S TRIUMPHAL ARCH RELIQUARY AND CROSS BASE, *c.* 828. Chased silver on wooden core. Height 28 cm. Until the French Revolution preserved in the Treasury of St Servatius at Maastricht. Pen and wash drawing, seventeenth century, from Jesuit seventeenth–eighteenth-century collection of inscriptions and Antique monuments, Paris, Bibliothèque Nationale, MS. Fr. 10440, folio 45. (Photograph: Bibliothèque Nationale, Paris.)

Lit: B. de Montesquiou-Fézensac, 'L'Arc de triomphe d'Einhardus', *Cahiers archéologiques*, IV, 1949, 79 ff; 'L'Arc d'Eginhard', *Cahiers archéologiques*, VIII, 1956, 147 ff; 'L'Arc de triomphe d'Eginhard', *Karolingische und ottonische Kunst*, Weisbaden, 1957, 43 ff. Compare Charlemagne's 'Tables', for which see F. N. Estey, 'Charlemagne's Silver Celestial Table', *Speculum*, XVIII, 1943, 112 ff.

94. GOLDEN ALTAR OF S. AMBROGIO, MILAN, *c.* 850. Figures of archangels and of the donor Angilbert and the master craftsman Wolvinius. (Photograph: Bildarchiv Foto Marburg.)

Lit: see notes on illustration 8.

95. THE GATEWAY OF LORSCH ABBEY, *c.* 800. (Photograph: Bildarchiv Foto Marburg.)

Lit: R. Krautheimer, 'The Carolingian Revival of Early Christian Architecture', *Art Bulletin,* XXIV, 1942, 1 ff; E. Gall. 'L'Abbaye carolingienne de Lorsch', *Mémorial d'un voyage d'études de la société nationale des antiquaires de France en Rhenanie,* ed. R. Louis, Paris, 1953, 57 ff; H. Walbe and W. Meyer-Barkhausen, *Die Torhalle in Lorsch*, Heppenheim, 1953; K. J. Conant, *Carolingian and Romanesque Architecture, 800–1200*, Harmondsworth, 1959, 18.

96. ST CYRIAKUS, GERNRODE, begun 961. (Photograph: Bildarchiv Foto Marburg.)

The western apse is a later addition to the church founded by the Margrave Gero in 961. Money was provided for the work by the Empress Theophano (died 991).

Lit: P. Frankl, *Die frühmittelalterliche und romanische Baukunst*, 52 f; L. Grote, *Die Stiftskirche zu Gernrode*, Burg-bei-Magdeburg, 1932; E. Hempel, *Geschich -te der deutschen Baukunst*, Munich, 1949, 44 ff.

97. GROUND-PLAN OF ST MICHAEL'S CHURCH, HILDESHEIM, *c.* 1000. (After Grodecki.)

The church was begun by Bishop Bernward about 1001, and was complete in 1033.

Lit: P. Frankl, *Die frühmittelalterliche und romanische Baukunst*, Wildpark-

Potsdam, 1926, 66 ff; H. Beseler and H. Roggenkamp, *Die Michaeliskirche in Hildesheim*, Berlin, 1954; L. Grodecki, *L'Architecture ottonienne; au seuil de l'art roman*, Paris, 1958.

98. WEST FRONT OF JUMIÈGES ABBEY, 1037–66. (Photograph: Bildarchiv Foto Marburg.)

Lit: L.-M. Michon and R. Martin du Gard, *L'Abbaye de Jumièges*, Petites monographies des grands édifices de la France, Paris, 1935; T. S. R. Boase, *English Art 1100–1216*, Oxford, 1953, 2 ff.

99. NORTH TRANSEPT PORCH, KELSO ABBEY, *c.* 1170. (Photograph: Crown copyright: Ministry of the Environment, Edinburgh.)

The design of the church, with western transepts and tower, has Carolingian antecedents. The transept façade, as a whole, recalls traditional designs like the façade of St Pantaleon at Cologne, while in its fenestration and rich textures it resembles recent work such as the tower at Bury St Edmunds. The Kelso porch gable is decorated in a manner similar to the Romanesque gables on the north and south flanks of the west façade of Lincoln Cathedral. The high upright format of the porch recalls that of the porch represented on the façade of Battle Abbey in the seal of the Abbey, for which see W. de G. Birch, *Catalogue of Seals in the Department of Manuscripts in the British Museum*, I, Pl. x, No. 2616. Compare the clean lines and trim quality of the porch with the porches of classical design in south French churches, at St-Restitut, Drôme, and St-Gabriel, Bouches-du-Rhone, for which see J. Gantner M. Pobé, *Romanesque Art in France*, London, 1956, Pls. 72 and 86.

Lit: T. S. R. Boase, *English Art 1100–1216*, Oxford, 1953, 151 f; *The County of Roxburgh*, I, Royal Commission on the Ancient Monuments of Scotland, Edinburgh, 1956, 240 ff.

100. WEST FRONT OF S. MICHELE, PAVIA, *c.* 1100–1160. (Photograph: Mansell Collection.)

Lit: A. K. Porter, *Lombard Architecture*, New Haven, 1915–17, III, 199 ff.

101. INTERIOR OF THE NAVE OF SOUTHWELL MINSTER, *c.* 1150. (Photograph: Crown copyright. National Monuments Record.)

Lit: G. Webb, *Architecture in Britain: The Middle Ages*, Harmondsworth, 1956, 52 f.

102. WEST FRONT OF ST-GILLES-DU-GARD, *c.* 1170. (Photograph: James Austin, Cambridge.)

Lit: R. Hamann, *Die Abteikirche von St-Gilles und ihre künstlerische Nachfolge*, Berlin, 1955.

103. INTERIOR OF CLUNY ABBEY, View from the ambulatory. Ambulatory, *c.* 1095. Church built, *c.* 1088–1130. Watercolour drawing by J.-B. Lallemand, *c.* 1773. Paris, Bibliothèque Nationale, Cabinet des estampes. (Photograph: Bibliothèque Nationale, Paris.)

Lit: For Cluny see J. Evans, *The Romanesque Architecture of the Order of Cluny*, Cambridge, 1938; J. Evans, *Cluniac Art in the Romanesque Period*, Cambridge, 1950; K. J. Conant, *Carolingian and Romanesque Architecture, 800–1200*, Harmondsworth, 1959, 107 ff; K. J. Conant, *Cluny: Les Églises et la maison du chef d'ordre*, Massachusetts, Macon, 1968.

104. CAPRICCIO By Robert Adam. 1782. London, Sir John Soane's Museum. (Photograph: Sir John Soane's Museum.)

Lit: A. T. Bolton, *The Architecture of Robert and James Adam (1758–1794)*, London, 1922, I, 75 ff.

105. THE STORY OF ROMULUS AND REMUS, THE FRANKS CASKET, *c.* 700. Whalebone. Length 22·9 cm. London, The British Museum. The right side panel of

the casket is in the Bargello, Florence. (Photograph: by permission of the Trustees of the British Museum.)

For other English versions of the wolf and the twins, see J. Brøndsted, *Early English Ornament*, London and Copenhagen, 1924, 96, Fig. 79.

Lit: O. M. Dalton, *Catalogue of the Ivory Carvings of the Christian Era*, British Museum, London, 1909, No. 30, 27 ff; G. Baldwin Brown, *The Arts in Early England*, VI, Part I, London, 1930, 18 ff.

106. THE STORY OF WELAND THE SMITH, AND THE ADORATION OF THE MAGI. The Franks Casket. *c.* 700. (Photograph: by permission of the Trustees of the British Museum.)

Lit: P. W. Souers, 'The Magi on the Franks Casket', *Harvard Studies and Notes in Philology and Literature*, XIX, 1937, 249 ff; P. W. Souers, 'The Wayland Scene in the Franks Casket', *Speculum*, XVIII, 1943, 104 ff.

107. FUNERARY STELE OF HORSEMAN, HORNHAUSEN, Saxony, *c.* 700. Halle, Landesmuseum für Vorgeschichte. (Photograph: Bildarchiv Foto Marburg.)

Lit: F. Rademacher, 'Frühkarolingische Grabsteine im Landesmuseum zu Bonn', *Bonner Jahrbücher*, 1939, 265 ff; K. Böhner, 'Der fränkische Grabstein von Niederdollendorf am Rhein', *Germania*, 1944–50, 63.

108. SARCOPHAGUS OF SS. SERGIUS AND BACCHUS, made for Abbot Boniface, 1179. From the Church of St Sylvester at Nogara. Verona Museum. (Photograph: Alinari.)

The scene of the martyrdom of the saints looks remarkably like the death of the Witnesses Enoch and Elias in a group of mid-thirteenth-century illustrated Apocalypses – the Morgan, Bodleian, and Paris Apocalypses.

Lit: A. Venturi, *Storia dell'arte italiana*, III, 226 f; R. Jullian, *L'Éveil de la sculpture italienne*, Paris, 1945, 174 f.

109. BATTLE SCENE, ABERLEMNO CROSS-SLAB. Early eighth century. Sandstone. Height 228·6 cm. Width 127 cm. Aberlemno Churchyard, Angus, Scotland (Photograph: Crown copyright. Ministry of the Environment, Edinburgh.)

Lit: J. Romilly Allen, *The Early Christian Monuments of Scotland*, Edinburgh, 1903, Part III, 209 ff; I. Henderson, *The Picts*, London, 1967, 134 ff.

110. INTERIOR OF TRANSEPT, SANTIAGO DE COMPOSTELA, *c.* 1120. (Photograph: Foto Mas.)

Lit: A. K. Porter, *Romanesque Sculpture of the Pilgrimage Roads*, Boston, 1923, I, 193 f; W. M. Whitehill, *Spanish Romanesque Architecture of the Eleventh Century*, Oxford, 1941, reprinted 1968, 266 ff; K. J. Conant, *Carolingian and Romanesque Architecture, 800 to 1200*, Harmondsworth, 1959, 99 f. For the cult of St James, see T. R. Kendrick, *St James in Spain*, London, 1960.

111. THE JOURNEY TO EMMAUS, S. DOMINGO DE SILOS, *c.* 1100, or second quarter of twelfth century. Stone relief on the north-west pier of cloister, Santo Domingo de Silos. (Photograph: Foto Mas.)

Lit: Dom E. Roulin, 'Les cloîtres de l'abbaye de Silos', *Revue de l'art chrétien*, 1909, LIX, 75 ff; A. K. Porter, *Romanesque Sculpture of the Pilgrimage Roads*, I, 44 ff; M. Schapiro, 'From Mozarabic to Romanesque at Silos', *Art Bulletin*, XXI, 1939, 313 ff; W. M. Whitehill, *Spanish Romanesque Architecture of the Eleventh Century*, Oxford, 1941, 155 ff; J. Gudiol Ricart and J. A. Gaya Nuno, *Ars Hispaniae*, V, 236 f.

112. THE EAST END OF ST MARTIN'S CHURCH, TOURS. Tenth, eleventh, and thirteenth centuries. The late-nineteenth-century excavations of the chevet, drawn by Jules Masquelez.

Lit: C. K. Hersey, 'The Church of Saint-Martin at Tours (903–1150)', *Art Bulletin*, XXV, 1943, 1 ff.

113. THE BATTLE OF HASTINGS, THE BAYEUX TAPESTRY, *c.* 1077. (Photograph: from *The Bayeux Tapestry* by Frank Stenton, published by Phaidon Press.)

The incident illustrated is the death of Leofwine and Gyrth, King Harold's brothers. The bottom margin is filled with the mutilated bodies of soldiers killed in battle.

114. SIGURD AND THE WOLF(?), 1016–35 (?). Stone relief. Height 69·5 cm. Length 52 cm. (Photograph: by courtesy of the Winchester Excavations Committee.)

This fragment of a narrative frieze was found in 1965 in the rubble of the eastern crypt of the Old Minster, Winchester – demolished 1093–4.

Lit: M. Biddle, 'A Late Saxon Frieze Sculpture from the Old Minster', in 'Excavations at Winchester, 1965. Appendix', *The Antiquaries Journal*, XLVI, 1966, 329 ff.

115. JACOB GOING TO MEET ESAU. Second quarter of the eleventh century. Illumination on vellum. 32·7 × 22·2 cm. Aelfric's Anglo-Saxon paraphrase of the Pentateuch and Joshua, London, British Museum Cotton MS. Claudius B. iv, folio 50*vo* (Photograph: by permission of the Trustees of the British Museum.)

Lit: For this Manuscript see S. J. Crawford, *The Old English Version of the Heptateuch*, Early English Text Society, 1922; G. Henderson, 'Late-Antique Influences in Some English Mediaeval Illustrations of Genesis', *Journal of the Warburg and Courtauld Institutes*, XXV, 1962, 172 ff; O. Pächt, *The Rise of Pictorial Narrative in Twelfth Century England*, Oxford, 1962, 5 ff; G. Henderson, 'The Joshua Cycle in B. M. Cotton MS. Claudius B. iv', *Journal of the British Archaeological Association*, XXXI, 1968, 38 ff.

116. JACOB'S MEETING WITH ESAU. Illumination on vellum. British Museum Cotton MS. Claudius B. iv, folio 51. (Photograph: by permission of the Trustees of the British Museum.)

Compare the prostrate figure of Heraclius in illustration 132, and also the prostrate Saul on folio 386*vo* of the First Bible of Charles the Bald, for which see W. Koehler, *Die karolingischen Miniaturen*, I, 1, *Die Schule von Tours*, Pl. 1, 74; see also the prostrate figure before a small structure with tiled roof shaped like a truncated pediment, on the front of a walrus ivory box in the Victoria and Albert Museum, for which see M. H. Longhurst, *English Ivories*, London, 1926, 31 and Pl. 34.

117. THE BURIAL OF JOSEPH. Illumination on vellum. London, British Museum, Cotton MS. Claudius B. iv, folio 72*vo*. (Photograph: by permission of the Trustees of the British Museum.

Lit: F. Wormald, 'Continental Influence on English Medieval Illumination', *Transactions of the Fourth International Congress of Bibliophiles*, London, 1967, 4 f.

118. THE WHORE OF BABYLON, VALENCIENNES APOCALYPSE. Early ninth century. Illumination on vellum. 27 × 20 cm. Valenciennes, Bibliothèque municipale, MS. 99, folio 31. (Photograph: Roualt, Paris.)

Lit: H. Omont, *Bulletin de la société française pour la reproduction des manuscrits à peintures,* 6e année, 1922; M. R. James, *The Apocalypse in Art*, The Schweich Lectures of the British Academy, 1927, London, 1931, 37.

119. THE WHORE OF BABYLON, BAMBERG APOCALYPSE, Reichenau. Early eleventh century. Illumination on vellum. 29·5 × 20·4 cm. Bamberg, Staatsbibliothek Bibl. 140, folio 43. (Photograph: Staatsbibliothek Bamberg.)

Lit: H. Wölfflin, *Die Bamberger Apokalypse*, Munich, 1921; A. Fauser, *Die Bamberger Apokalypse*, Bamberg, 1958.

120. THE HISTORY OF ADAM AND EVE, Tours. Second quarter of the ninth century. Illumination on vellum. 51 × 36 cm. The Moûtiers-Grandval Bible, London,

British Museum Add. MS. 10546, folio 5*vo*. (Photograph: by permission of the Trustees of the British Museum.)

In the late sixteenth century this manuscript belonged to the monastery of Moûtiers-Grandval near Basle.

Lit: W. Koehler, *Die karolingischen Miniaturen*, I, 2, *Die Schule von Tours*, 13 ff, and 118 ff.

121. THE HISTORY OF ADAM AND EVE, Tours, 844–51. Illumination on vellum. 49·5 × 37·5 cm. The First Bible of Charles the Bald, Paris, Bibliothèque Nationale MS. Lat. 1, folio 10*vo*. (Photograph: Bibliothèque Nationale, Paris.)

Lit: W. Koehler, *Die karolingischen Miniaturen*, I, 2, *Die Schule von Tours*, 27 ff.

122. SCENES FROM THE LIFE OF MOSES, Canterbury, *c*. 1200. Illumination on vellum. 48 × 32·5 cm. Paris, Bibliothèque Nationale, MS. Lat. 8846, folio 2 (Photograph: Bibliothèque Nationale, Paris.)

Lit: T. S. R. Boase, *English Art: 1100–1216*, Oxford, 1953, 289 f; M. Rickert, *Painting in Britain: The Middle Ages*, 2nd ed., Harmondsworth, 1965, 93 f.

123. SCENES FROM THE LIFE OF MOSES, *c*. 1150. Illumination on vellum. 39·4 × 28 cm. New York, J. Pierpont Morgan Library, MS. 724. (Photograph: J. Pierpont Morgan Library.)

Compare Goliath (bottom centre) with the knight on the Basset Seal, illustration 91.

Lit: M. R. James, 'Four Leaves of an English Psalter, 12th century', *The Walpole Society*, XXV, 1936–7. 1 ff; H. Swarzenski, 'Unknown Bible Pictures by W. de Brailes and Some Notes on Early English Bible Illustration', *Journal of the Walters Art Gallery, Baltimore*, I, 1938, 67 ff.

124. THE CHILDREN OF ISRAEL CROSSING THE RED SEA, late eleventh century. Wall painting in the Church of St-Julien at Tours, from a watercolour drawing by L. Ypermann, 1892, Paris, Musée des monuments français. (Photograph: Archives photographiques.)

Lit: A Grabar, 'Fresques romanes copiées sur les miniatures du Pentateuque de Tours', *Cahiers archéologiques*, IX, 1957, 329 ff.

125. INTERIOR OF THE ABBEY CHURCH OF ST-SAVIN, *c*. 1060–1115. (Photograph: Hirmer Fotoarchiv.)

Lit: E. Maillard, *L'Église de Saint-Savin-sur-Gartempe*, Petites monographies des grands édifices de la France, Paris, 1926; K. J. Conant, *Carolingian and Romanesque Architecture, 800–1200*, Harmondsworth, 1959, 160 f; *Poitou roman*, introd. R. Crozet, Zodiaque, La nuit des temps, 2nd ed., 1962, 128 ff.

126. THE BUILDING OF THE TOWER OF BABEL, ST-SAVIN. Early twelfth century. Wall painting.

Lit: G. Gaillard, *Les Fresques de Saint-Savin*, Paris, 1944; P. Deschamps, M. Thibout, and A. Grabar, 'Observations sur les fresques de Saint-Savin', *Cahiers archéologiques*, IV, 1949, 134 ff; H. Focillon, *Peintures romanes des églises de France*, Paris, 1950; P. Deschamps and M. Thibout, *La Peinture murale de France*, Paris, 1951, 72 ff; G. Henderson, 'The Sources of the Genesis Cycle at Saint-Savin-sur-Gartempe', *Journal of the British Archaeological Association*, XXVI, 1963, 11 ff.

127. THE WOMAN IN FLIGHT FROM THE DRAGON, BAMBERG APOCALYPSE. Early eleventh century. Illumination on vellum. Bamberg, Staatsbibliothek, Bibl. 140, folio 31*vo*. (Photograph: Staatsbibliothek Bamberg.)

Lit: See note on illustration 119.

128. THE FALL OF PRIDE. Late ninth century. Drawing on vellum. 26·4 × 21 cm. Psychomachia of Prudentius, Bern Stadtbibliothek, MS. 264, folio 44*vo*. (Photograph: Burgerbibliothek, Bern.)

Lit: R. Stettiner, *Die Illustrierten Prudentius Handschriften*, Berlin, 1905, 70 ff.

129. APOCALYPSE TYMPANUM, MOISSAC, *c.* 1115. (Photograph: Bildarchiv Foto Marburg.)

Lit: M. Schapiro, 'Two Romanesque Drawings in Auxerre and Some Iconographic Problems', *Studies in Art and Literature for Belle da Costa Greene*, Princeton, 1954, 331 ff. See also note on illustration 54.

130. THEOPHILUS TYMPANUM, SOUILLAC, *c.* 1125. (Photograph: Bildarchiv Foto Marburg.)

Lit: See note on illustration 57. For the Theophilus legend see H. L. D. Ward, *Catalogue of Romances in the British Museum*, II, 1893, 595; Sir G. W. Dasent, *Theophilus in Icelandic, Low German, and other Tongues*, London, 1845,; E. Mâle, *L'Art religieux de XII⁰ siècle en France*, Paris, 1922, 434; E. Mâle, *L'Art religieux du XIII⁰ siècle en France*, Paris, 1902, 297.

131. THE CREATION, *c.* 1050. Drawing on vellum. London, British Museum, Cotton MS. Tiberius C. vi, folio 7*vo.* (Photograph: by permission of the Trustees of the British Museum.)

Lit: See note on illustration 50.

132. THE EXALTATION OF THE CROSS. Probably from Mont-St-Michel, *c.* 1050–65. Illumination on vellum. Height 19·8 cm. A Sacramentary, New York, J. Pierpont Morgan Library, MS. 641, folio 155*vo.* (Photograph: The Pierpont Morgan Library.)

The top miniature shows the repetition of Constantine's vision of the Cross in the sky to the Emperor Heraclius at Jerusalem, A.D. 630.

Lit: J. J. G. Alexander, *Norman Illumination at Mont St Michel, 966–1100*, Oxford, 1970, 127 ff. and 288 ff.

133. APSE MOSAIC, S. PUDENZIANA, ROME. 401–17. (Photograph: Alinari.)

Lit: O. Wulff, *Altchristliche Kunst*, Berlin, 1918, 328 f; W. Koehler, *Forschungen zur Kirchengeschichte und zur christlichen Kunst*, J. Ficker zum 70. Geburtstag dargebracht, Leipzig, 1931, 167.

134. PROCESSIONAL CROSS. Seventh or eighth century. Silver (gilt) with precious stones, glass pastes and gold glass medallion. Height 142·5 cm. Brescia, Museo civico. (Photograph: Alinari.)

Lit: A. Venturi, *Storia dell'arte italiana*, Milan, 1901, I, 555; P. Toesca, *Storia dell'arte italiana*, Rome, 1927, I, 65, 79, 323, 332, 1146; H. Wentzel, 'Die Kaiser-Kamee am Gemmenkreuz in Brescia', *Mitteilungen des deutschen archaeologischen Instituts, Römische Abteilung*, LXII, 1955, 53 ff.

135. CROSS OF LOTHAIR, *c.* 1000. Gold, filigree, precious stones, cloisonné enamel. Height 49·8 cm. At the centre is an Antique sardonyx cameo of Augustus; on the stem a rock crystal, with bust of Lothair II (?) (855–69), cut in the same technique as the Lothair Crystal, see illustration 72. Aachen Minster Treasury. (Photograph: Bildarchiv Foto Marburg.)

Lit: H. Schnitzler, *Dom zu Aachen*, 1950, XIX; P. E. Schramm and F. Mütherich, *Denkmale der deutschen Könige und Kaiser*, No. 106, 155.

136. THE CROSS OF ELIGIUS AND THE GOLD ALTAR OF CHARLES THE BALD. Early seventh century, and *c.* 870. Detail from panel painting, *The Mass of St Giles*, *c.* 1500 London, National Gallery. (Photograph: reproduced by courtesy of the Trustees of the National Gallery.)

Compare the gold altar with the extant gold altars at Milan and Paris, illustrations 8 and 94, and 12.

Lit: For the painting, see M. Davies, *Early Netherlandish School*, National Gallery Catalogue, 1945, No. 4681, 72 ff.

For Eligius, *c.* 588–659, Bishop of Noyon, see Thieme-Becker, *Allgemeines Lexikon der bildenden Künstler von der Antike bis zur Gegenwart*, Leipzig, X, 1914,

459; also see *Monumenta Germaniae historica: scriptorum rerum Merovingicarum*, IV, 1902, 634 ff.

For his metalwork, see C. de Linas, *Orfèvrerie mérovingienne: les oeuvres de Saint-Eloi et la verroterie cloisonnée*, Paris, 1864, 60 ff; Sir M. Conway, 'The Abbey of Saint-Denis and its Ancient Treasures', *Archaeoligia*, LXVI, 1914-15, 124 ff; J. J. Marquet de Vasselot, *Bibliographie de l'orfèvrerie et de l'émaillerie française*, Paris, 1925, 87, 100, 108, 109, 173, 176, 177, 185; B. de Montesquiou-Fézensac, 'Une épave de trésor de Saint-Denis. Fragment retrouvé de la croix de Saint-Eloi', *Mélanges en hommage à la mémoire de Fr. Martroye*, Paris, 1940, 213 ff.

For the gold altar, see P. E. Schramm and F. Mütherich, *Denkmale der deutsch-en Könige und Kaiser*, No. 48, 132.

137. THE ADORATION OF THE LAMB, ST-SEVER APOCALYPSE, 1028-72. Illumination on vellum. 36·5 × 27·9 cm. Paris, Bibliothèque Nationale, MS. Lat. 8878, folios 120*vo*, 121. (Photograph: Bibliothèque Nationale, Paris.)

Lit: W. Neuss, *Die Apokalypse des hl. Johannes in der altspanischen und altchristlichen Bibel-Illustration*, Münster, 1931, 34 ff and 237 ff.

138. THE LAMB UNSEALING THE BOOK, Reims (?), between 870 and 875. Illumination on vellum. 44·8 × 34·5 cm. Bible of S. Paolo fuori le Mura, folio 307*vo*. (Photograph: Basilica Photograph.)

This Manuscript was written by Ingobertus for Charles the Bald. The angels in the illustration are the angels of the seven churches. In heaven the Lamb unseals the book, unveiling the hidden nature of the Father.

For this Apocalypse scene see J. Croquison, 'Une Vision eschatologique carolingienne, *Cahiers archéologiques*, IV, 1949, 105 ff. Also W. Koehler, *Die karolingischen Miniaturen*, I, 2, *Die Schule von Tours*, 136 ff.

Lit: J. O. Westwood, *The Bible of the Monastery of St Paul near Rome*, Oxford, 1876; P. E. Schramm and F. Mütherich, *Denkmale der deutschen Könige und Kaiser*, No. 56, 136 f.

139. READING DESK OF ST RADEGONDE, before 587. Wood. Length 26 cm. Width 19 cm. Abbey of Sainte-Croix, Poitiers. (Photograph: Roger Viollet, Paris.)

140. THE RUTHWELL CROSS, front. Parish church, Ruthwell. (Photograph: Crown copyright. Ministry of the Environment, Edinburgh.)

Lit: See note on illustration 63; also E. Kantorowicz, 'The Archer in the Ruthwell Cross', *Art Bulletin*, XLII, 1960, 57 ff; M. Schapiro, 'The Bowman and the Bird on the Ruthwell Cross and Other Works', *Art Bulletin*, XLV, 1963, 351 ff.

141. GOD ENTHRONED WITH THE SYMBOLS OF THE FOUR EVANGELISTS, second quarter of the ninth century. Illumination on vellum. 29·4 × 23·3 cm. Berlin, Lat. Theol. Fol. 733, folio 17*vo*. (Photograph: Staatsbibliothek Preussischer Kulturbesitz Handschriftenabteilung.)

Compare the small rosette motif with that on Einhard's Arch Reliquary, illustration 93.

Lit: See note on illustration 64.

142. PORTRAIT OF RABANUS MAURUS AT THE FOOT OF THE CROSS, Fulda, *c.* 840. Illumination on vellum. 40·3 × 30·7 cm. Vienna, Österreichische Nationalbibliothek, Cod. 652, folio 33*vo*. (Photograph: Österreichische Nationalbibliothek, Vienna.)

Rabanus Maurus composed an epitaph for Einhard, died 840. For Einhard's contribution to the iconography of the Cross, see illustration 93.

Lit: For the text of Rabanus Maurus's book, see J.-P. Migne, *Patrologia Latina*, CVII, col. 132 and *Figura* XXVIII. For the sister manuscript in the Vatican, see P. E. Schramm and F. Mütherich, *Denkmale der deutschen Könige und Kaiser*, No. 22, 121 f.

143. ENGLISH IVORY CROSS, c. 1150. Walrus ivory. Height 57·7 cm. Breadth 36·2 cm. New York, The Metropolitan Museum of Art. (Photograph: The Metropolitan Museum of Art, New York.)

Lit: W. Mersmann, 'Das Elfenbeinkreuz der Sammlung Topic-Mimara', *Wallraf Richartz-Jahrbuch*, XXV, 1963, 7 ff; T. P. F. Hoving, 'The Bury St Edmunds Cross', *Metropolitan Museum of Art Bulletin*, XXII, 1964, 317 ff; S. Longland, 'Pilate Answered: What I Have Written I Have Written', *Metropolitan Museum of Art Bulletin*, XXVI, 1968, 410 ff; S. Longland, 'A Literary Aspect of the Bury St Edmunds Cross', *Metropolitan Museum Journal* II, 1969, 45 ff; S. Longland, 'The Bury St Edmunds Cross', *The Connoisseur*, CLXXII, 1969, 163 ff; Catalogue, *The Year 1200*, A Centennial Exhibition at the Metropolitan Museum of Art, 1970, No. 60, 52 f.

144. RELIQUARY CROSS. Eleventh or twelfth century, forming ivory case for a (lost) gold box containing a relic of the True Cross. Height 11·9 cm. Breadth 4·6 cm. London, Victoria and Albert Museum (Photograph: Crown copyright. Victoria and Albert Museum.)

Compare the archer with that at the head of the Ruthwell Cross, illustration 140.

Lit: J. Beckwith, 'A Rediscovered English Reliquary Cross', *Victoria and Albert Museum Bulletin*, II, 1966, 117 ff; B. Raw, 'The Archer, the Eagle, and the Lamb', *Journal of the Warburg and Courtauld Institutes*, XXX, 1967, 391 ff.

145. THE CRUCIFIXION, Mosan, 1140–50. Copper gilt with champlevé enamel. 10·2 cm. square. New York, The Metropolitan Museum of Art, gift of J. Pierpont Morgan, 1917. (Photograph: The Metropolitan Museum of Art, New York.)

Lit: H. P. Mitchell, 'Some Enamels of the School of Godefroid de Claire', *Burlington Magazine*, XXXIV, 1919, 85 ff, 165 ff; XXXV, 1919, 34 ff, 92 ff, 217 ff; XXXVI, 1920, 18 ff, 128 ff; P. Lasko, 'The Pentecost Panel and Godefroid de Claire', *The Connoisseur Year Book*, 1966, 45 ff.

146. PEDESTAL OF THE ST-BERTIN CROSS, Mosan, c. 1180. Gilt bronze. The domed base and the sides of the pillar are covered with plaques of champlevé enamel. Height, 30·7 cm. Saint-Omer, Museum. (Photograph: Giraudon, Paris.)

Lit: L. Deschamps de Pas, 'Le Pied du croix de St-Bertin', *Annales archéologiques*, XVIII, 1858, 1 ff; S. Collon-Gevaert, *Histoire des arts du métal en Belgique*, 1951, 162 ff. For Abbot Suger's great cross see E. Panofsky, *Abbot Suger on the Abbey Church of St-Denis and its Art Treasures*, Princeton, 1946, 56 f; R. B. Green, 'Ex ungue leonem', *Essays in Honor of Erwin Panofsky*, ed. M. Meiss, New York, 1961, 157 ff; P. Verdier, 'What Do We Know of the Great Cross of Suger in Saint-Denis?', *Gesta*, IX, 2, 1970, 12 ff.

147. THE VOLTO SANTO OF LUCCA. Thirteenth century (?) replica of older image. Poly chromed wood. Lucca, Cathedral. (Photograph: Mansell Collection.)

Lit: A. Guerra, *Storia del Volto Santo*, Lucca, 1881; E. Panofsky, 'Das Braunschweiger Domkruzifix und das "Volto Santo" zu Lucca', *Festschrift für Adolph Goldschmidt*, 1923, 37 ff; A. K. Porter, *Spanish Romanesque Sculpture*, II, Florence and Paris, 1928, 8 ff. See also R. Haussherr, *Zeitschrift für Kunstwissenschaft*, XVI, 1962, 129 ff.

148. CRUCIFIXION, SACRAMENTARY OF CHARLES THE BALD, c. 870. Illumination on vellum. 26·9 × 19·9 cm. Paris, Bibliothèque Nationale, MS. Lat. 1141, folio 6vo. (Photograph: Bibliothèque Nationale, Paris.)

Lit: V. Leroquais, *Les Sacramentaires et les missels manuscrits des bibliothèques publiques de France*, I, Paris, 1924, 35 ff; A. M. Friend, 'Two Manuscripts of the School of S. Denis', *Speculum*, I, 1926, 59 ff; J. Croquison, 'Le "Sacramentaire

Charlemagne" ', *Cahiers archéologiques*, VI, 1952, 55 ff. See also C. Beutler, *Bildwerke zwischen Antike und Mittelalter*, Düsseldorf, 1964, 34 ff.

149. BOOK COVER WITH CRUCIFIXION, Liège. First half of the eleventh century. Ivory. 17 × 11 cm. Tongres, Église de Notre-Dame. (Photograph: copyright A. C. L. Bruxelles.)

For the Carolingian antecedents of this ivory, see for example the book cover showing the Crucifixion in London, the Victoria and Albert Museum, *Early Medieval Art in the North*, H.M. Stationery Office, 1949, Pl. 8 (No. 250).

Lit: M. Laurent, *Les Ivoires prégothiques conservés en Belgique*, Brussels, 1912, 89 f; A. Goldschmidt, *Die Elfenbeinskulpturen aus der Zeit der karolingische und sächsische Kaiser*, II, No. 57; J. Schwartz, 'Quelques sources antiques d'ivoires carolingiens', *Cahiers archéologiques*, XI, 1960, 145 ff.

150. CRUCIFIX OF ARCHBISHOP GERO, 969–76. Wood. Height of whole figure 187 cm. Cologne, Cathedral. (Photograph: Bildarchiv Foto Marburg.)

Lit: H.-U. Haedeke, 'Das Gerokreuz im Dom zu Köln und seine Nachfolge im 11. Jahrhundert', *Kölner Domblatt*, XIV-XV, 1958, 42 ff.

Books for Further Reading

GENERAL SURVEYS AND CATALOGUES, AND REGIONAL STUDIES:

M. Hauttmann's *Die Kunst des frühen Mittelalters*, Propyläen-Kunstgeschichte, VI (Berlin, 1929), contains a useful pictorial survey of early medieval art, including architecture. H. Swarzenski's *Monuments of Romanesque Art* (2nd ed., London, 1967), provides a brief but authoritative catalogue of early medieval manuscripts, ivories, and metalwork, and makes an important contribution to the appreciation of early medieval art by its impressive illustrations. Manuscripts, precious metalwork and other objects of supreme artistic and historical value are examined in two indispensable works, P. E. Schramm, *Die deutschen Kaiser und Könige in Bildern ihrer Zeit 751–1152* (Leipzig, 1928), and P. E. Schramm and F. Mütherich, *Denkmale der deutschen Könige und Kaiser* (Munich, 1962).

The chapters on 'Continental Art in the Last Centuries B.C.' and 'Insular La Tène' in N. K. Sandars's Pelican History of Art, *Prehistoric Art in Europe* (Harmondsworth, 1968), provide a stimulating introduction to the 'Celtic' art style which lives on into the early medieval period. B. Salin, *Die altgermanische Thierornamentik* (Stockholm, 1904, new ed., 1935), contains the standard analysis and classification of design in Germanic metalwork at the beginning of the medieval period. M. and L. De Paor's *Early Christian Ireland*, Ancient Peoples and Places (2nd ed., London, 1960), gives a sensitive and balanced account of the Irish contribution to early medieval art. D. M. Wilson and O. Klindt-Jensen's *Viking Art* (London, 1966), provides a scholarly and thorough survey of Viking stone and wood sculpture and metalwork, with excellent diagrams and plates. The vast range of early medieval art in Italy is usefully surveyed in P. Toesca's standard work, *Storia dell'arte italiana*, I, *Il Medioevo* (Turin, 1927). H. Jantzen's *Ottonische Kunst* (Munich, 1947), deals efficiently with the history of German art in the brilliant period leading to the Romanesque style. J. Evans's *Art in Medieval France* (Oxford 1948, revised ed., 1957), gives a sympathetic picture of the cultural wealth of medieval France from the tenth century onwards. T. S. R. Boase's *English Art 1100–1216* (Oxford, 1953), is an excellent interpretative and factual guide to Romanesque art in Britain, and includes important comments on Scottish Romanesque. The first part of *Romanesque and Gothic Art, Studies in Western Art*, Acts of the XX International Congress of the History of Art, I (Princeton, 1963), contains important papers on aspects of early medieval art by F. Wormald, F. Mütherich, M. Schapiro, and a notable paper (67ff.) by O. Pächt on 'The Pre-Carolingian Roots of Early Romanesque Art'.

PAINTING:

E. A. Lowe's *Codices Latini antiquiores* (Oxford, 1934–), an authoritative catalogue with facsimiles, provides the basis for the study of pre-Carolingian manuscripts. A major study of early illuminated books, including the great insular Gospel Books, with important plates, is E. H. Zimmermann, *Vorkarolingische Miniaturen*, (Berlin, 1916). On manuscripts from the Court and other workshops in the Carolingian age, W. Koehler, *Die karolingischen Miniaturen* (Berlin, 1930-), is indispensable. A. Goldschmidt's *German Illumination* (New York and Paris, 1928), reproduces a useful selection of illuminated books, up to the eleventh century. G. Swarzenski, *Die Salzburger Malerei* (Leipzig, 1913), is an important study of Romanesque illumination in Germany. G. Cames, *Byzance et la peinture romane de Germanie* (Paris, 1966), draws attention to the special cultural pressures which influenced art in twelfth-century Germany. For early medieval Spanish illumination, two books by W. Neuss provide firm guides to the complexities of style and iconography, namely *Die katalanische Bibelillustration um die Wende des ersten Jahrtausends und die altspanische Buchmalerei* (Bonn and Leipzig, 1922), and *Die Apokalypse des hl. Johannes in der altspanischen und altchristlichen Bibel-Illustration* (Münster, 1931). M. Salmi, *Italian Miniatures* (London, 1957), is a useful survey of the main trends in Italian book illumination. E. B. Garrison's *Studies in the History of Mediaeval Italian Painting*, Florence, 1953-, deal with a wide range of detailed problems in the history of Italian Romanesque painting. J. Porcher, *L'Enluminure française* (Paris, 1959), summarizes the achievement of French illuminators. J. Porcher's catalogue to the Exhibition *Manuscrits à peintures du VIIe au XIIe siècle* (Paris, 1954), has important entries on Romanesque illumination. F. Wormald's *English Drawings of the Tenth and Eleventh Centuries* (London, 1952), is an admirable introduction to the late phase of Old English book illustrations, at once readable and precise. The best short guide to English Romanesque illumination is F. Wormald's paper on 'The Development of English Illumination in the Twelfth Century', *Journal of the British Archaeological Association*, 3rd series, VIII, 1943. Stimulating analysis of iconography is found in O. Pächt, *The Rise of Pictorial Narrative in Twelfth-Century England* (Oxford, 1962). E. W. Anthony's *Romanesque Frescoes* (Princeton, 1951) provides a useful survey of wall paintings throughout Europe. The splendour of Spanish Romanesque painting is well conveyed by the plates in W. W. S. Cook and J. Gudiol Ricart, *Pintura e imagineria Romanicas, Ars Hispaniae*, VI (Madrid, 1950).

SCULPTURE:

A. Goldschmidt's *Die Elfenbeinskulpturen aus der Zeit der karolingischen und sächsischen Kaiser* (Berlin, 1914), is the indispensable standard work on early medieval ivory carving. The most ambitious monuments of early medieval metalwork are discussed in A. Goldschmidt's *Die deutschen Bronzetüren des frühen Mittelalters* (Marburg, 1926), and other aspects of German metalwork are dealt with by J. Braun, *Meisterwerke der deutschen Goldschmiedekunst der vorgotischen Zeit* (Munich, 1922). A useful survey of German Romanesque stone sculpture is provided by H. Beenken, *Romanische Skulptur in Deutschland (11. und 12. Jahrhundert)* (Leipzig, 1924). A. Haseloff's *Pre-Romanesque Sculpture in Italy* (Florence, 1930) is a short guide, with good plates, to the beginnings of Italian medieval sculpture. R. Jullian, *L'Éveil de la sculpture italienne* (Paris, 1945), brings the story up to the Romanesque period, and has a useful selection of plates with many details. Striking illustrations of Spanish Romanesque sculpture appear in J. Gudiol Ricart and J. A. Gaya Nuno, *Arquitectura y escultura Romanicas, Ars Hispaniae,* V (Madrid, 1948). P. Deschamps, *French Romanesque Sculpture* (Florence, 1930), does like service for France. A. Kingsley Porter's *Romanesque Sculptures of the Pilgrimage Roads* (Boston, 1923), contains a very large collection of plates of sculpture in various regions of France. J. Evans's *Cluniac Art of the Romanesque Period* (Cambridge, 1950), is an attractive study of monastic sculpture, set firmly in the context of the whole life of the Benedictine Order in France.

The major writer on French Romanesque sculpture is M. Schapiro, for whose studies of individual monuments see the notes on the plates. Also important is the monograph on *Gislebertus, Sculptor of Autun* (London, 1961), by D. Grivot and G. Zarnecki. The best guides to English Romanesque sculptures are the short but concentrated studies by G. Zarnecki, *English Romanesque Sculpture 1066–1140* (London, 1951), and *Later English Romanesque Sculpture, 1140–1210* (London, 1953). M. Blindheim's *Norwegian Romanesque Decorative Sculpture, 1090–1210* (London, 1965), is an excellent introduction to the special character of Romanesque stone and wood sculpture in the far north of Europe.

ARCHITECTURE:

K. J. Conant's Pelican History, *Carolingian and Romanesque Architecture*, 2nd ed., (Harmondsworth, 1966), gives an enthusiastic but detailed and coherent account of the development of European medieval architecture up to the dawn of the Gothic style. Lombardy, an important creative area, is discussed in a standard survey by A. Kingsley Porter, *Lombard Architecture* (New Haven, 1915–17). A solid detailed study of the types of design found in various parts of France is provided by R. C. de Lasteyrie, *L'Architecture religieuse en France à l'époque romane* (Paris, 1912). Much useful information is contained in J. Evans's *The Romanesque Architecture of the Order of Cluny* (Cambridge, 1938). L. Grodecki's *L'Architecture ottonienne* (Paris, 1958), is a highly interesting and important study of German architecture on the verge of the Romanesque. W. M. Whitehill's *Spanish Romanesque Architecture of the Eleventh Century* (Oxford, 1941, repr. 1965), has few illustrations but an excellent informative text. The standard work on Old English architecture is H. McC. Taylor and J. Taylor's *Anglo-Saxon Architecture* (Cambridge, 1965). G. Webb's Pelican History, *Architecture in Britain: The Middle Ages*, (Harmondsworth, 1956), gives a readable incisive account of the important developments in eleventh- and twelfth-century English architecture.

The following is a brief selection of books on various other aspects of the history of the period:

M. Deanesley's *A History of Early Medieval Europe 476–911* (London, 1956), is a useful concise factual account of early medieval history. The basic study of Church history in the Middle Ages is the grand-scale work by A. Fliche and V. Martin, *Histoire de l'église depuis les origines jusqu'à nos jours* (Paris, 1934–). M. L. W. Laistner's *Christianity and Pagan Culture in the Later Roman Empire* (Ithaca, New York, 1951), is an important account of the mixture of cultures out of which medieval ideas were to grow. N. K. Chadwick's *Poetry and Letters in Early Christian Gaul* (London, 1955), is a memorable study of Early Christian civilization at its best. The standard reference work on all categories of medieval Latin literature is M. Manitius, *Geschichte der lateinischen Literatur des Mittelalters*, (Munich, 1911–31). M. L. W. Laistner's *Thought and Letters in Western Europe A.D. 500 to 900*, 1931, new ed., London, 1957), provides an excellent summary of trends. A fascinating source book for the first stage of medieval society is Gregory of Tours's *History of the Franks*, ed. R. Buchner (Darmstadt, 1955), or in the English version ed. O. M. Dalton (Oxford, 1927). J. Wallace-Hadrill's *The Long-Haired Kings* (London, 1962), vividly depicts the workings of the Merovingian monarchy. One of the great original works of the early Middle Ages, Bede's *Ecclesiastical History*, ed. C. Plummer (Oxford, 1896), is a fundamentally important guide to the development of English Christian civilization. The influence of English culture on Western Europe is traced in the important book by W. Levison, *England and the Continent in the Eighth Century* (Oxford, 1949, repr. 1966). K. Hughes's *The Church in Early Irish* Society (London, 1966), is an admirable study of early Christian conditions in Ireland, full of insights. All aspects of the political and cultural impact of Charlemagne are analysed by an impressive array of specialists in the magnificent volumes on *Karl der Grosse, Lebenswerk und Nachleben*, ed. W. Braunfels (Düsseldorf, 1965-8). A masterly survey of Charlemagne's achievements is D. Bullough's *The Age of Charlemagne* (Elek Books, 1965), with apt and striking plates. E. Duckett's *Alcuin, Friend of Charlemagne* (New York, 1951) and *Carolingian Portraits* (University of Michigan Press, 1962), are elegant and learned evocations of the promoters of Carolingian civilization. P. E. Schramm's *Kaiser, Rom und Renovatio* (Leipzig, 1929, repr. Darmstadt, 1957), is a fundamentally important work of interpretation of the political and cultural ideas of the Ottonian Age. *The Making of the Middle Ages* by R. W. Southern (London, 1959), is an attractive introduction to the leading men and the leading ideas in tenth-, eleventh-, and twelfth-century Europe. W. Ullmann's *The Growth of Papal Government* (London, 1955), deals authoritatively with legal and political aspects of the Church. Important vernacular literary developments in the Romanesque age are studied by R. Menéndez Pidal in *La Chanson de Roland et la tradition épique des Francs*, (2nd ed., Paris, 1960).

Index